FORMATION OF
REPUBLIC OF JINNAHPUR

FORMATION OF REPUBLIC OF JINNAHPUR

An Inevitable Solution

Syed Jamaluddin

Author of **DIVIDE PAKISTAN TO ELIMINATE TERRORISM**

iUniverse, Inc.

New York Bloomington Shanghai

Formation Of Republic Of Jinnahpur
An Inevitable Solution

iUniverse books may be ordered through booksellers or by contacting:

iUniverse
1663 Liberty Drive
Bloomington, IN 47403
www.iuniverse.com
1-800-Authors (1-800-288-4677)

Because of the dynamic nature of the Internet, any Web addresses or links contained in this book may have changed since publication and may no longer be valid.

The views expressed in this work are solely those of the author and do not necessarily reflect the views of the publisher, and the publisher hereby disclaims any responsibility for them.

The author Syed Jamaluddin is not member of any political party in Pakistan. Similarly, Syed Jamaluddin is neither member nor supporter of MQM-Muttahida/Mohajir Qaumi Movement which is a political party registered in Pakistan. Syed Jamaluddin is a freelance political analyst and his views are based on his best possible judgment of political circumstances in Pakistan and South Asia. His opinion about formation of Republic of Jinnahpur is purely based on facts and figures which, in his judgment, are true and correct under the prevailing political scenario inside Pakistan. Syed Jamaluddin hereby extends his apology to those Pakistanis who may feel hurt with certain contents of this book.

ISBN: 978-0-595-51453-3 (pbk)
ISBN: 978-0-595-61907-8 (ebk)

Printed in the United States of America

dedicated to

Muhammad Ali Jinnah
Zulfiqar Ali Bhutto
Shaikh Mujeebur Rehman
Bacha Khan
G.M. Syed
Akbar Bugti
Altaf Hussain
Kofi Annan

CONTENTS

PREFACE

"All conflicts are identity conflicts" said John Paul Lederach, Professor of International Peacebuilding at The Joan B. Kroc Institute for International Peace Studies, University of Notre Dame, Indiana, USA. This statement is, in my opinion, very conclusive to explain the very nature and significance of all conflicts existing either at international level or regional level. All such conflicts are basically 'identity conflicts'.

In recent years, scholars have taken an intense interest in questions concerning identity. In comparative politics, "identity" plays a central role in work on nationalism and ethnic conflict. In international relations, the idea of "state identity" is at the heart of constructivist critiques of realism and analyses of state sovereignty. And in political theory, questions of "identity" mark numerous arguments on gender, sexuality, nationality, ethnicity, and culture in relation to liberalism and its alternatives. Compared to recent scholarship in history and the humanities, however, political scientists remain undecided when it comes to work on identities. Despite this vastly increased and broad-ranging interest in "identity," the concept itself remains a controversy.

A "failed state" is one that has a "shattered social and political structure". In the words of former Secretary-General of the United Nations, Boutros Boutros-Ghali: 'A feature of such conflicts is the collapse of state institutions, especially the police and judiciary, with resulting paralysis of governance, a breakdown of law and order, and general banditry and chaos. Not only are the functions of government suspended, but its assets are destroyed or looted and experienced officials are killed or flee the country. This is rarely the case in inter-state wars. It means that international intervention must extend beyond military and humanitarian tasks and must include the promotion of international reconciliation and the re-establishment of effective government.'"

The Telegraph newspaper has reported recently in an editorial that Pakistan is a failed state hosting both nuclear weapons and alQaeda's core leadership; a unique combination which makes it the world's most dangerous country. According to the paper, if threats to global security in terms of terrorism, nuclear weapons and the spread of failed states are considered, Pakistan stands at the nexus of all three phenomena. Whoever emerges from the present political maelstrom to lead Pakistan will have to deal with the country's unofficial status as al-Qaeda's heartland, the paper adds. According to the Telegraph, the Pakistani state is so weak that armed Islamist groups have a free rein over large areas. In Balochistan, an ethnic insurgency is underway. In Karachi, Pakistan's largest city and the commercial capital, a ruthless political machine linked to organised crime, is in charge, while Peshawar is seen as the hotbed of Islamist zealotry.

Therefore, Pakistan for all practical purposes is very close to disintegration, and could most definitely be termed as a 'failed state'.

Noted philosopher and political activist Noam Chomsky also recently said that Pakistan was a "paradigm example of a failed state" that had undergone an "extremely dangerous form of radical Islamisation." The country was now in danger of "collapsing" as it grappled with rebellion, militancy and extremism that was "getting worse". Asked to draw a parallel between the situation in Pakistan and the characteristics of a failed state highlighted in his book "Failed States", Chomsky said, "I am afraid to say Pakistan is the paradigm example of a failed state and has been for a long time. It has had military rule, violence and oppression." Since the 1980s, the country had undergone an extremely dangerous form of radical Islamisation, which had undermined a good part of the society, under the Zia-ul-Haq tyranny, he said. "Now it is in danger of collapsing, there is a rebellion in Balochistan, the (Federally Administered Tribal Areas) territories are out of control and always have been and it is getting worse.

In view of this accepted and recognized fact that Pakistan is going to disintegrate any time from now, it is important that all nations living under siege of presently undivided Pakistan's military dictatorship should begin efforts for their respective liberation as envisioned by me in my earlier book titled "DIVIDE PAKISTAN TO ELIMINATE TERRORISM".

Being a member of a family which had migrated from India in early 50s and settled in Karachi, the port city of presently undivided Pakistan, it has now become my duty to caution my friends and brothers back in Pakistan particularly in Karachi to stop dreaming about a united Pakistan. To implement my vision of dividing Pakistan and forming 6 new countries in South Asia by disintegrating Pakistan, I would like to start this campaign by proposing formation of REPUBLIC OF JINNAHPUR. This book shall highlight reasons, causes and necessary elements for the formation of Republic of Jinnahpur. This is my humble prayer that Karachi should soon become Republic of Jinnahpur. Ameen.

Formation of Republic of Jinnahpur is inevitable as soon as possible before the Pakistan Army decides to launch yet another 1992-like genocide in Karachi. I suggest to Mr. Altaf Hussain, leader of MQM which is the single most influential political force of 'Mohajirs' (Migrants from India who had settled in Pakistan at the time of breakup of United India in 1947) to utilize these precious moments of his life by giving a call for formation of Republic of Jinnahpur by launching Jinnahpur Liberation Movement under the banner of MQM. I hope the people of Karachi will loudly say "YES" to his call.

Syed Jamaluddin

www.dividepakistan.blogspot.com

www.jinnahpur.blogspot.com

dividepakistan@gmail.com

jinnahpur@gmail.com

CONCEPT OF IDENTITY

I feel that the meaning of "identity" as we currently use it is not well captured by dictionary definitions. Our present idea of "identity" is a fairly recent social construct, and a rather complicated one too. Even though everyone knows how to use the word properly in everyday life, it proves quite difficult to give a short and adequate summary statement that covers the full range of its present meanings. Given the centrality of the concept to so much recent research, it would be useful to have a concise statement of the meaning of the word in simple language that does justice to its present significance.

"Identity" in its present form has a double sense. It refers at the same time to social and religious categories and to the sources of an individual's self-respect or dignity. There may be no necessary linkage between these things. In ordinary language, at least, one can use "identity" to refer to personal characteristics or attributes that cannot naturally be expressed in terms of a social or religious category, and in some contexts certain categories can be described as "identities" even though no one sees them as central to their personal identity. For instance, a Punjabi person living in Pakistan may describe himself more a *Punjabi* than a Muslim because such person feels that by identifying himself as a *Punjabi* would truly reflect his identity as compared to be considered merely a Muslim because a Bangladeshi is also a Muslim and so a Malaysian or an Afghan.

Some of the renowned scholars have described "identity" in the following words:

1. Identity is "people's concepts of who they are, of what sort of people they are, and how they relate to others" (Hogg and Abrams 1988, 2).

2. Identity is used in this book to describe the way individuals and groups define themselves and are defined by others on the basis of race, ethnicity, religion, language, and culture" (Deng 1995, 1).

3. Identity refers to the ways in which individuals and collectivities are distinguished in their social relations with other individuals and collectivities" (Jenkins 1996, 4).

4. National identity describes that condition in which a mass of people have made the same identification with national symbols (Bloom 1990, 52).

5. Identities are relatively stable, role-specific understandings and expectations about self (Wendt 1992, 397)

6. Social identities are sets of meanings that an actor attributes to itself while taking the perspective of others, that is, as a social object (Wendt 1994, 395).

7. By social identity, I mean the desire for group distinction, dignity, and place within historically specific discourses (or frames of understanding) about the character, structure, and boundaries of the polity and the economy (Herrigel 1993, 371)

8. The term [identity] (by convention) references mutually constructed and evolving images of self and other (Katzenstein 1996, 59)

9. Identities are prescriptive representations of political actors themselves and of their relationships to each other" (Kowert and Legro 1996, 453)

10. My identity is defined by the commitments and identifications which provide the frame or horizon within which I can try to determine from case to case what is good, or valuable, or what ought to be done, or what I endorse or oppose (Taylor 1989, 27)

11. Yet what if identity is conceived not as a boundary to be maintained but as a nexus of relations and transactions actively engaging a subject? (Clifford 1988, 344)

12. Identity is any source of action not explicable from biophysical regularities, and to which observers can attribute meaning" (White 1992, 6)

13. Indeed, identity is objectively defined as location in a certain world and can be subjectively appropriated only along with that world. (Berger and Luckmann 1966, 132)

14. Identity emerges as a kind of unsettled space, or an unresolved question in that space, between a number of intersecting discourses. (Hall 1989)

The moment a person or a group begins to subjugate multilayered identities in favour of one particular identity, especially if that identity is acquired politically and asserted as a nationality primarily in opposition to some other group, rather than used for self expression and internal cultural bonding, it becomes a sure recipe for civil strife and inter-group enmity likely to tear any society. In this regard it is quite revealing that those who lead such movements are often those who do not live at the center of their community's cultural life. Rather, westernised, culturally uprooted, and alienated people such as Muhammad Ali Jinnah (founder of Pakistan) more prone to playing this leadership role in this game of competitive zero sum identity assertion and denigration of other groups.

Had the super-Anglicised Jinnah lived a little longer after creating Pakistan, in all likelihood he would have migrated to London because Pakistan was created out of his obsession to one-up "Hindu leaders", rather than to provide a real haven for Muslims. He certainly could not have survived the regime of military dictators like Ayoub Khan or Ziaul Haq and religious fundamentalists that he indirectly helped bring to power in the name of creating a land for the socalled pure people (Pak). In the process he jeopardised the safety and well-being of millions of Muslims whose identity he claimed to safeguard from "Hindu domination".

Today, Indian Muslims, who make up 15 percent of the total Indian population, are a vulnerable and mistrusted minority in India, whereas in the unpartitioned India the 35 percent Muslim community would have had tremendous bargaining power. The idea behind the Partition was that Muslims could not live in a Hindu-majority India and as a consequence of this fake concept, Two-Nation Thoery was introduced which was a great blunder of the 20th century. The Partition devised by Jinnah left many more million Muslims living in India than could be absorbed in Pakistan, even after the near total ethnic cleansing of Hindus in territories that became Pakistan.

It is no coincidence that the Urdu-speaking Muslims of India who were the most enthusiastic supporters of the demand for Pakistan are virtually at war with the nation-state of their own making, as also with other ethnic communities of Pakistan. They are still called Mohajirs (migrants), indicating that they continue to be treated as aliens and provoke a great deal of hostility in Pakistan. In the 1940s it was their Muslim identity which came to dominate all their other identities, leading to their demand for a Partition. Subsequently, in an all Muslim state, it is their identity as migrants from India which has pitched them in a murderous battle against other groups in Pakistan. As we see in Pakistan and in many other parts of the world, the process of ethnic cleansing is inherently unstable. Pakistan's Muslims soon came to perceive dangers to their own group from other Muslims with other criteria to establish additional diverse identities: Sindhis, Mohajirs, Baluchis, Punjabis, Shi'ites and Sunnis. This begins a never ending process of division. This book of mine is basically proposing a repair to the damage caused by the Two-Nation Theory back in 1947.

Whenever someone's assertion of identity is loaded with overblown praise for one's own group, and hatred for some other group, whenever competition and tit-for-tat becomes the real motivating factors in identity consolidation and political struggle in nations, whenever our leaders try to make us paranoid or aggressive vis a vis others in asserting a particular aspect of our identity (whether based on caste, religion, gender, language or region), we should subject such ideas and leaders to thorough scrutiny and check out whether we are being manipulated into imagining dangers from others or is there a real objective basis for it. Such leaders are in all likelihood leading us towards harming others to achieve their own self-determined goals rather than protecting our legitimate interests. Such assertions lead to increasing fragmentation and civil strife without real benefit to anyone. And the moment we begin to succumb to hate propaganda against another group, it is important to pause and subject ourselves to thorough self-examination. Why is our own sense of self so fragile that we need to fear and hate others merely because they are somewhat different from us? Predominance of negative ethnocentric sentiments against others is a sure sign of a fragile, fractured, and uprooted identity. Hatred of others is usually a sign of self-contempt. Those who really like themselves, are comfortable being themselves, are not prone to hatred and aggression towards others. What Punjab is doing in Pakistan against poor Urdu-speaking (Mohajirs) is surely condemnable but mere condemnation will not solve the crisis. Time has already run out for any compromise or inter-ethnic dialogue. Time has come for securing a comprehensive identity of Urdu-speaking people of Pakistan through an independent state called REPUBLIC OF JINNAHPUR.

At the time of Partition in 1947, who went where and how are they doing? Pakistanis and Indians outside South Asia

The beginning

In the space of a few months during the Partition of India in 1947, twenty million people were displaced, a million died, seventy-five thousand women were said to have been abducted, raped, and families were divided, properties lost, homes destroyed and countries (India and Pakistan) exchanged. Excluding the internally displaced, today South Asia has the fourth largest concentration of refugees in the world. Going back to 1940s, Partition's refugees/migrants during the last five decades have had a long and complex history in the course of reaching respective homelands, some of them more than once (in the 1940s-60s and then in 1970s onwards) and some of them found themselves disowned by it in 1971 when Bangladesh came into being. Those who could afford, turned diasporic, those who could not, await repatriation to Pakistan and still others have decided on lives of constant border crossings.

By December 1951, 6,597,000 refugees had moved from India to West Pakistan, and 7,94,127 refugees moved to what was then East Pakistan. Of the Indian Muslims headed for Pakistan during 1947-48, 95.9% of the migrants from Assam, West Bengal and Bihar moved to East Pakistan and 3.2% to Karachi. According to the 1951 census, 66.69% of the migrants in East Pakistan came from West Bengal, 14.50% from Bihar, 11.84% from Assam and 6.97% from other places in India. A passport and visa scheme was introduced only on 15 October 1952. But travel documents were not even required until 1953-54, several years after India and Pakistan became two separate countries. Several government employees opted for Pakistan, although some changed their minds later and returned to India. Following riots in Khulna and Calcutta in January 1964 and as a reaction, in Jamshedpur and Rourkela in March 1964, there was a yet another spate of migrations in both directions. After the December 1971 India-Pakistan war Pakistan was no longer a migrant destination.

When the autonomy movement picked up in the 1960s some 'Biharis' openly sided with the Pakistan regime. By December 1970, attacks on non-Bengali shops and properties by Bengali mobs were quite common in Dhaka and Chittagong. Many were killed at Chittagong, Jessore, Khulna, Rangpur, Saidpur and Mymensingh in early March 1971, even before the military action. Subsequently the Bangladesh government declared them to be Pakistanis who should be returned to their home country. Of the 534,792 Biharis who applied for repatriation only 118,866 were accepted by the Pakistan government. Since the early 1970s, the Bihari Muslim diaspora in the U.K. and U.S.A. intervened to salvage the Biharis from their existence in the 66 refugee camps across Bangladesh, initially through voluntary organizations, then the Asian Committee of the British Refugee Council and the Mecca based Rabita al Alam al Islam. In February 1972, Ghulam Sarvar, the editor of Sangam (Patna) floated the Bihari Bachao (Save the Biharis) Committee, which urged the Indian government to allow the uprooted Biharis to return to Bihar. While some of them did, others made Bihar a temporary base, en route to Pakistan, via Nepal, Sri Lanka, Burma and Thailand.

It may be mentioned that earliest group of immigrants from South Asia to the U.S.A. were Punjabi men who settled mainly in California's agricultural valleys in the 1910s and 1920s and constructed a "Hindu" ethnic identity which in those days simply meant "from Hindustan or India", even though 90% of the men were Sikhs and 8% were Muslims. They married Mexican and Mexican American women. After Partition, there was a rupture among California's "Hindus". In ethnic representations at county fairs, a "Pakistani Queen" joined the "Hindu Queen" and many Muslim-fathered families renamed themselves "Spanish Pakistanis". On the east coast, in 1951, the New York based Pakistan League of America intervened against the deportation of "illegal" Pakistanis working as agricultural, factory, hotel and restaurant workers in New York, New Jersey, Michigan and California, and worked for a separate country quota for Pakistanis in the context of "millions" having been rendered homeless and refugees by Partition.

Across the Atlantic, in Southall, London, the fallout of Partition was found to be "as intense" as on the subcontinent and had tangible consequences in the public sphere. Thus Pakistani Southallians were only entitled to associate membership in the powerful Indian Workers' Association. Muslims set up their separate community organizations, either inclusively Muslim or specifically Pakistani or Bangladeshi. An anthropological study of London's Punjabi Hindus which did not solicit thoughts on the Partition found its memory underpinning the narratives of both migrants and their British born children. Despite the increasing public privileging of an Islamic identity, diaspora Pakistanis continue to valorize their national roots.

The Stranded Pakistani General Repatriation Committee[SPGRC], formed in 1977, links the Bihari muhajirs in the 66 refugee camps and has had representatives in London, Chicago and Paris. Its overseas support network comes from the Bihar Muslim, rather than just the muhajir diaspora. The focus has been on working out the funding of their repatriation as a "humanitarian", rather than a "political" project. The SPGRC has during its career authored several, simultaneous recastings of the muhajirs. As 'refugees' threatening to do a Vietnamese, by moving from coast to coast to get across their statelessness to an unmoved UN, which slots them instead as "displaced persons". As 'Muslim Refugees' to get the support of the Mecca based Rabita al Alam al Islam. And trilingually, as Stranded/Mehsoor/Aatkay Pora Pakistanis to address their case more widely in English, Urdu and Bengali. While it shares the MQM's perspective that it was migrants from undivided India's Muslim minority provinces who created Pakistan there is a significant difference. It squarely blames the politics of the Muslim League for the uprooting of the Biharis and their being sacrificed three times over: in 1946, 1947 and 1971, and retrospectively idealizes Bihar, the pre-1947 homeland. In this 1980s reconstruction of the Pakistan movement, it is emphasized that the bulk of the railway employees opted for East Pakistan only in response to Jinnah's call to get Pakistan going.

According to Tariq Meer, an organizer of the MQM in Europe, following the army crackdown in Sindh in 1992, in the space of a couple of months "thousands" had gone underground to escape death and torture, "hundreds" claimed refugee status in Britain alone, and "hundreds" more had gone to the U.S. and Germany. "Much of our work (these days) is dealing with governments across the world checking with us about the claims for asylum and refuge ... We are beginning to get inquiries also from countries like Australia, New Zealand, Japan, Thailand and many others". Many also escaped to Afghanistan to look for ways out from there. About a year later the MQM protested to the British Home Office, the French and German Interior Ministries, that the refusal to consider the political asylum applications of the MQM cadres was in serious conflict with the UN conventions of 1951 that dealt with the rights of the refugees. The British Home Office, on its part, had turned down the applications because the MQM had become a coalition partner of the government in 1997. The MQM then argued that the army had launched its operation against its cadres in 1992, despite its being a coalition partner of the Nawaz Sharif government.18 The U.S. and Canadian governments too have over the years been in touch with the MQM to check out political asylum applications.19 Meanwhile several MQM leaders on the run have been in hiding in the Gulf and the U.S. since 1992. Occasionally, whenever possible, their supporters arrange for them to meet the diasporic constituency. However, many hold back from coming out in the open as MQM supporters for fear of repercussions on their families back home. There are of course others, who either reject its politics or have come to distance themselves from its "terrorism", after having initially supported it, or are plain indifferent to its career, domestic or diasporic. Significantly, in a couple of cases Pakistani community organizations have split along muhajir/Punjabi lines in the 1990s.

The hardening of ethnic boundaries in Pakistan has over the years tightened the definition of muhajir, to produce "a revised category" which incorporates Urdu-speaking Pakistanis above all, to the exclusion of other ethnic groups who were similarly uprooted at independence. Thus migrants from East Punjab gradually came to be labelled primarily as 'Punjabi' rather than muhajir, a description which was reserved more and more for refugees coming from northern India. Of the approximately one million muhajirs who settled in Sindh by 1951, 85 % were Urdu speakers from the pre-1947 provinces where Muslims were in the minority. Initially they were dominant in the Muslim League and the government. Not long after however, the party self-destructed and virtually vanished. With the late

1950s domination of the army in the Pakistani polity, the muhajirs came to be edged out by the Punjabis. Around 1984 when the Muhajir Qaumi Mahaz was formed, it cut into the Jamat e Islami's support among the migrants in Sindh. More recently the MQM has been described as "an excellent example of a movement that is diasporic, transnational and anti-state", with a leadership in exile in London, since the army operations began in 1992.

According to the MQM leader Altaf Hussain, guiding the movement from its international secretariat is expensive but adequately funded by supporters the world over. His outreach inside and outside Pakistan is maintained with a combination of telephonic speeches and video addresses, with titles like Hum Door Nahi (I Am Not That Far Away). In 1996 the Overseas MQM had nineteen branches in the U.S.A. (started in 1988 and afresh in 1991) and two in Canada. In its estimate about 15% and 10% of the Pakistani diaspora in Chicago and New York are muhajirs, and some 10% of this strand is post-1992. The introductory comments of the 1994 Chicago annual banquet edition of MQM Vision, described diasporic muhajirs as its "natural constituency", who could provide "decisive" support in restoring human rights in Pakistan.

Some support has been forthcoming. In 1995 the Coalition of Muslim Organizations of the greater Houston area, an umbrella group of 15 organizations in Texas wrote an open letter signed by 1,821 community members to all Pakistani leaders to resolve the Sindh situation with "an open mind" and passed a resolution against the massacre of citizens in Karachi. The Overseas MQM was on the panel of a seminar organized by the Pak-American Task Force for the Solidarity of Pakistan in 1995, in Detroit. Likewise, in June 1995 the United Muslims of America (UMA), together with the Pakistan Association of the San Francisco Bay Area and the American Muslim Alliance, San Francisco organised a forum titled, "Why Is Karachi Bleeding?" Rifat Mahmood, the UMA chairman, emphasized that though muhajirs had built Pakistan for all Pakistanis, there were still so many of them stranded in Bangladesh. A resolution was passed to involve all political parties, "including the MQM", in a conference to sort things out.26 A similar resolution was passed by the organizers of the forum on 19 August 1995, at the Pakistan Independence Day Festival at the Golden Gate park, San Francisco. Around December 1995, the UMA made an offer to send a team of "highly skilled and qualified arbitrators of eminent American Muslims to facilitate and enhance the peace negotiation" in Sindh. The following year too, at the 49th Pakistan Independence Day celebration at the Golden Gate, there was a pointed rewind to the 1940 Lahore resolution and a similar offer was repeated. On the east coast Dr Shafi Bezar, who headed the International Council for Repatriation of Pakistanis from Bangladesh in the 1980s in New York, floated the Mohajir International Forum in 1995. This has links with the community in New York, Chicago and California.

The focus of the overseas MQM has been on making a human rights case of happenings in Sindh. In addition to its website updates, its twin videos, Extrajudicial Execution and The Genocide include close-ups of reports of Amnesty International, Asia Watch, World Organisation Against Torture and excerpts from U.S. State Department reports. Also scenes of tanks rolling on the streets of Karachi, morgue sequences, bereaved families and crowds at the funeral of Altaf Hussain's brother and nephew. In 1996 the MQM published A Catalogue of the Victims (The Mohajir Nation) of State Crime, a 134 pages account detailing state action against MQM supporters, its leaders and rank and file during 1995. Death Warrant was an appeal to "the world conscience" against the persecution of a "22 million strong" nation. Similarly Genocide of the Mohajir Nation and Mohajir Rights Are Human Rights carry supportive copies of reports of international human rights organisations and western governments and stress that the MQM had been vindicated in national and provincial elections in urban Sindh in 1988, 1990 and 1993. However, several of the human rights groups invoked by the MQM have also expressed their concern about its own human rights abuses, all of which is deflected as "concocted" preludes to legitimizing state repression. More recently the MQM organized protests in London, the U.S. (New York, Washington and Chicago), Canada, Germany, South Africa, Australia, Belgium and a couple of other countries to "internationalize" government atrocities against muhajirs, "6,000" of whom had been killed since 1992, in a terrain that it compares with Bosnia and Kosovo. Altaf Hussain added that he was only emulating the Pakistani government trying to internationalize the Kashmir issue through its action in Kargil. 30 The MQM tracks muhajirs as being crushed by the state right from the assassination of Liaquat Ali Khan, but is more focused against the post-1992 operations.

A major demand made by the MQM in 1987 was that muhajirs be recognized as the fifth nationality (panchvi qaum), along with the Punjabis, Pathans, Balochs and Sindhis and that non-Sindhis and non-muhajirs should not be allowed to buy property in Sindh. Today its position is that if "national integration" is to be forged it is "imperative to recognize and accept the constitutional rights of Sindhi, Punjabi, Pakhtoon, Mohajir, Baloch, Saraiki, Brohi, Makrani and all other nationalities, fraternities, lingual, cultural and religious units". Not long ago however, around 1994, the MQM had moved close to creating a province comprising the southern Sindh cities of Hyderabad, Karachi, Mirpur and Thatta. This "reduced notion of Pakistan", i.e., Urdudesh/Muhajiristan/Jinnahpur has been attributed to second generation muhajirs. A couple of months ago the MQM had warned of 'another Bangladesh' in case the Nawaz Sharif government extended job quotas on a rural-urban basis to pit the Sindhis against the muhajirs. Simultaneously however, Altaf Hussain stated that if Sindh continued to be "ruled from Punjab" then there would be no choice left but to demand the right to self determination, as written into the 1940 Lahore resolution. But he added that the basic disagreement between the MQM and the Jeay Sindh Qaumi Mahaz (part of the World Sindhi Conference formation to be discussed below) is that "they demand a separate 'Sindho Desh', whereas the MQM aims for full provincial autonomy for Sindh within the (geographical) framework of Pakistan". A point often made by the MQM leader, Altaf Hussain, not too long ago was that when the muhajirs had a country they sought freedom; now that they have freedom they are seeking a country.

["Watan thaa to azadi dhoondta thaa; Ab azad hoon to watan dhoondta hoon"].

The WSC's stand regarding the repatriation of Biharis from Bangladesh has been that of opposing it stiffly. Thus in the late 1980s it sent a backgrounder on the Biharis to Lord Ennals of International Alert and the Asian Refugee Council to put its point of view across. In its recall the Biharis had migrated to East Pakistan "of their own free will in search of a better life". But "instead of merging with the native population they tried to impose their language and culture" on the Bengalis and later established terrorist organizations called Al Shams and Al Badr which were active in the massacre of Bengalis in 1971 and then went on to become "unwanted parasites". It was ironic, according to its then chairman, Halepota, that the MQM had emerged along similar lines and with the intention of turning Sindhis into a minority, to make them "aliens in their own homeland". This continues to be the WSC position and its meeting in London on 29th August 1999 passed a resolution both against the repatriation of Biharis to Sindh and for the return of "illegal migrants" to their countries of origin.

But very recently and perhaps significantly, the chairman of the WSC, Dr Safdar Sarki noted, that it was a positive sign that Altaf Hussain had for the first time "explicitly and resolutely expressed his views on the injustice and wickedness inflicted upon Sindh and Sindhis after the creation of Pakistan" by Punjabis [see above]. In response, he added that the Sindhis had never trampled the rights of the Urdu-speaking population, nor had they shut their doors to "the new settlers" in 1947. He also recalled that G.M.Syed had seen in the MQM the debut of lower and middle class leadership among the Urdu-speaking people, but regretted that subsequently the MQM was turned against the Sindhis by "Punjabi agents". That, he regarded as the "biggest mistake of the MQM in its history". Was it not time, that the Urdu-speakers called themselves Sindhis, fifty years after migration and when all of them were born in Sindh?

Have we not seen a similar trend all over the world? Especially in the UK and USA, many immigrants have accepted local identities in one way or other, and many people proudly call themselves "British" or "American". The same holds true for immigrants from Africa, China, and Latin America, who made UK or USA their home. They keep their languages and cultures intact and practice their customs. Yet, they are part of the host nations. Why don't we accommodate a comparable scheme in the case of Sindh? Thus, for Sarki the possibility of retrieving the legacies of Shah Latif and G.M.Syed towards resolving Partition's migrant history is to be sought in the pedagogy of diasporic formations.

Forefathers
Compared to overseas communities of other origins, the total number of people of South Asian descent who are living outside South Asia is quite small. Exact figures are difficult to come by because of major national differences in census taking. But a decade ago the total number of South Asians living outside Pakistan, India, Bangladesh, Nepal and Sri Lanka was about 8.6 million, i.e. fewer than 1% of the combined populations of these South Asian countries. Very briefly, the first wave of migration from the subcontinent started around 1830 and lasted until 1920 and consisted of indentured labour recruited for the plantations and railways that were being established in the British and French colonies. The second wave of emigration from the subcontinent occurred between 1920 and 1939 when small groups of traders and white collar migrants travelled to British East Africa, South Africa and Malaya. The third period of emigration began after the Second World War and includes the following strands. Workers in the lowest levels in factories, foundries and textile mills in the expanding British economy. Across the Atlantic, South Asian immigration to both the U.S.A. and Canada has been two-phased. One dating from the early twentieth century and more staggered and discontinuous, comprising in the main of the labouring and agricultural class and the second, around the mid-1960s, of mainly middle class professionals. Following shifts in the world economy around the mid-1980s, migrants from smaller towns and less privileged backgrounds are now working at restaurants, news-stands and grocery stores or driving taxicabs. In addition since the oil price rise in 1973 there has been a wave of migrants to the Middle East, totaling between three and four million South Asian workers. On the whole, South Asians comprise 0.5% of the U.S. population and about 2% of the Canadian population.

According to one estimate South Asian Muslims in the U.S. add up to between 250,000 and 450,000, with about 160,000 Indians, 80,000 Pakistanis and 10,000 Bangladeshis. Quite the reverse of the U.S., where Muslims from the Middle East are in a majority, it is South Asians who predominate in Canada as they do in Britain. Early South Asian Muslim immigrants were mostly farm labourers from Punjab and moved to the U.S. from western Canada, settling in California, Oregon and Washington. In the 1920s and the 1930s, sailors, small traders and factory workers from Bengal in particular Sylhet, settled in New York, New Jersey and Connecticut, with a few moving to industrial centres like Boston and Detroit. Several students who enrolled in American universities in the 1950s and 1960s just stayed on. The largest and most "homogeneous group of Indian Muslims belong to Hyderabad. Numerically, Gujratis and Mahrashtrians come next, followed by Muslims from Assam, Bengal and Bihar. Though widely dispersed in the U.S., there are large concentrations in California, Illinois, New York, New Jersey, Connecticut and more recently in Texas, Florida and Georgia.

Within this formation the emergence of the American Federation of Muslims From India [AFMI} in 1989 was equally a statement on the tokenism faced in the Indian community at large and the non-Indian preoccupations of the umma, despite the fact that Indians add up to 12.5–13% of the community. Based in Detroit, it has regional presidents in California, Illinois, Massachusetts, Nebraska, Texas, Washington DC and Canada and an international liaison committee covering USA, Germany, Australia, Saudi Arabia, Kuwait and the UK. Its intervention against the Hindutva project is summed up in its statement submitted to the Indian prime minister, Narasimha Rao in 1993 in which it summed up that India stood torn between "those who want to turn the 46 years old republic into a Hindu state ... and those who are keen to establish secularism". During the 1993 elections, it identified UP as the battleground between fascist and secular forces. In its perception what had sharpened the struggle was the fact that the citizenship of Indian Muslims was "still under suspicion" years after Partition. Together with other Indian American Muslim organisations it campaigned during 1994 for the release of Muslims held without trial after the 1992-3 riots under TADA (Terrorist and Disruptive and Activities Act). In 1994 it forged an alliance with the International Dalit Sena, led by Ram Vilas Paswan of the Janata Dal. It has simultaneously been taking on the Hindutva ensemble in the U.S. through its newsletters and advertisements in Indian American newspapers "to counter the myths and lies propagated by Hindu extremists".

Between 1994 and 1996 AFMI has organized educational meets in Delhi, Lucknow and Patna to achieve its target of 100% literacy for Indian Muslims by the year 2005. It has also urged the US government to allocate "say 10-15%" of US investment specifically for minority entrepreneurs. However, its response to economic liberalization has been uncritical in its expectation that it will generate immense "opportunities" for Muslims. And though its electoral watch was centred on north India it did not engage with the shifts that have occurred within the community both at the levels of leadership and agenda, in particular the movements for affirmative action among the subaltern Muslim biradaris since the 1990s. These movements have not only challenged the ashraf leadership for having led the Pakistan movement and subsequently focused on "emotive" issues mobilizing around communitarian-identitarian symbols, but emphasized the lower caste pre-conversion roots of 90% of the community. At least in Bihar, the dalit and backward Muslims have intervened to inscribe their agency by keeping track of AFMI's projects. Thus the All India Backward Muslim Morcha pointedly gave its literature to its delegation visiting India. And the Amarat e Ahle Ansar associated with the Pasmanda Muslim Mahaz passed a resolution against AFMI for seeking reservation for "all" Muslims.

Other organizations that have focused on contesting Hindutva and funding relief and legal aid to Muslims arrested in the aftermath of riots of 1992-3 ("about 80%" of the "65,000 TADA detenus" were Muslims) and in general campaigned for the human rights of Indian Muslims include the Indian Muslim Relief Committee of the Islamic Society of North America(IMRC), the Consultative Committee of Indian Muslims in the U.S. and Canada (CCIM), and the Association of Indian Muslims of America (AIM).8 3 According to AIM, which represents over "100,000" Indian Muslims in North America, though 60 million Muslims had rejected the two-nation theory and stayed on in India in 1947, they have been victims of the backlash of the formation of Pakistan during the past several decades. Thus Indian Muslims are stereotyped as being fundamentalist and "intolerant of the Hindu majority" both in the Indian and North American press. Ever since the making of Pakistan, notwithstanding their having cleared that "agnipariksha", they have been on the receiving end of "unrelenting economic discrimination, injustices, humiliation, intimidation, carnage of violent riots and considerable loss of life and property". AIM intends to forge links with progressive Indians and has been working on establishing links with Pakistani Americans. It supports the search for a "new leadership" among progressive Indian Muslims who "should definitely not wage campaigns on symbolic issues like the Shah Bano affair or the Satanic Verses issue". More importantly it holds that the "state of siege" in the Muslim community needs to be broken. In January 1995 some AIM office bearers on a visit to England held meetings with the Indian Muslim Federation (IMF), the largest organization of Indian Muslims in the UK, and the Union of Muslim

Organizations of UK to work on joint campaigns and projects aimed at improving the situation of Muslims in India. However, two years ago, the IMF (which had earlier organized protests against the Bhagalpur riot in 1989) appeared divided over its approach to the Bharatiya Janata Party, though it was still dominated by people who supported the Janata Dal or the Congress.

The Canadian Council of South Asian Christians, established in 1991, includes Christians from Bangladesh, India, Pakistan and Sri Lanka, and has been working on overcoming their exclusion and discriminatory treatment both within the South Asian and wider Canadian community. It aims at dialogue with non-Christian South Asian organizations "to create a better understanding between the communities". A representative mention may be made of one of its community service awards in 1996. The recipient was Shadab Khokhar of the International Christian Awaz, for his five year long campaign against religious persecution in Pakistan under the blasphemy law. Through his initiative protest rallies were launched in Toronto and Ottawa in 1991 and 1993. A memorandum of understanding was signed between the Canadian government and Awaz, as result of which 200 families migrated to Canada by the end of 1996. Last year the National Association of the Asian Indian Christians protested to the UN to increase international pressure on the BJP-led government to rein in right-wing Hindu groups who had made several attacks on the community in India. The Bangladesh Hindu, Buddhist and Christian Unity Council, UK, it may be mentioned here is in touch with the World Sindhi Congress which has taken a stand against the rise of religious fundamentalism and called for the immediate abolition of the blasphemy law in Pakistan.

The elite Indian American organizations include the Association of Indians in America, the Federation of Indian Associations [which split into the FIA, the Federation of Hindu Associations and the FIA-Indian Origin between 1994-7] and the National Federation of Indian American Associations. They are known to have made efforts to win greater US government support for India (and less favour to Pakistan), an effort that has occasionally made the Indian community support right wing politicians. In general, the leadership of the Indian immigrant community is conservative. It has not sought to form alliances with other ethnic groups. In the late 1980s, for instance, Chinese and Koreans in the New York area made tentative moves towards a pan-Asian combination against racial discrimination but there was no response from the Indians. In fact most Indian immigrants express open prejudice against African Americans and Hispanics and non-white migrants. By contrast, many South Asian immigrants in both Canada and Britain have chosen an alternative strategy, identifying themselves as 'black'. It has been argued the Indian immigrant bourgeoisie remembers the history of the Indian community in the U.S. largely in terms of its own history since the mid-twentieth century. This selective memory that deletes the pre-first world war subaltern immigrants (the farmers, railroad builders, workers and political refugees) from its narrative, is seen to flow from its model minority self-image, one that seriously limits its understanding of racism and its response to other communities. By contrast, the history of the pre-first world war immigrants is summed up as more radical in its awareness of the scope of western imperialism and the diaspora generated by it. While this perspective does not mean to devalue the importance of a minority group's efforts at creating a voice of itself, it points to its intense racism towards other communities and its denial of the existence of marginalized Indians: the illegal migrants, the ill-paid labourers and domestic workers, gays, lesbians and battered women.

During the past two decades the Hindu right has been doing intensive propaganda among the Indian immigrants in the US, UK and Canada. It is against this backdrop that we documented the intervention of some Indian American Muslims and will, later in this section consider that of some leftist groups. But first a look at the Vishwa Hindu Parishad of America (VHP-A). It is registered in thirteen states, mostly on the East Coast and has a membership of around 2000. At the local level it has "contacts" with about 10,000 families.

Much of its work focuses on children's educational programmes and youth camps. It publishes literature on the "Hindu way of life" and runs its social service projects mostly in India. But its influence extends well beyond its enrolment. According to one summing up, in the US religious identity becomes a way of evading racial marginality. Moreover, support for a strong nationalist state at home is seen to promise a better status in the terrain migrated to. Unsurprisingly contemporary Hindu nationalism articulates "a genteel multi-culturalist presence in the US with militant supremacism in India".

At the "First Dharma Sansad in the Western Hemisphere" organized by the VHP-A in Pennsylvania in August 1998 the achievements catalogued included the setting up of the Hindu University of America in Orlando and the expansion of the Hindu Students Council (HSC) to "almost fifty campuses". It was added that, "it is because of the brilliant work of some of the very bright people of the HSC, (that) the Hindu Dharma has a major presence on the Internet and the World Wide Web". The report of the Sansad detailed the antecedents of the contemporary "Hindu Diaspora" to include the Buddhist dispersal at "the time of Emperor Ashoka" and subsequently that of the Vaishnavs in South East Asia. "Then came the darker time of foreign invasions … then came another Diaspora in the nineteenth century, the forced one, when the British took Hindus [completely overlooking the 15% of the jahazis who were Muslims] to their colonies". It sees the "most recent", i.e. the second half of the twentieth century one as likely to bring about "more far reaching effects than any other Diaspora". The resolutions passed were unmistakably homogenizing in intent. "The VHP-A should be the voice of Hindus in the western hemisphere. All religious, spiritual, cultural organizations, temples and ashrams should associate, endorse and/or affiliate with the VHP-A, to make the Hindu Voice more effective" (original emphasis). It also resolved to publish "an authentic history book of India and its heritage for the benefit of the young generation of Hindus in the Western Hemisphere".

"Youth Ready to Induct Time Tested Hindu Values in Modern Society", reads the title of a report on a youth conference in Boston in June 1998. The Hindu Heritage Day in Houston that May spent "some serious moments at the mention of the more than 40 Kashmiri Hindus" killed around that time, "just for being Hindus". The same issue of Hindu Vishwa carries an e-mail reminding readers that "there may be so many Hindus from Afghanistan, in the US & Europe who are waiting for some help from us" and that the Taliban had imposed jizya on Hindus. It also carried a notice that the Global Hindu Electronic Networks (GHEN) was adding eleven new Amar Chitra Kathas to Freeindia.org, an educational website which is a project of the HSC. The new additions included Shivaji, Valmiki, Vidyasagar, Mirabai, Parshuram, Prithviraj Chauhan, Harishchandra, Ganesha, Kumbakarana, Draupadi and Rana Pratap.55 Significantly over the last few years in universities and community centres in Britain, the VHP has been targeting Hindu Asian youth with the slogan, "Better to be a Hindu Asian than a British Asian" and projecting Hindutva as the answer to the Muslim fundamentalism sweeping the college campuses.

In response to the spread of the Hindutva movement in North America, the Forum of Indian Leftists (FOIL) was formed in 1995 as an organization of overseas Indians to intervene "in the crisis generated by neo-liberal economics and communalism—crises that find expression in the diasporic Indian community and in the Indian nation". It collaborates with other progressive individuals and groups active on similar issues in Europe, North America and the South Asian subcontinent. The focus on India was explained by drawing attention to the fact that "there are certain issues that are bound by the nation-state and its products overseas which are not identical with those of South Asia as such". It feels that if other South Asians later want to become a part of it it would "change accordingly". Its pamphlet series include subjects like structural adjustments, new capital flows into South Asia Area Studies and the Indian left's support for liberalization. Among its projects are the coordination of a speakers bureau of intellectual-activists, putting together a cultural collective and a progressive South Asia exchange web project. Also a media project to appear in specific centrist newspapers such as India Abroad, India Tribune and India West. It envisages summer school internships to link second generation students with radical non-governmental organizations and leftists in India. In 1997 it organized a Youth Solidarity Summer programme in Atlanta, on the occasion of fifty years of Indian independence and Pakistani nationhood, to offer progressive perspectives on South Asian history, identity and politics. This was to address a "growing" and "stark need" for "alternative engagements with South Asia" so that the second generation can learn about contemporary South Asia as well as the complexities of the diaspora. As it summarizes, on the one hand reified notions of South Asian "tradition" and "culture" are transmitted by immigrant parents. On the other, the only South Asian studies offerings on the university circuit are most often informed by orientalizing perspectives or erasures of the knowledge of popular struggles for economic, religious and gender equality in South Asia.

A few days after the destruction of the Babri Masjid, the Coalition Against Communalism (CAC) was formed in the Bay Area in 1992. According to one of its members, the right wingers in the South Asian community are among the most effective organizers. "At the drop of a hat they can get 40 people into a room to sit writing letters expressing outrage about something or the other. So the idea was to form something to counter that. And to say that there is an alternative point of view". The group has Indians and Bangladeshis and some Pakistanis. But its focus was mainly on India, "because Indian communalism was, at that point" the problem that bothered them "the most". In 1998 a BJP Government Watch group emerged in the US to monitor the HSC.59 The recent right wing take over of institutions of research like the Indian Council of Historical Research and the withdrawal of two volumes of the "Towards Freedom" documents series from the publishers evoked web-site interventions such as "Akhbar" and "South Asia Documents". There was an appeal to take up the matter in academic associations and area studies centres to express concern on this subject to the Indian government.60 There are several bibliographical resource pages against communalism on the internet. Significantly the web-site of the BJP is in fact operated from the US.

Based in the US, SAMAR (South Asian Magazine for Action and Reflection) is published twice a year. The term "South Asian", it elaborates, is chosen "to bring attention to the fact that South Asians are a group of people with a shared history and that this history provides a common basis for understanding of our place in the contemporary world". It's statement goes on to add that "whereas most other South Asian magazines are based on differences of region, religion and nationality within South Asia", it has chosen to base itself "on a South Asian collectivity that is now spread out across the globe" (emphasis added). Ranged against the contemporary rightward political drift, it sees its basic commitment as social and economic justice both in North America and South Asia. In 1998 it began producing a regular radio programme as part of the Asia Pacific Forum in New York (WBAI 99.5 FM). Subjects covered included the Indian elections and nuclear test explosions in the subcontinent and the taxi workers' mobilization and strike (see below) in New York.

The Lease Drivers Coalition (LDC), a community-based organisation of the Committee Against Asian Violence (CAAAV,1986), which grew out of feminist and leftist Asian American politics, was formed in 1992 and organizes South Asians who form 50% of the New York's 30,000 yellow cab drivers. Subsequently called the New York Taxi Workers Alliance (NYTWA), the focus is on negotiating the racialized police force, the exploitative garage owners, the Taxi and Limousine Commission (TLC) inspectors and courts. Most drivers work about 84 hours a week in 12-hour shifts. In 1997 some drivers invested in citizens band radio networks to bond themselves linguistically (about 31/40 are Punjabi networks and around 5 Bengali). The organizing committee members meet two or three times each month, and general members meet once in every two months. Initially the bulk of the its roughly 700 members were Pakistanis. On 13 May 1998 the NYTWA co-organised a taxi strike in New York, during which 97% of the drivers are believed to have been off the streets against 17 new anti-worker laws proposed by the TLC. The LDC profiled itself as being different from other unions and driver organizations in that it had "equal respect for Bangladeshi, Indians and Pakistanis". This solidarity making is conceptualized as a prelude to linking up with drivers of "all other communities", such as African Americans, Latinos, Europeans and non-coloured Americans.

The Canadian counterpart of the South Asian movement is said to have "a somewhat older history" than the American one. Thus for example, the proliferation of South Asian materials emanating from Canada (films, music, cultural events, journals, anthologies) has yet to be matched in the US. This has been attributed to two factors. The significantly larger concentrations of South Asian populations are in large Canadian metropolitan centers such as Toronto, Vancouver and Montreal. And the unconscious promotion of ethnic identities through Canada's declared "mosaic" policy in multicultural affairs.64 In Toronto, the post-1960s

South Asian diaspora has recently expanded with the arrival of 100,000 Tamils, many of them asylum seekers. Here progressive activists, some of whom belong to the South Asian Committee of the New Democratic Party have been forging a collective. This includes the Progressive Pakistani Committee, the North American Sikh League, the Tamil Eelam Society, the Canadian Council of South Asian of South Asian Christians (mentioned earlier) and the Scarborough Muslim Association. The agenda is to think through participation in Canadian politics as well as to intervene against racism both among South Asians and other metropolitan communities.

The South Asia Solidarity Group (SASG) supports people's struggles against exploitation and oppression in South Asia and strengthening the links between these struggles and those of Asian communities in Britain. In Britain its activities have included supporting Asian women workers demanding basic rights, organizing against racist attacks and opposing racism in health and education policies, as well as fighting repressive immigration and asylum laws. It also produces and distributes written material. One of the events in its campaign of saying no war and fascism in India and Pakistan included distribution of leaflets on mass scale and collecting signatures at the World Cup final at Lord's cricket ground two years ago. Its quarterly, Inquilab, carries articles takes on debates among the left in South Asia and Britain. Its conference on "Globalization, Identity and Resistance" in October 1997, to mark 50 years of the end of British rule in South Asia drew nearly 200 participants, both activists and academics from South Asia, Britain and Canada. The workshops examined themes such as workers' struggles and globalization; cultural production and globalization; gender and nationalism; nationalism and refugees; communal/fascist parties rooted in the denominational politics of Partition; and national liberation struggles in Kashmir, Baluchistan, Sri Lanka and of the Jumma people in Bangladesh. "In a period when erstwhile progressive writers and intellectuals are becoming apologists for imperialism", the organizers highlighted the significance of bringing together a coherent critique of globalization. As a follow-up the SASG is "beginning to examine the growth of communalism in the Asian community in Britain It is also working on developing a coherent left perspective on workers' struggles in Britain. As it see it, "this will involve working with a wide network of groups and identifying possibilities for unity".

A random look at the letters to the editor columns of newspapers in the Gulf and a couple of interviews indicate that ethnic and communal politics flowing from the Partition experience and the nation states defined by it, avidly engage the South Asian community and explain fund-raising initiatives and political affilitations. What became sharply evident, since the early 1990s in particular, at several levels and in different ways, both in the subcontinent and the South Asian diaspora is that the denominational nation-making projects of the 1920s–1940s are still around and are being worked on/bypassed/questioned/transcended. It is a contested field, but given the combination of transnational practices and trans-border technologies, as also the different, gendered layers of the Partition diaspora itself, it is imperative for social scientists and activists to track events, trends and debates in the subcontinent as well as in the diaspora.

Thus for example, the South Asia Citizen's Web has emerged as an "independent space on the net to promote dialogue and information exchange between and about South Asian citizens' initiatives [located in Bangladesh, India, Pakistan, Sri Lanka and in their diasporic communities]" (emphasis added). Likewise, the website of the Bombay based journal Communalism Combat notes that its subscribers include anti-communal Indian groups in the US, Canada and UK. Similarly, more and more non-governmental organizations in South Asia are beginning to forge regional networks to tackle issues like mass movements of refugees and cross-border migration. In 1994 the South Asian Human Rights community acquired a profile to work on discrimination against minorities, women's rights, torture and extra-judicial killings. It should be added that one of the resolutions of the six year old Pakistan-India Peoples' Forum For Peace and Democracy at its 1995 session in New Delhi decided that "in future such people to people meetings should include Indian and Pakistani diaspora."

The Pakistan-India People's Forum is an attempt at making the constituency for a subcontinental peace movement visible. It is ranged against state-sponsored ideologies of demonizing the other that inform the "national security" agendas of the post-Partition nation states. Its five joint conferences in Delhi, Lahore, Calcutta, Peshawar and Bangalore in 1995-2000 attended by representatives of trade unions and mass organizations, academics, artists and activists got support from members of the Pakistan-Indian Diaspora. Regarding Kashmir, it aims at getting past the assumption that post-colonial nation-state boundaries are sacred and that it is just a territorial dispute. This is seen as basic to reducing communal and ethnic tension in the subcontinent and scaling down defence expenditure and militarism Its re-definition of political nationhood contests the minimizing of contact between the people by governments that impose restrictions on travel between the two countries and on the duration of each stay. The Forum is therefore working for the granting of visas with greater ease, the reduction of costs of telecommunications and postal exchange and facilitating the free exchange of journals and information. It also proposes the joint preparation of resource books and pamphlets and literature, alternate people-to-people television channels and joint cultural productions and securing the rights of cross-border migrant labour. Given the connections that are made between the "border question" and the "communal question" this is going to be uphill going. Significant headway has however been made in linking up the women's movements in Pakistan and India. This will expand to include drawing up a charter of women's rights. The expectation is that Muslim women in Pakistan, Bangladesh and Sri Lanka supporting this charter will support Muslim women in India and women in Pakistan will get support in their demands for women's rights beyond the present focus on marriage, divorce and personal laws.

CONCEPT OF ETHNICITY IN THE CONTEXT OF PAKISTAN

Ethnicity is not a new phenomenon in world politics of today. Almost all the important countries around the world have dealt with ethnicity within their specific political environment. After the nation building efforts of Bismarck and Garibaldi succeeded in Europe during the 19th century, the European States were mainly considered mono-national states, where the influence of any sub-national ethnic groups was largely neglected. After the end of the Second World War, with numerous multinational multiethnic colonised nations becoming independent, the issue of ethnicity assumed enormous scholarly significance.

Many of the post-colonial states have faced the problem of ethnicity in one form or the other ever since. In many cases, ethnic assertion has assumed violent forms. Since the end of the Cold War and the dissolution of the Soviet Union, the reassertion of the ethnic movements, especially in violent forms, across the globe has forced many states to look at it more closely. Ethnicity has its own significance and thus can never be ignored or forgotten.

Before coming to the ethnic problems in pakistan, it will be helpful to define ethnicity. The word 'ethnic' is derived from the Greek word 'ethnikos'; which referred to (a) non-Christian 'pagans' (b) major population groups sharing common cultural and racial traits; primitive cultures. Ethnicity denotes the group behaviour of members seeking a common ancestry with inherent individual variations. It is also a reflection of one's own perception of one self as the member of the particular group. According to the Prof. Dawa Norbu, "an ethnic group is discrete social organization within which mass mobilization and social communication may be affected. And ethnicity provided the potent raw material for nationalism that makes sense only to the members of that ethnic group. its primary function is to differentiate the group members from the generalised others".

Out of 132 countries in 1992, there were only a dozen which could be considered homogeneous; 25 had a single ethnic group accounting for 90% of the total population while another 25 countries had an ethnic majority of 75%. 31 coun-

23

tries had a single ethnic group accounting for 50 to 75 % of the total population whereas in 39 countries no single group exceeded half of the total population. In a few European and Latin American cases, one single cases, one single ethnic group would account for 75 % of the total population.

The Pakistan Case

The country Pakistan comes under the third level, with one dominant ethnic group accounting for 50 to 75 % of the population, as the Punjabis are around 56 % of the total population. In the case of Pakistan, the regional assertion based on the ethnic identities came to the fore in more pronounced ways in the 1990s. Ethnic disaffection was simmering in Baluchistan and NWFP since the 1970s. Similarly, the Urdu-speaking nation of Pakistan were accepted as an important political force even by the military dictatorship of Pakistan in the recent times. Existence of such political force was evidenced especially in Karachi and the twin city of Hyderabad. The Sindhi assertion has along been there since 1950s. All this has to be studied against the background of the separatism within Pakistan that climaxed in the formation of Bangladesh in 1971.

Historical Background

To examine the ethnicity in Pakistan, we will have to search for its root in the Pakistan movement. It was a movement of a special nature though based on serious flaws committed by the socalled Muslim political leaders who had pretended to be the saviours of Muslims of India. Led by the Muslim League under leadership of Mohammed Ali Jinnah, the muslims of British India were fraudulently fed with the fond hope of an Islamic State as opposed to the secular, democratic ideals of State advocated by the Indian National Congress, which sought to unify diversities. Well, in my opinion, Muhammad Ali Jinnah's concept was also similar to Indian National Congress, however, the subsequent political leadership in Pakistan manipulated a new concept as if Pakistan was formed on the principles of Islam. While the Congress Party organised constructive programmes like, women welfare, eradication of illiteracy, untouchability, decentralisation of power and so on, the leaders of the Pakistan movement jumped to the anti-Congress agenda and their strategy of exploitation of the religious sentiments which culminated in Direct Action Day in August 1946. The idea of 'Islamic State' overstepped all other secular concerns and after the foundation of the State of Pakistan on August 14, 1947, there was no further impetus to build a nation out of several disparate ethnic groups. The demand for an Islamic Pakistan was essentially a demand for political empowerment, and was therefore not so religious in intent. As such,

'Islam' did not act any more as a binding force once Pakistan came into existence. It is of little surprise that the most prominent of India's Ulema and religious leaders, notably those in the Jamaat-i-Ulama-i-Hind (party of Indian Ulema) did not look favourably upon Muslim Communalism and instead supported the Congress Party's notion of United India.

After independence, the positive programmatic policies of the Congress Party were incorporated into the Indian Constitution as the guidelines of a welfare state. In contrast, the ideological foundation of Pakistan as a unified Muslim nation could not take roots in the minds of the people in Pakistan for the sole reason that Pakistan was an artificial country made as a result of a conspiracy by the Punjabi landlords who had acted at the behest of their British Masters to crush and divide the Mulsim strength in the United India. The failure of the process of drafting of a constitution for the state of Pakistan revealed the irreconcilable differences among various groups seeking to impose their World-view on the people of Pakistan. This lack of consensus marked the nature of the Pakistani polity ever since.

Pakistan movement was very strong in Muslim minority provinces; where Muslims feared Hindu domination most. Pakistan, however, was created in the Muslim majority provinces of northwestern India and Bengal. Ethnic, linguistic and cultural distinctions set them apart. The socio-cultural outlook of the Muslim populations of the Muslim minority provinces (Bihar, U.P, M.P, Hyderabad) had very little similarity with the Muslims in Sindh, Baluchistan, NWFP and even in Punjab. The Sindhis, Punjabis, Bengalis, Biharis, or Hyderabadis followed different customs. they were different people who had more in common with their Hindu neighbours than with muslims of other provinces. The founding fathers of Pakistan had hoped, however, that the cementing force of Islam would maintain the integrity and unity of the country despite the presence of various ethnic groups. However, this dream could not come true as Bangladesh for formed in 1971 while other separitist movements are still alive in the remaining Pakistan.

After the death of both Muhammad Ali Jinnah and Liaquat Ali Khan, the Muslim League virtually became leaderless. The League leadership was heavily dominated by Urdu-speaking people. Just after independence, out of 27 top posts of the country including P.M, C.M, Governor, Attorney General etc., Urdu-speaking numbered about 18. They were very well-educated in comparison to the other ethnic groups. The educational superiority of Urd-speaking nation over Punjabis in particular paved way for ethnic discrimination at that time because Punjabis began to hate the Urdu-speaking people instead of becoming like them. The Punjabis started making plans as to how to eliminate Urdu-speaking people from the main scenario and ultimately the Punjabis adopted a policy of ethnic imbalance in order to marginalize Urdu-speaking nation.

Not only this, the Punjabi also did not like the Bengali nation who were culturally much stronger than Punjabis in Pakistan and numerically preponderant. However, one-sided discriminatory economic policies made by Punjabi lobby left East Pakistan (Bangladesh) in a state of suffering. Authoritarianism became associated with economic disparity. Ayub Khan's (1958-1967) rule especially harboured an ethnic bias. According to Mahbubul Haq, 1968, twenty two families controlled two thirds of Pakistan's industrial assets : 80 % of banking and 70 % of insurance. Majority of them were from West Pakistan. this hatred and the sense of discrimination against the Bengalis culminated in the bifurcation of Pakistan in December 1971. It was the first direct manifestation of the anguish of major ethnic groups against the dominant ethnic groups, i.e., Punjabi, Sindhi, Pathan, Mohajir (Urdu-speaking) and Baluchi, apart from many small groups like Saraiki, Hindko, Zikri etc.

The rise of Zulfikar Ali Bhutto and the PPP to power in 1971 presented Pakistan with another opportunity to define national identity in secular socio-economic terms. But he miserably failed to embrace democratic norms, thus shaking the foundations of newly established paramilitary democracy and federalism in Pakistan. Bhutto could not tolerate his PPP's political disaster in 1970 elections in Baluchistan as well as NWFP (Pakhtoonistan).

The Case of Baluchi and Pathan Assertion

Baluchistan is the largest province of Pakistan in terms of its geographic size constituting 43% of the total population. Even if the name would suggest that the province is named after the principal ethnic community, the Balochi, in Baluchistan, the Baloch make up less than half of the population of the province. In fact Balochi population residing in Karachi outnumber the Balochi population living in Balochistan itself. The reason is that Z.A Bhutto allowed massive migration of Baloch nation from Balochistan to Karachi in order to balance the ethnicity in Karachi to facilitate political existence of PPP within the Urban Sindh. Balochis are divided into several tribes and clans and organized on the lines of traditional semi-feudal Sardari System. Firstly Z.A.Bhutto played the sardars against each other for their own interest and finally in 1976 he declared the system abolished. Subsequently, Balochi leader Ghaus Bakhsh Bijenjo gave the theory of four nationalities. Z.A.Bhutto motivated by desire to dominate Balochistan and NWFP (Pakhtoonistan), dismissed the elected provincial governments and put the Baloch nationalist leaders on trial before the special Hyderabad Tribunal. These measures were seen in Balochistan and NWFP (Pakhtoonistan) as an assault on the autonomy of the provinces. The resistance in Balochistan soon developed into a civil war. Bhutto ordered the armed forces to suppress the Balochi dissidents. The war against Balochis lasted almost three years and many Balochis were forced to flee Afghanistan. The war resulted in the martyrdom of 10,000 Balochis and ill-fated death of 3300 Pakistani army soldiers. The Shah of Iran (who will be remembered as one of the cruel human beings in the history of Muslim heads of state) also came to the help of Bhutto in suppressing the Balochi nationalities as he was afraid that the freedom fight of great Baloch nation might involve the Iranian Balochis too.

Again in October 1992, ethnic tempers ran high and clashes took place between the Balochis and second largest ethnic group, the Pathans in Balochistan, when 12 new wards were included in the Quetta Municipal Corporation. Pathans dubbed the decisions as faulty because according to them it was meant to outnumber Pathan councilors against Baloch to ensure the election of a Baloch mayor.

After the Chagai nuclear tests by Pakistan in June 1998, some Balochi students hijacked one PIA plane to register their disapproval and draw international attention to the prevailing sense of discrimination in Pakistan against Baloch people and Baluchistan. The Afghan crisis in early 1980s also triggered ethnic tension between the Pathans and the Balochis.

The idea of an independent Pakhtoonistan is very old. The origins of this idea lie in the nostalgic association of the Pathans with the empire of Ahmed Shah Durrani, a Pathan, who gained control over the entire area from Persia to Delhi during the late 18th century. This empire did not last long. But the memory of this empire lingers in the popular memory and this has provided the legacy for those advocating Pakhtoonistan. Apart from this the major ethnic group in Afghanistan, the Pathans are willing to support any movement for autonomy for Pathans in Pakistan. Continued neglect of NWFP (Pakhtoonistan) by central leadership in Islamabad gives further legitimacy to the movement for ethnic assertion, which might assume disintegrative proportion. The gradual decline of Pathan representation in administration and especially security agencies, has created lot of resentment among the Pathans. In 1968 Pathans were almost 40% of the top military elite, thus getting the bigger share than the Punjabis (35%). Ayub Khan was himself a Pathan. For sometime, the large presence of Pathans in the state apparatus made it difficult for the advocates of autonomous or independent Pakhtoonistan to convince the younger educated middle classes to believe that they were being ruled by other ethnic group. But later on the steps taken by the central administration contributed to their fear of gradual marginalisation in the hands of the Punjabis.

The massive influx of Afghan refuges into Balochistan and NWFP (Pakhtoonistan) in the wake of the Afghan war revived the Pakistani fears of an eventual revival of the Baloch and Pathan separatism in the 1980s. This in fact distributed the ethnic equation in Balochistan leading to Baloch assertion for they were being 'minoritised' (outnumbered by Pathans). Similarly in NWFP (Pakhtoonistan), the huge Pathan-refugee population added to the confidence of the Pathans for renewed assertion. During this period, regional parties were welcomed into alliances with mainstream national parties and such coalition succeeded in blunting the edge of ethnic assertion effectively for sometime till irreconcilable differences tore them apart leading to ethnic assertion by the regional parties again.

Thus, after the 1998 elections the Awami National Party (ANP) having considerable Pathan following, made an alliance with the PPP and in 1990 formed a coalition government with the Islamic Jumoori Ittehad (IJI), and again with PML-N in 1997. This alliance broke down when the government of Nawaz Sharif refused to rename the NWFP as Pakthunkhwa. This marked apparently the return of the strategy of ethnic mobilization by the ANP. Begum Nasim Wali (the wife of Wali Khan) declared in an interview: "I want an identity. I want the name to change so that Pathans may be identified on the map of Pakistan". She emphasised that Pakthunkhwa was "the 3000 year old name of this area: the name used by Ahmed Shah Abdali who said he forgot everything including the throne of Delhi but not Pakthunkhwa". ANP is also against the Kalabagh Dam project whose royalties the Pathans say is bound to go in Punjabi pockets. In 2008's elections, ANP is back to power in NWFP (Pakhtoonistan). It has to be seen if ANP makes efforts towards formation of an independent Pakhtoonistan or remain as a "beggar" in front of the Punjabi leadership in the name of United Pakistan.

The Urdu-speaking Nation (Mohajirs)

Another serious ethnic tension, going on in Karachi since last several years, is the one between the Sindhis and the Urdu-speaking nation termed as "Mohajirs" (Migrants). The Mohajirs are the people who migrated to Pakistan mainly from gangetic belt of India, in 1947. The Mohajirs were not only in politics but also dominant in administration in Pakistan during the initial years until they became victim of cruel and brutal Punjabi bureacracy combined with Punjabi military dictatorship.

Z. A. Bhutto's PPP came to power in 1971. The Sindh saw it as the empowerment of Sindhi nationalism. At the same time Mohajirs correctly saw Bhutto as Anti-Mohajir. Bhutto showed his mental backwardness and hatred against the Urdu-speaking Mohajirs by making learning of sindhi language compulsory in schools by passing the Sindhi Language Bill. It forced bureaucrats to use Sindhi as an official language. Mohajirs protested against this. Bhutto introduced a quota system under which 1.4 % of the posts in Central Administration was given to rural Sindhis (Sindhi hinterland) through the 1973 Constitution. This affected the Mohajir preponderance in the Civil Service of the province. Following table shows the percentage of ethnic groups in Sindh province:

Table-1

Ethnic Groups In Sindh

Ethnic Group	Total	Urban	Rural
Mohajirs (Urdu-speaking)	4.1	54.4	2.2
Sindhi	55.7	20.0	81.5
Punjabi	10.6	14.0	8.2
Pathans	13.6	7.9	0.5
Baluchis	16.0	3.7	7.6

Mohajir ethnic consciousness found expression first in 1986 in the form of student activism, but very soon it consolidated into a political party—the Mohajir Qaumi Movement (MQM). Soon after its appearance, the MQM swept into power in the Urban centers of Sindh, taking over the Mayorship of Karachi and Hyderabad in 1988. This led to confrontation and the province of Sindh became the battleground for violence and armed conflict. Army launched operation clean up in 1992 to clean Sindh of dacoits and anti-social elements. During the operation, MQM activists were harassed and fake-encounters occurred. Army also engineered split within MQM and the split away group was known as MQM—Haqiqi faction, which acted as an arm of the security agencies of the Pakistani State. The main MQM party was then known as MQM—Altaf Hussain faction. The leader of MQM—A, Altaf Hussain, had to leave Pakistan and since then he is living in London, United Kingdom. During the last decade, encounters between the two MQM factions and as well as between MQM—A and the Police and security forces took tens of thousands of lives in Karachi.

There are many other small ethnic groups in the country and many linguistic groups as well. Various smaller linguistic groups often complain that they are not receiving proper treatment from the center.

Table-2

Language distribution in Pakistan

	Percentage	No. of speakers
Punjabi	48.17	54.4
Poshto	13.14	20.0
Sindhi	11.17	14.0
Sirake	9.83	7.9
Urdu	7.60	9.7
Baluchi	3.02	3.8
Hindko	2.43	3.1
Brahvi	1.21	1.5
Others	2.81	3.6

Among the above mentioned linguistic groups, Sariki-speaking people have proclaimed their independent ethnic identity within Punjab. They have demanded that Punjab should be bifurcated and Sarikistan should be constituted.

As far as fulfillment of regional aspiration is concerned, after the secession of Bangladesh, Punjab emerged as the single powerful province. Indeed, this was made possible by continuous political conspiracies invented by the cunning Punjabi leadership which included Mumtaz Daultana, Nawabzada Nasrullah Khan, Mamdot and Punjabi military dictators.

Pakistan is a multi-ethnic and multi-lingual country. There are also so many multiethnic, linguistic and racial groups in India, however, the problems of ethno-linguistic assertion has been successfully managed through the mechanism available for resolution of such tensions within the Indian constitutional framework. Unlike India, the leaders of Pakistan could not evolve a healthy democratic culture. The party responsible for formation of Pakistan was not sufficiently democratised to lead Pakistan to a truly representative form of democracy. The conflicting forces of unity and diversity could not be balanced due to prevalence of acute ethnic and linguistic variations and lack of mutual interdependence of national and regional sub-systems. The frequent outbreak of federal provincial and inter-provincial crisis such as the the one-unit act, the Pakhtoon-Baluch struggle for maximum autonomy and the Sindh-Urdu controversy in Sindh continued to disturb the federal equilibrium. In my opinion, the only way to repair this damage is disintegration of Pakistan and formation of 5 or 6 new states in South Asia as proposed in my book titled "DIVIDE PAKISTAN TO ELIMINATE TERRORISM".

WHAT I AM SAYING

What I am saying is very simple. Urdu-speaking people living in Karachi, Hyderabad, Sukkur and other cities in the province of Sindh (Pakistan) deserve their own country. An independent country for Urdu-speaking people will solve their economic problems on one hand and provide an environment of freedom from the military dictatorship of Punjab province on the other. Time has now come that the cruel domination of Punjab must end by all means. The Punjabi military has been ruling Pakistan ever since its inception. The Urdu-speaking great leaders who had struggled for the freedom of Pakistan were brutally murdered as part of the Punjabi conspiracy to hijack the country. It has become inevitable now that Punjab should no longer be given the right or power to continue its control on other smaller provinces of Pakistan. At least Sindhis, Pathans and Balochis have some of their regional identities but the Urdu-speaking people have been compelled to become Sindhis which is not possible. Urdu-speaking people have their own identity and worth. It is not possible for Urdu-speaking people to become part of Sindh. This attempt to make Urdu-speaking people part of Sindh has always failed. This fact that Urdu-speaking people are independent in their thinking and are able to represent themselves more effectively if they are independent, should be accepted and recognized by the whole world. One cannot force a French person to become German or a Czech citizen to become Spanish or a Polish citizen to become Russian, similarly, one should also not force an Urdu-speaking citizen to become Sindhi. Urdu language is much different from Sindhi language. Not only language, there is glaring difference in terms of culture, traditions, national character, vision, approach, mindset and above all religious thinking. Indeed Sindhis are brothers of Urdu-speaking people in their joint effort to get rid of Punjab's political domination through achieving independence of Jinnahpur and Sindhudesh. Urdu-speaking people cannot be forced to stay with Sindhis forever and without their own right of freedom. Both Urdu-speaking people and Sindhis deserve their respective identities through formation of Jinnahpur and Sindhudesh. Both these nations are not ready to remain under the umbrella of socalled Pakistan which is nothing but a political colony of Punjab. This colony must, therefore, disintegrate without any further delay.

If other separatist movements in the world are accepted and acknowledged world-wide, movement for a free and independent state for Urdu-speaking people currently living under dictatorial siege of Pakistan army should also be embraced by the United States of America and other Western nations. If Kosovo can get independence in 21st century, why not Urdu-speaking people of Pakistan can get their own country called Republic of Jinnahpur. Urdu-speaking people are also intelligent, educated, hardworking and politically sound to fight for their independence in the 21st century. Urdu-sepaking people should not be under estimated or considered as any regional minority of Pakistan. Urdu-speaking people represent the most educated class in the presently undivided Pakistan. When it come to educational statistics of Pakistan in the field of education, the contribution of Urdu-speaking people is upto 80%. It must be noted that Pakistan without Urdu-speaking people is nothing but a jungle of illiterates from Punjab and people in uniform who have hijacked this country for the economic betterment of military dictators along with Punjabi bureacracy and their families.

Republic of Jinnahpur shall be an economic capital of South Asia which will beat Dubai and Singapore on one hand and become a great place for foreign investment on the other. The deserving people of Republic of Jinnahpur will have job opportunities because of billions of dollars of foreign investment which is at present hindred because of terrorist activities sponsored by Inter-Services Intelligence (ISI) and other military sponsored organizations. Such terrorist activities conducted by Pakistan's ISI and other military sponsored militant organizations have rather blocked the economic progress of Karachi which in turn have created hurdles for the deserving educated Urdu-speaking class to invite foreign investment into Karachi. It is only possible if Karachi gets its independence and formation of Republic of Jinnahpur shall ensure that the deserving Urdu-speaking people will get their right of progress and prosperity under the banner of an independent country called Republic of Jinnahpur.

Pakistan has been declared a failed state and therefore remaining part of Pakistan means declaring ourselves as failed too. Urdu-speaking people of Karachi cannot be classified as failed because it is due to them that Pakistan has been surviving so far. Had there been no educated class making contribution towards Pakistan's economic growth in the last 60 years, Pakistan would not have reached to the level where it is now. However, due to its political failure and its inability to remain as a sovereign state, Pakistan is very close to its disintegration. In such a situation, it would not be ideal for Urdu-speaking people to remain intact with Pakistan. Rather, it is important that Urdu-speaking people should initiate their fight for freedom while Pathans, Balochis and Sindhis should follow suit. Republic of

Jinnahpur can establish a precedence for freedom of all nations currently suffering under the military siege of Punjab.

When I say "Punjab", I do not intend to include those great people of Punjab who consider themselves as Ghulaman-e-Ahl-e-Bait (Servants of Holy Prophet Muhammad SA, His beloved daughter Hazrat Bibi Fatima AS, His loyal son-in-law Hazrat Ali AS, His beloved grand sons Hassan AS and Hussain AS) and also the Seraiki nation who were wrongfully made part of Punjab province by the cruel Punjabi politicians in order to gain monetary gains by manipulating the total population of Punjab province. Even after 60 years, the Seraiki belt has been economically kept backward while poor Punjabi servants of Ahl-e-Bait were deprived of their constitutional right of serving in the Pakistan Army because of Wahabi-oriented policies made by Asian Hitler called General Zia-ul-Haq back in 1979 which kept Shia and true Barelvi Sunni Muslims away from army jobs. The doors of Republic of Jinnahpur shall remain open for such Punjabi brothers forever.

As for the Pathans, Balochis and Sindhis, I would like to convey my message to them that they should also get up from long sleep. The Punjabi military killed several Pathan freedom fighters, Baloch freedom fighters and even stabbed Zulfiqar Ali Bhutto who had brought back home 90,000 Punjabi Prisoners of War. The brutality of Punjabi military can be evaluated on the basis of their one single act that they stabbed and killed Zulfiqar Ali Bhutto who was their rescuer from Indian prison. Not only this, the Punjabi military recently killed Benazir Bhutto in order to wipe her off from the political scene to keep the status quo alive. The murder of Bhuttos should be sufficient for the Sindhis to wake up and get their own independence from Pakistan by forming Sindhudesh. Similarly, independent Pakhtoonistan and Balochistan should also appear on the world map in the nearest future.

The Urdu-speaking people are peace-loving people in true perspective. They dont want any confrontation, however, they have their right to defend themselves against the brutality of Punjabi army. The Urdu-speaking people shall not become victim of yet another *Operation Cleanup* which was once conducted by Punjabi army in 1992. Nawaz Sharif and his Punjabi political team of hypocrites cannot succeed in their conspiracy to regain substantial power again although they have just swallowed a bitter pill of shaking hands with Asif Zardari, a Sindhi man and spouse of Shaheed Benazir Bhutto. It is important that Asif Zardari should immediately understand conspiracy and hidden agenda of Nawaz Sharif and his political team of hypocrites who do not possess any sympathy or love for any nation otherthan typical Wahabi minded Punjabis. Nawaz Sharif is only waiting for the right time to confront Asif Zardari and as such Nawaz Sharif will definitely attempt to get into Pakistan's National Assembly through a by-election and thereafter challenge Asif Zardari and Bhuttos' Sindh-based political party called Peoples' Party. I cannot accept for any reason that Nawaz Sharif or his political team of hypocrites would ever accept any Sindhi, Pathan, Baloch or Urdu-speaking person to become Pakistan's prime minister. This is impossible for any Punjabi hypocrite like Nawaz Sharif to extend his hand for cooperation or affection towards any Sindhi, Pathan, Baloch or Urdu-speaking person in the name of socalled political reconciliation. I ask all the politicians from Pakhtoonistan, Balochistan, Seraiki belt and Sindhudesh not to believe Nawaz Sharif and his false promises of mutual cooperation or other similar sweet slogans. A snake is always a snake. Nawaz Sharif cannot be trusted.

I want all Urdu-speaking people living in Karachi, Hyderabad, Sukkur and other parts of Sindh to become active members of JINNAHPUR LIBERATION MOVEMENT. This movement shall be non-militant and non-violent in reality. This movement shall be run by Urdu-speaking intellectuals, educationists, workers, students, businessmen and politicians. This movement shall be peaceful and totally committed for creating international awareness about the great demand for an independent state called Republic of Jinnahpur by the Urdu-speaking people living under military siege of Pakistan army.

FORMATION OF REPUBLIC OF JINNAHPUR-AN INEVITABLE OPTION

According to my proposed plan, the Southern port city of Pakistan called Karachi shall become the Republic of Jinnahpur. This proposed formation of Republic of Jinnahpur shall be in line with the anticipated plan towards Pakistan's disintegration in the best interest of world's peace and elimination of terrorism as envisioned by me in my earlier book titled "DIVIDE PAKISTAN TO ELIMINATE TERRORISM". The name Republic of Jinnahpur is given in view of the fact that Muhammad Ali Jinnah who was leader of Muslim League back in 1940s in the United India and who had struggled for the formation of Pakistan was born in Karachi on December 25, 1876. Muhammad Ali Jinnah's mausoleum is also in Karachi.

Muhammad Ali Jinnah was a man with untiring efforts, indomitable will, and dauntless courage. He united the Indian Muslims under the banner of the Muslim League and carved out a homeland for them, despite stiff opposition from the Hindu Congress and the British Government.

His father Jinnah Poonja was an Ismaili Khoja of Kathiawar, a prosperous business community. Muhammad Ali Jinnah received his early education at the Sindh Madrasa and later at the Mission School, Karachi. He went to England for further studies in 1892 at the age of 16. In 1896, Jinnah qualified for the Bar and was called to the Bar in 1897. Muhammad Ali Jinnah started his political career in 1906 when he attended the Calcutta session of the All India National Congress in the capacity of Private Secretary to the President of the Congress. In 1910, he was elected to the Imperial Legislative Council. He sponsored the Waqf Validating Bill, which brought him in touch with other Muslim leaders. In March 1913, Jinnah joined the All India Muslim League.

Jinnah was a fragile man with an iron will. He had the habit of spending time alone, in peace and quiet, and this increased his ability to concentrate on studies and his career. Jinnah was a brilliant constitutional lawyer. He was not excited by the charm of words but later realized that they were his own strength and best trait through which he could always communicate effectively and win arguments. He became hard-working and developed faith in himself. His honesty towards himself and others brought him many friends as well as a few rivals but he didn't care as long as he knew he was right. During that time, and for the rest of his life, his companion and his closest relation was his sister, Fatima Jinnah, who was a mentor, a partner and a friend to Jinnah. Jinnah sent his sister to "Bandra Convent School" where every Sunday, he traveled from Bombay to Bandra, on a horse back to visit her. This shows his love and affection for his sister which lasted till his last breath. However, socalled Pakistan's most famous and most cruel military dictator Field Marshal Ayoub Khan confronted Fatima Jinnah which caused political turmoil in Pakistan even felt today.

Karachi had lost its economic dynamism as a consequence of a series of ill-advised actions taken by a succession of Pakistani leaders over a period of last 60 years. It all began with the decision of President Ayub Khan to move the country's capital from Karachi to a new city he was to call Islamabad. That move deprived Karachi's well-educated, well-trained, highly experienced work force of jobs in the government sector.

A significant number of these people belonged to the Mohajir community. This community had come to Karachi, pulled by the promise of a better life in the capital city of the country they or their parents had fought hard to create. The move of the capital, therefore, was more than an economic loss. It was also a kind of betrayal.

The second shock was felt by the city a decade after the decision by Pakistan's first military leader to relocate the country's capital. While Ayub Khan punctured the public sector, Zulfikar Ali Bhutto inflicted an equally serious blow on the city's private economy. A series of nationalizations of privately held assets ordered by Bhutto devastated private enterprise in the city. Even when Ayub Khan took with him government functionaries to Rawalpindi-Islamabad, there was still a great deal of economic life left in Karachi.

Some of it was, in fact, the consequence of the model of economic development the military administration had pursued in the sixties. This model had produced a vibrant private economy. In the 1960s, Pakistan developed banking and insurance industry that was remarkable in its scope, depth and reach for a country at its stage of development.

This was not the only part of private enterprise that had grown under the patronage of Ayub Khan. The Karachi Stock Exchange also worked remarkably well. It was able to draw capital from the increasingly prosperous upper and middle-income groups into industry, commerce and finance. KSE's market capitalization increased significantly during the period of Ayub Khan. During that time established as well as new entrepreneurs used "initial public offerings" IPOs to mobilize private savings.

Karachi's economy would have survived the departure of the civil servants from the city had Zulfikar Ali Bhutto not killed private entrepreneurship. That Bhutto played that role in Karachi's economic travails is surprising since his affection for the city was not hidden from view and manifested itself in many different ways. Not well tutored in economics, he seemed not to have realized that by killing the private sector he was killing the goose that had laid so many golden eggs in the city.

Bhutto's nationalization of large-scale industry, finance, insurance and large-scale commerce drained modern sector jobs from the city's economy. Once again, the burden of this change in public policy fell on the shoulders of the Mohajir community. After Bhutto's departure, another national leader stepped in the late seventies and eighties to adopt policies that compounded Karachi's growing problems. The new military president's approach to Karachi's growing economic and political difficulties was not motivated by any desire to find solutions for the city's failing economy. Ziaul Haq sought a political opportunity for himself from the city's difficulties. Ziaul Haq tried to hijack the single most powerful political force of Mohajirs called MQM in order to fulfil his own evil political designs, but, this never happened as he wanted.

In my opinion, the MQM, in its formative period, was a reactionary movement in the sense that it was reacting against the established economic, political and social order. The organization adopted the policy of addressing issues concerning economic persecution committed by the political leadership from Punjab. MQM gave awareness to urdu-speaking people of urban Sindh about their constitutional rights and freedom to exist. However, the hidden elements of the military establishment played their own role by bringing Mohajirs and Pathans living in Karachi face-to-face in a confronting style. This was indeed a great conspiracy. There was little social interaction between these two nations. While the loss of opportunities in both public and private sectors had turned a segment of the Mohajir nation towards the politics of violence, the Pushtuns were still reasonably satisfied with their situation. This changed suddenly with an incident at Sohrab-Goth.

The Sohrab Goth community of Pushtuns owes its origin to an entrepreneur who set up a store in the village of that name in Karachi's outskirts, selling imported merchandise smuggled into the country. Soon Sohrab Goth became the site of a "Bara" market, so called because of a similar market near Peshawar, which also sold smuggled goods.

In 1981, thousands of refugees from Afghanistan moved to Karachi and settled in the vicinity of Sohrab Goth. With the Afghans came drugs and weapons and Sohrab Goth became a part of a long supply chain. This chain linked the poppy producing areas in Afghanistan, small drug processing plants in Pakistan's tribal areas, and smuggling centres such as Sohrab Goth that fed the international drug markets.

Islamabad came under intense pressure from a number of foreign governments and agencies to move against this community of Pushtuns. This was done on December 12, 1986, when the government sent bulldozers to demolish the shops and houses that were alleged to be a part of the long drug chain. Reaction to the operation came quickly; two days later, on December 16, hundreds of Sohrab Goth residents descended on Orangi, a community of mostly Mohajir residents.

What ensued was ethnic violence of the type Pakistan had not known in its history. It left 170 dead and thousands injured. For several days, the government seemed to have lost control over Karachi's outskirts. The army was called in to bring peace to the city. Karachi now had another angry group to contend with— the Pushtun community.

While the Mohajir nation's anger was channelled into political violence by the MQM, the Pushtuns sought solace in religion. Radical Islam along with a number of its institutions—in particular "deeni madressahs"—had arrived in Karachi along with the Mohajir nation in 1947, at the time of Pakistan's birth. But it was not until the late eighties that it became a formidable political force. That happened for a number of reasons and Sohrab Goth was only one of them. It was rather first step towards of making of Taliban by the most cruel and brutal military dictator called General Ziaul Haq inside Karachi.

The other contributing factors included the first war in Afghanistan, the arrival of political zealots who had fought in that war, and the preaching in the religious seminaries by conservative ulema. As is now well-recognized, radical Islam has flourished in situations of economic distress; in the late 1980s and most of 1990s Karachi faced serious economic difficulties. It presented a good opportunity for radical Islam to take root. In my other book titled "DIVIDE PAKISTAN

TO ELIMINATE TERRORISM", I have described in detail the mechanism of Tablighi Jamaat (preaching group) and its functions.

Three raging storms have hovered over Karachi's sky for several years now. These are the storms caused by economic difficulties faced by the young and the failure of the city to provide basic services, by ethnic rivalries that cannot be contained by the political system, and, finally, by the arrival of radical Islam. Will these storms clear and bring light into Karachi once again? The answer to that question depends on how faster Republic of Jinnahpur is formed.

Jinnahpur's major political force is none other than MOHAJIR QAUMI MOVEMENT *(Political Movement of migrants from India)* (MQM) although it has been renamed some years ago as MUTTAHIDA QAUMI MOVEMENT *(Allied Nations Movement)* in order to find some space in the political scenario of presently undivided Pakistan. The main leader of this movement is ALTAF HUSSAIN who was forced to leave presently undivided Pakistan back in 1991 as a consequence of a military crack down on political workers of MQM by the then government of Punjabi politician Nawaz Sharif who has been well-known for his hatred and persecution against the Urdu-speaking nation living in Karachi.

In the words of ALTAF HUSSAIN, Pakistani establishment, secret agencies and the power-hungry mafia have been working on a three-pronged strategy to eliminate Mohajirs, crush their representative political party, MQM and to conquer Karachi. Elaborating different facets of this strategy in a thought-provoking lecture at the MQM's International Secretariat in London on *December 15, 1998*, Altaf Hussain listed them as:

1-Isolation: That Mohajirs in general and the MQM in particular is cut off from all other ethnic groups;

2-Criminalisation: That Mohajirs instead of being accepted as law-abiding citizens are classified and treated as criminals. Moreover, MQM, instead of being treated as a political party, struggling for the rights of Mohajirs is portrayed as a group of gangsters and terrorists who are treated as habitual offenders;

3-Demoralisation: That the Mohajirs in general and the MQM workers in particular are disheartened and discouraged with a mala fide motive to create sort of an overall depression among them to reduce the real strength of MQM;

According to ALTAF HUSSIAN, the Military Establishment, secret agencies and power mafia have been working consistently to physically eliminate Mohajirs, crush the MQM and capture Karachi. Governor's rule, establishment of summary military courts under Article 245 of socalled Constitution of presently undivided Pakistan, State-wide repressive operation against the MQM and the propaganda campaign through media trial has always been reflecting the ugly strategy of the rulers of presently undivided Pakistan.

In the said lecture of December 15, 1998, attended by intellectuals, writers, teachers and political analysts, ALTAF HUSSAIN detailed injustices meted out to Mohajirs in various walks of life after the creation of presently undivided Pakistan. Explaining as to why the MQM was opposed and State operations were carried out against it, Altaf Hussain elaborated the above-mentioned three-pronged strategy from all possible angles and the rationale behind it. Altaf Hussain said Mohajirs in Pakistan have won freedom from the feudal shackles long ago, which have crippled other societal groups. Politically alive, Mohajirs live their lives according to their own will, while the majority of the ethnic groups in Pakistan are still forced to live in slavery, physically and mentally, to that crippling feudal oligarchy. He said the feudal oligarchy (sardars, jagirdars and waderas) in Pakistan have created a kind of family to permanently rule the country.

According to ALTAF HUSSAIN, since, the Mohajirs did not belong to that "family", they were regarded as a threat to their familial rule and systematic steps were taken during various governments to push Mohajirs out of the system. This process commenced right after the assassination of the first Pakistani Prime Minister, Liaquat Ali Khan. For example, the capital was shifted from Karachi to Punjab, Mohajirs were forcibly retired from bureaucracy and other government departments, educational institutions, industries and banks, established by Mohajirs were nationalised, chances to higher education and jobs were eliminated for them by introducing "quota system" *(selective allocation system)* in Sindh and linguistic riots were masterminded. All these steps were aimed at paralysing Mohajirs as a community so that they are left incapable to challenge the monstrous feudal system prevalent in presently undivided Pakistan.

Moreover, ALTAF HUSSAIN was of the opinion that these unbowing Mohajirs became ever more threatening for the feudal system when they decided to unite under the MQM banner as the party emerged as the sole representative of Mohajirs in the country. It was the only party with no feudal in its ranks and the leadership blossomed from the lower and middle classes. The prospect of seeing these "downtrodden" in the representative assemblies sent shudders up the feudal spine. They were afraid of a ripple effect of this Mohajir phenomenon in the poor Sindhis, Baloch, Punjabis, Pakhtoons, Kashmiris and Seraikis, which could spell the end of feudalism in Pakistan. This fear of losing control forced the Military Establishment to propel a propaganda campaign aimed at creating a Mohajir ghost to frighten other ethnic groups in the country. And to prove that the Mohajirs were against all other communities, the Military sponsored Establishment agents masterminded Punjabi-Mohajir and Pakhtoon-Mohajir riots in Karachi. Tragedies like Sohrab Goth on October 31, 1986 and Aligarh and Qasba Colony on December 14, 1986 were part of the same scheme after which thousands of MQM leaders and workers were arrested and put behind bars. Recently, the famous May 12, 2007 Karachi massacre during the MQM rally is also continuation of such schemes sponsored by none other than military controlled intelligence agencies of presently undivided Pakistan. The double-edged scheme aimed at creating fissures between the Mohajirs and non-Mohajirs on the one hand and scaring the Mohajirs to leave MQM on the other. An attempt which failed to materialise.

These anti-MQM moves pumped an impetus when the MQM won a heavy mandate in Karachi and Hyderabad in the 1987 local bodies elections. Groups were formed, consisting of terrorists and criminals, to attack Mohajir dwellings. After failing to cripple the MQM through manufactured Punjabi-Mohajir and Pakhtoon-Mohajir riots, the Establishment tried to create a rift between the Mohajirs and Sindhis and for that purpose, on 30 September 1988, Hyderabad Massacre was carried out through paid agents. This attempt to isolate and destroy the MQM, like the previous, failed and the party emerged in the 1988 general elections as the country's third largest, Sindh's second largest and the largest in urban Sindh. Again in 2002 and now in 2008, MQM has emrged as a political force of Mohajirs.

However, despite the fact that MQM is still a strong political force of Mohajirs in Karachi, certain decisions by its leader ALTAF HUSSAIN to remain part of presently undivided Pakistan is totally baseless. Having realized for many years the reality of presently undivided Pakistan's military dictatorship and the traditional feudals sitting in the National Assembly of this country and socalled Provincial Assemblies who do not recognize the real power and rights of Mohajirs so much so that those discriminatory policies are still in existence against Mohajirs, there is no justification for MQM to remain loyal to presenlty undivided Pakistan.

In a historic Constitutional Petition No. 46 of 1994 filed by MQM in Supreme Court of presently undivided Pakistan against Federation of Pakistan and the Province of Sindh, MQM's presentation of facts truly reflect about the genuine grievances of Mohajir nation. The following constitutional petition of MQM is an apparent evidence to my proposed solution that formation of Republic of

Jinnahpur has become inevitable. The rights of Mohajirs can only be safeguarded and protected through an independent state called Republic of Jinnahpur. Staying with Pakistan is a political and emotional burden on the shoulders of Mohajir nation which they can never get rid of unless an independent country called Republic of Jinnahpur becomes a reality.

Following is the extract of the MQM's historic petition:

IN THE SUPREME COURT OF PAKISTAN
ORIGINAL JURISDICTION
Constitutional Petition No. of 1994

MQM (Mohajir Qoumi Movement), Central Office, 494/8, Azizabad, commonly known
as "90", (Nine Zero), Karachi, Through, Senator Ishtiaq Azher, Convenor Central Coordination Committee of MQM.
PETITIONER

VERSUS

1. **Federation of Pakista**n, through Secretary to the Government of Pakistan, Ministry of Interior, Secretariat, Islamabad.
2. **The Province of Sindh**, through Secretary to the Government of Sindh, Home Department, Karachi, Sindh.
RESPONDENTS

1-That the MQM (Mohajir Qoumi Movement) is the third largest political party of Pakistan on the strength of its membership of Provincial Assembly and Federal Parliament since the last many years. The Respondents are the Federation of Pakistan and the Province of Sindh.

2-That the grievance of the Petitioner, as explained in detail hereinafter, is that contrary to the Constitutional mandate contained in several provisions of our Organic Basic Law, the Petitioner has been prevented from operating and functioning as a major political party of the country. It will be submitted that the *raison d'etre* of this deprivation has been the realisation and fear of the political leadership of the Government at the level of the Federation and the Province of Sindh, that with the vast public support with the MQM it was logically destined to be in a position to seriously challenge the supremacy and hegemony of the Pakistan Peoples Party to continue in incumbency. As such direct and indirect misuse of state controlled authority has been resorted to by the said Respondents to crush, annihilate and demolish the MQM as a viable political party of the country.

3-That in order to fundamentally comprehend the issues involved in this petition certain basic yet well known facts have to be submitted. This will enable this honourable Court to be in a position to evaluate properly the gross and inhuman treatment meted out to the MQM and to its leadership and workers by and at the hands of the Respondents. So shocking is the heinous nature of this mayhem perpetrated on the Petitioner and its supporters that it has resulted in rendering the very foundations of representative Government in Pakistan moribund, substanceless and of a farcical nature.

4-That the actions of the Respondents in accomplishing this unspeakable task is so comprehensively violative of the Constitutional protections dealing with Fundamental Rights that the scheme envisaged to operate a successful and viable parliamentary democracy has been utterly destroyed. That the fundamental rights trampled upon in this manner are Articles 9, 10, 14, 15, 16, 17, 18, 19, 22, 25, and 27. In addition the theoretical *grundnorms* of the Constitution contained in Articles 2, 2A and 4 have also been violated and contravened.

5-That so inhuman and drastic has been the denial of the Petitioner's Fundamental Rights that several recognized international human rights organisations have directly or indirectly acknowledged the tyranny inflicted upon the Petitioner such as Amnesty International, which issued a special circular on 5 April, 1994, and in their Annual Report 994 contained such assertions. Since Pakistan is also a signatory to the Universal Declaration of Human Rights 1948, the International Convention on Civil and Political Rights 1966, the United Nations Convention Against Torture and other Cruel, Inhuman and Degrading Treatment 1984 and the Convention for the Protection of all Persons in any form of Detention and Imprisonment, 1988, the aforesaid violations also render the Government of Pakistan as an Offender of International Law and that of the Law of the United Nations. No civilised country's government at the close of the twentieth Century can be allowed by accepted Conventions of International Law to violate such basic International Instruments of universal applicability and validity with impunity. This court has already held that Universal Norms of International Human Rights Law are to be respected by all countries of the world including Pakistan. It is therefore, submitted that the eventual adjudication of this matter necessarily involves keeping in view the contemporary respect for human dignity and the sanctity of genuine democracy.

6-That before adverting to the narration of facts necessary for evaluating this matter, briefly some statistics are to be noticed which give a true picture of the political strength of the MQM. In 1990, General Elections the MQM won 28 seats in the Provincial Assembly of Sindh which has in all 100 directly elected seats which means that it obtained nearly 30% of the total seats. However, the total number of votes of the people secured by the MQM were nearly twice as many as secured by the remaining candidates since a vast majority of such seats belonged to the rural areas which are thinly populated. Similarly in the National legislature, the MQM secured 15 seats, 12 of them from Karachi, the country's largest commercial centre and its biggest city. It also had three Senators. It formed a part of the Government in Sindh where it was assigned eight Ministerial departments and six Provincial Advisorships. Similarly, at the Centre the MQM had two Ministers. In addition the last Municipal Elections were held in 1987, in which the MQM swept the polls in both Karachi and Hyderabad. In both the cities it got its members elected as unopposed Mayors namely Dr. Farooq Sattar and Aftab Ahmed Shaikh from Karachi and Hyderabad respectively. In the 1993 elections the MQM on one day's notice was able to secure victory in all the Provincial Assembly seats of Sindh from Karachi and as many as 27 altogether. In the latest elections for the Senate the MQM was again successful as now its total stands at five. In the National context this makes the MQM the third largest political party of Pakistan after the Pakistan Peoples Party and Muslim League led by Mr. Nawaz Sharif. In view of the fact that its majority of followers are located in the principal Metropolitan areas of Sindh in the Southern part of the country which are next to the sea, it therefore, represents a most important area of the country.

7-That while on the basis of present seats in the National Assembly the Pakistan Peoples Party which has largely essentially obtained rural constituencies can claim to be the single largest political party in Sindh, the Petitioner has been disputing such assertions since census figures of 1961, 1972 and 1981 were engineered in a manner in which, in order to achieve a gerrymandering of electoral constituencies and to effect pre-devised consequences of distribution of resources and allocation of funds, the population of people of different places and areas were shown to be less than they actually were. At a minimum according to the document issued by the Petitioner, entitled **MQM Demands Fundamental & Constitutional Rights for Mohajir**s, the doctoring of this nature has reduced as far as Mohajirs are concerned who constitute core of MQM, their population by at least 50%. 1991, when the last census was being held it was made subject to same machination. For example the population of Nau Shero Feroz a village in interior Sindh was calculated to be 6.4 million and that of Karachi as being 6.8 million! NO wonder these results were so unbelievable that census was aborted. However, keeping in mind that the population of Sindh province is approximately over 3 Crores (30 Million), and that of Karachi alone being more than half of it, it is reasonable to projectively calculate that the Mohajirs constitute about 60% of the population of Sindh because of their vast presence in the cities of Hyderabad, Sukkur and elsewhere. Respondent No. 1, has therefore, deliberately, failed to continue or complete the census constitutionally mandated, since it is aware that the results would not be to its liking. The Petitioner conversely is insistent that accurate census on accepted scientific lines be completed since by its own calculation reinforced by available data its own projected population figures will stand scrutiny while the inaccurate claims, particularly of Pakistan Peoples Party of being the majority party of the province of Sindh demolished.

8-That the sequence of essential facts which led to the calling in of the Armed Forces to which the civilian administration in Sindh and Karachi were apparently unable to achieve is described in the next part of this petition. The scheme adopted in this petition is to divide the presentation in the format of different parts and sections so that the vast and enormous nature of the Petitioner's submission and its clearly unusual nature is capable of being comprehended with facility.

The scheme adopted for this purpose hereinafter is follows:-

(a) PART I. This contains factual details and introductory materials and submissions. The material contained in this part is in addition to averments made above in paragraphs 1 through 8.

(b) PART II. This segment contains Petitioner's submissions on the violations of Article 17.

(c) PART III,

SECTION A. It contains Petitioner's submissions on violations of Articles 9, 10, 14, 15, 17, 19, 22, 25 and 27.

SECTION B. This part contains the Petitioner's submissions on the Fundamental Rights contained in the phrase "Political Justice" which occurs in the Objectives Resolution and is a part of the Constitution under Article 2 A, and which has been so interpreted by recent pronouncements of this Court.

(d) PART IV. The Petitioner's submissions on violations of Article 18 as sources and means of livelihood of the rank and file of the followers and members of the MQM were intentionally destroyed by the Respondents.

(e) PART V. Persistent Genocide.

(f) PART VI. Mr. Altaf Hussain's statements and stand on behalf of the MQM.

(g) PART VII. Conclusions and Prayers.

II That in this petition details of several matters have been intentionally not given since the Court might like to hear them in camera proceedings; as such appropriate requests will be made at the relevant time.

PART I
INTRODUCTORY

1-That it is necessary briefly to give the historical genesis of MQM as a political party. MQM which stands for the phrase Mohajir Qoumi Movement and was formed in March 1984 in Karachi. Two years later, on 8 August 1986, it held its first public meeting at Nishtar Park Karachi, in which nearly 0.2 million people turned up. For a new political party this represented such massive public support in the biggest city of the country, that alarm bells rang in the corridors of power and in the attitude and thinking of the political parties of the country. Particularly disturbed was the Pakistan Peoples Party which since its inception had been claiming to represent the entirety of the province of Sindh.

2-That the party's creation had been preceded by various facts and events which had resulted in the feeling and awareness that those who constituted ultimately the MQM had been victimised by the State administration. Mohajirs, are immigrants from India who came to Pakistan in 1947 or—thereafter with the intent to be considered as free and equal citizens of the new State of Pakistan as conceived of in the Pakistan Resolution and as directly promised by the Father of the Nation, the Quaid-e-Azam Muhammad Ali Jinnah, when he spoke to the Constituent Assembly of Pakistan on 10 August 1947. Even more than the local people who lived in the provinces now comprising Pakistan, the Mohajirs came to the motherland at great sacrifice of lives, family and property. Over 2 million lives of Mohajirs were lost while struggling for creation of a new country. Indeed the creation of Pakistan had been in part, due to, the immense turmoil and sufferings inflicted upon the would be Mohajirs. It is well known that in 1946, realising the impending creation of Pakistan unparalleled atrocities were inflicted on millions of Muslims in Hindu majority areas. For example, in the State of Bihar such tyranny led to death of thousands of Muslims and scores of women jumped into wells along with their babies to save themselves from dishonour, and the Quaid-e-Azam Muhammad Ali Jinnah was constrained to show the photographs of such massacres to the British Viceroy which accelerated the realisation of Pakistan.

3-That despite this colossal contribution that the Mohajir community had made for the creation of Pakistan several Federal Governments meted out discriminatory treatment to them. Amongst the worst instances of discrimination and victimisation occurred when during the first Government of the Pakistan Peoples Party after the passing of the Martial Law Order 114, 1300 civil servants were sacked, mostly Mohajirs. As such a clear attempt was made by the Government to weed out in large numbers Mohajir bureaucrats to deprive them of being a part of an important instrumentality of the State. Simultaneously, Mr. Bhutto's Government provided for a "quota" system under which the local population of Sindh was accorded 40% of positions to urban areas in all government jobs and 60% of this formula was made applicable to the rural areas of Sindh. As analysed elsewhere in this petition, this policy or formula had no national application thereby emphasising that it was directed solely against the Mohajir community of Sindh. It may be mentioned that a high percentage of Mohajir community has settled in Sindh, mostly in the cities of Karachi, Hyderabad and Sukkur etc. This means that this action was essentially and entirely directed to deprive the Mohajir community of obtaining services on the basis of merit.

4-That it is noteworthy to emphasise that in July 1972, when the Peoples Party formed Government both at the Federal level and in the Province of Sindh, the legislative Assembly of the Province passed a Law by which in addition to giving the Sindhi language official status, it made it compulsory for all kinds of civil servants to know this language. When it led to riots the mandatory requirement of the knowledge of Sindhi for such people was initially dispensed with for twelve years.

5-That since discrimination of this kind started against the Mohajir community in educational institutions which continued during martial law the All Pakistan Mohajir Students Organisation (APMSO) was formally created by Mr. Altaf Hussain on June 11, 1978. Thereafter, when this student organisation was unable to totally safeguard the interests of its community the political movement for realising the Constitutional and legal rights of Mohajirs began in 1984 as described above.

6-That a central theme in the creation of these organisations by Mr. Altaf Hussain was the ideology that democracy can only be successfully run by the middle and poor educated classes. It is well known that Pakistan's National politics is dominated by a feudal elite and hierarchy. This class could not possibly countenance their replacement by people belonging to lower social orders as such they have ganged up along with the elite in the Establishment to keep the protagonist of such democratic ideas out of the corridors of powers. As an example of this phenomenon, it can be seen from published documents and media reports, that whereas the principal political parties of the country contain and boast of leadership which consists of Nawabs, Nawabzadas, Khans, Pirs, Sardars, Jagirdars, Waderas and industrialists, the MQM has attracted and successfully fielded candidates of lower and middle classes. Moreover in the electioneering process where as the former category of people spends millions of rupees, the MQM candidates and leaders hardly spent a few hundred. Thus it has been the fear of political elimination that has coalesced the political leadership of other political parties with the Establishment to keep the success of the MQM to minimum proportions. It has been a determined policy, as analysed in this petition, that the MQM was to be cut down to size by whatever means possible.

7-That in this background and atmosphere in which the Mohajirs in general and the poor people in particular gathered under the flag of the MQM and under the dynamic leadership of Mr. Altaf Hussain in 1984, when he formed this party; this new entrant into the political scene of Pakistan swept the very first election in which it participated in 1987. Thereafter the MQM maintained its political development which is analysed later in this petition.

8-That after the lifting of the Martial Law on the 31 December 1985, the political Waderas of Sindh who had strong connections with the political bourgeoisie of the province began the patronisation of criminal and goonda elements and started a reign of terror. Under this conspiracy large scale docoities were indulged in the rural areas from where the majority of the members of the Peoples Party came. Matters became so bad that transportation and travel through these areas became very hazardous which led to other crimes such as kidnapping for ransom of even foreigners such as engineers from China.

9-That in this situation, without resort to any clear legal provision of the Constitution, in June 1992, "Operation Clean Up" was launched by calling in the Armed Forces ostensibly to apprehend these robbers and dacoites working in the rural areas of Sindh. But as the MQM believed at that time, and as latter events proved, the "authorities" had in fact started this "Clean-Up" to demolish the political strength and might of MQM. The Petitioner believes that although at that time it was itself a part of both the Provincial and Federal Governments, the Establishment had been convinced by other political parties who had been wiped out, particularly in Karachi, that unless the MQM was physically prevented from becoming still stronger, it will be impossible to withstand its political might and challenge it in future. Even the present Prime Minister has admitted in an official address to the officers in training in Quetta earlier in 1994, that the problems of Sindh cannot be "solved" unless politically the vote bank of MQM is destroyed! As such being a part of the Government the MQM leadership was aware that the 1992 Operation had been moved at the behest and instance of elements who only pay lip service to the notion of genuine democracy.

10-That in line with proper democratic convention of representative Government, because of the events of June 19, 1992, the entirety of MQM membership in the Provincial Assembly of Sindh and in the National Assembly, as a mark of protest, tendered their resignations. In a country where political allegiance often goes with power and authority, this action of the MQM leadership speaks volumes for the political strength of this party.

11-That the above resignations en bloc were tendered on June 27. For the week that intervened between the advent of "Operation Clean-Up" and the departure of the MQM's members from the Assemblies, the Law Enforcement Agencies of the Respondents physically tried to kidnap and forcibly make such members change their political allegiance. A hue and cry was raised in the public and the press noted these terrible happenings which were blatantly occurring in the aftermath of the events of June 19. Such forcible change of political loyalties perpetrated on the members of Assemblies of MQM by the Respondents is unparalleled in the contemporary history of democracy. The respondents are thus guilty of the grossest violation of the Constitution and of relevant norms of contemporary International Laws.

12-That like any other political party the MQM had to take disciplinary action against some of its members for corruption or other anti-social activities. By 19 June 1992, when the military operation began, about 200 of such members of MQM had been turned out of organisation. These expelled members were collected by the Agencies working for the Respondents. By the time the "Operation Clean-Up" began these expelled members had been given the title of the "Haqiqi" group of the MQM. This group, as later events proved, was a group of terrorists, who appeared when the Army came, with the Respondent's support to eliminate the MQM.

13-That thereafter, as described in this petition, this "Haqiqi" group acted with full support of the Respondents and the local Army authorities to terrorise citizens of particularly Karachi so as to oust the political influence of the MQM and Mr. Altaf Hussain. They have also been masquerading as "the" MQM. However, their pitiful performance in the 1993 elections when they performed miserably while MQM won comprehensively establishes conclusively that it is the MQM which remains the paramount and legitimate representative of millions of people, in Sindh particularly in the cities of Karachi, Hyderabad and Sukkur.

14-That while in different ways the MQM and Mohajirs, who are chiefly identified by being Urdu speaking, the National language of Pakistan, have been victimised by the Governments of different times, their Fundamental Rights have been drastically interfered with since June of 1992. The matters have taken a turn for the worst since October 1993, when the Pakistan Peoples Party which feels directly threatened politically by the MQM has assumed powers both in Sindh and in Islamabad. This has led to a comprehensive denial of the Fundamental Rights of the Petitioner which is described in some detail hereinafter. The Petitioner has been thus constrained to file this petition since its effective functioning as a political party has been unlawfully put to an end to by the Respondents. Unless, therefore, the political and other rights guaranteed to the MQM and its members and supporters are restored by this Court as mandated by the Constitution the political functioning of the Petitioner will be impossible. This regretful eventuality would not only harm the country but its democratic future as well.

PART II

1-That the MQM has been denied its most fundamental basic political right guaranteed in the Constitution, namely, Article 17. Article 17 says:-

"Every citizen shall have the right to form associations or unions, subject to any reasonable restrictions imposed by law in the interest of (sovereignty or integrity of Pakistan, public order or morality)" (2) "Every citizen, not being in the service of Pakistan, shall have the right to form or be a member of a political party, subject to any reasonable restrictions imposed by the Law in the interest of sovereignty or integrity of Pakistan and such law shall provide that where the Federal Government declares that any political party has been formed or is operating in a manner prejudicial to the sovereignty or integrity of Pakistan, the Federal Government shall, within fifteen days of such declaration refer the matter to the Supreme Court whose decision on such reference shall be final."

2-That the scope, ambit and authorisation permitted to the political parties of the country came in for an exhaustive pronouncement by this Court in the first landmark case on this subject in *Benazir Bhutto Vs Federation of Pakistan,* 1988 SC. p 416. The *ratio decidendi* of this case was followed on the following issues by this

Court in the celebrated case of *Muhammad Nawaz Sharif Vs President of Pakista*n, 1993 SC. p 473.

3-That in these cases there; are Lengthy observations containing the jurisprudence of this Court on the extent of functioning of political parties. It was held that the term "operating" connotes the right not merely to form a political party but comprises other consequential rights including the right to approach the people for political dissemination of its programme and the right to participate in elections as well, and to form the Government should it gain a majority.

This Court further held in this case that any unlawful Governmental interference which led to frustrating 'such activity was an infringement of Article 17.

4-That other principles enunciated on this matter emphasise that the right to form an association included the right to carry out the policies and activities of such ;an association; conversely merely forming an association without being allowed to implement its goals was of no avail and tantamount to an infringement of Article 17 of the Constitution. This Court further pronounced that while working within the framework of the Constitution it was lawful for a political party to assert itself through its following and organisation and to utilise all available channels of mass communication to propagate its views in relation to the complex matters of legislation and administrative policies of the country. It was also determined that under Article 17 there is not only the guarantee to be a member of a political party but to be allowed to work for propagating and implementing the political platform of the particular party.

5-That indeed it was emphatically held in *Benazir Bhutto's Case*:-

"That indeed, our very State of Pakistan itself could never have come into existence if a political party (the Muslim League) was not allowed to function as a party, without let or hindrance". As early as in 1942 in a speech made by the Quaid-e-Azam (Muhammad Ali Jinnah) at a reception in Delhi on the occasion of his birthday on 25th December, he said "the position of Muslim India during the 200 years has been that of a ship without a rudder and without a captain, floating on the high seas full of rocks. For 200 years it remained floating, damaged, disorganised, demoralised, still floating. In 1936 with the co-operation of many others we salvaged the ship. Today the ship has wonderful rudder and a captain who is willing to serve and always to serve. Its engines are in perfect working order, and it has got its loyal crew and officers. In the course of last five years it has turned into a battleship. If members of Muslim League were allowed to contest elections only in their individual capacities and not as a "loyal crew" i.e. members of the Muslim League Party, there would have been no battle, no victory, no Pakistan." 1988 SC. at 467.

6-That it is respectfully submitted that the MQM has been denied to operate as a political party according to the principles outlined above by Respondents No 1 and 2. The manner and extent of this violation of Article 17 is very extensive and comprehensive in its effect. However, illustratively the following facts will highlight this sorrowful state of affairs.

7-That while generally the political regimes in powers have been continuously attempting to deprive the MQM of its due political status since it represented genuine lower and middle classes while its opponents were safeguarding essentially the interests of the feudal and the industrial, classes of the country, matters have greatly worsened in the last two and half years. Instances in particular that emphasise such conduct of respondent s No 1 and 2 are as follows:-

(a)-That it is a well known fact that in the last General Elections held in October 1993, the MQM was officially prevented to participate in the polls for the National Assembly held on 6-10-93. Despite the fact that these elections were held under the so-called neutral regime of Mr. Moin Qureshi, and were described to be fair and transparent, the following narration belies this myth. When the Government and the Election Commission announced that the next Elections in October 1993 will be "free", "fair" and "transparent", MQM also announced its intention to participate in the General Elections and filed the nomination papers for its candidates, not only from urban Sindh but also from Punjab, Balochistan and NWFP. In view of many facts narrated in this petition, the Petitioner was aware that its desire to do so would not be without hurdles and obstacles; still it wished to be a part of the democratic process the presence of which has been long denied to the: people of Pakistan by vested Jagirdars and Waderas who prominently figure in the two other major political parties of the country.

(b)-That sadly, however, once MQM filed nomination papers, the local Army personnel intervened and clearly demonstrated that unless compliance with their instructions was forthcoming, the MQM should be prepared to face dire consequences; indeed, there were many such occasions when Petitioner's candidates' lives were in manifest danger.

(c)-That while it is not the Petitioner's intent to give the entire catalogue of such occurrences since it fervently wishes to maintain the good image of the Army or its individual personnel that at the relevant time were posted in the relevant areas, some details are necessarily to be given to show the deprivation of the Petitioner of the protection of Article 17. Five days before the election, 5 of Petitioner's prominent workers were shot dead in cold blood by the Government sponsored terrorist group which calls itself "Haqiqi" in the presence and unfortunately under the apparent protection of the Army. On one occasion, a petitioners candidate, on a visit to his constituency was fired upon by the "Haqiqi" terrorists but he luckily escaped. On another occasion, another MQM candidate when visiting his constituency for electioneering, was stopped by the Army Officers accompanied by the members of "Haqiqi" group. The Army Officers ordered the MQM candidate to leave the area immediately and stop campaigning. Veteran MQM Senator Ishtiaque Azhar, over 70 years of age in another incident along with the local MQM candidate went to "Malir" to attend the funeral of one of Petitioner's workers, Taslim Siddiqui, who was murdered by the "Haqiqi" group, on 29 September, 1993, just before the General Elections for the National Assembly. The moment Senator Ishtiaque Azhar along with his companions reached "Malir", they were completely surrounded by the personnel of the Army and Rangers, charged with their weapons unlocked, ready to fire. A senior Army officer, came over and told Senator Ishtiaque Azhar to leave the area otherwise their funeral could be arranged instead (these incidents have already been reported to several authorities). However, undeterred by such occurrences, the MQM candidates continued with their campaign determined to participate in the elections.

(**d**)-That in this atmosphere a high ranking Army officer of the area who had been authorised by his superiors made contact with the leader of the MQM Mr. Altaf Hussain in London and told him that his party should only contest on four National Assembly seats while leaving the rest for the Haqiqi group and other pre-identified candidates. Karachi has 13 seats in the National Assembly and the MQM because of its vast following was expected to sweep perhaps all of these constituencies.

(**e**)-That after considering the truncated scope of elections that the future thus held the Petitioner approached the interim Prime Minister; sadly however, he seemed to admit his entire helplessness in the matter as according to him the overall administrative control of election management was with the local Army authorities. Subsequently, the acting President, Mr. Wasim Sajjad was also put into the picture. He too, though being sympathetic, acknowledged his lack of authority to do anything. Under these circumstances, MQM had no choice but to boycott the General Elections of October 1993. MQM also felt that by boycotting the General Elections of October 1993, the field would be left open for "Haqiqi". It would put to test their popularity amongst the people of urban Sindh by contesting the Elections virtually unopposed. However, as later results showed all the candidates thus "sponsored" and belonging to the "Haqiqi" group lost miserably and some even their deposits.

(f)-That when several parties of the International observers including from the SAARC, the EEC countries, and the United States reached Karachi to monitor the Elections, they were chiefly briefed by the local Army public relations officers and inaccurately told that the MQM was not contesting the Elections because they had lost popularity and feared heavy losses in the ensuing Elections. The International Observers thereafter went to the residence of Mr. Altaf Hussain (it only has 120 square yards of space) which is also the Central Office of MQM and suggested the party to contest elections from whichever Constituencies they were allowed by the local Army authorities MQM categorically denied the suggestions made by the Army about losing the popularity and told the International Observers that they would either contest from all the Constituencies or none at all, and as a matter of principle they should be allowed to contest from all the Constituencies according to democratic norms, if Elections which were claimed to be free, fair, transparent and democratic.

(g)-That the MQM boycott appeal was overwhelmingly successful; only two percent to five percent people turned up at the polling stations. Witnessing the success of boycott appeal, the International Observers realized that the authorities, the caretaker Government and the bureaucracy had misled them. Therefore, they pressurized the Government and the local Army authorities to allow the MQM the freedom to campaign and contest for the remaining Provincial Assembly Elections; otherwise they intimated that they will report that the elections were not free, fair and transparent. Under the pressure from these International Observers, who had come to monitor the elections, the same Army officers and indeed their superiors approached Mr. Altaf Hussain and agreed to lift all restrictions and allow free movements to his candidates in all the constituencies. After these assurances by the Army, MQM once aga in had the opportunity to show its popularity and strength by participating in the Provincial Assembly Elections on 9 October 1993 in which it won all its 27 seats on 24 hours notice with thumping majority despite the handicaps against it.

(h)-That in view of the submissions and facts given above, the forcible denial of the Petitioner to participate in the General Elections of 1993 clearly amounts to a denial of Article 17 of the Constitution. It also renders the composition of the present National Assembly legally devoid of legal legitimacy. The political atmosphere in which the 1993 Elections were held, and the events which followed this

Court's decision in Nawaz Sharif Case, leaves no doubt that the scheme to create a new Executive, was the result of an engineered election.

8-That subsequently even those MQM candidates who were elected to the Provincial Assembly of Sindh, have been meted out horrendous treatment by the Respondents 1 and 2 as well as by the Law Enforcement Agencies. The manner of the denial of their due process envisaged by Article 17 is very diversified, but even a few prominent details will establish how the MQM has been prevented from functioning as a political party. The instances that may be mentioned are :-

(a)-That Mr. Zulfiqar Haider who was elected from the Shah Faisal Colony PS 100 area was physically prevented from even, entering the constituency by the local Law Enforcement Agencies. The manner and diversity of this prevention of lawful performance of an elected member's constitutional duties is violative of Article 17 as interpreted by this Court in the landmark; cases referred to in this petition pertaining to 1988 and 1993. That the standard formula adopted by the Respondents No. 1 and 2 was that a look out was maintained for Mr. Haider and the moment he entered the constituency he was called and taken to the nearest Police Station. There he was ordered to leave the area otherwise they were going to arrest him in some criminal case. At times he was taken to the nearest Army camps and then directed to do likewise. Such actions of the Respondents have violated the Petitioner's right to work; and propagate for the welfare of the people; in addition this prohibition prevented the said Member of the Assembly from opening a working party office in the said constituency.

(b)-That similar unlawful manoeuvres were effected against other vocal and active members of the Petitioner's party such as, Muhammad Hussain, PS 94, Haroon Siddiqui, PS 95, Qazi Khalid PS 96, Hamiduz-Zafar PS 98, Farrukh Naeem PS 99, Kamran Jaffery PS 77, Mohiuddin PS 76, Rana Safdar PS 89, Shoeb Bukhari PS 80 and Afzal Anwar PS 78. That the compendium of consequences of this unlawful interference by Respondents 1 and 2 was that the MQM was prevented from utilising Available and established channels of complication to work for the political viability of the party in accordance with the accepted norms and practices of democratic governments. This violation infringes upon the rights of the petitioners guaranteed by Article 17 of the Constitution.

(c)-That another *modus operandi*, of the Respondents 1 and 2 was to demoralise the Members of the Provincial Assembly so that they not only cease to operate for the MQM but to terrorise them into yielding and succumbing to those that had the patronage of the powers that might be. A striking example of this pattern of infringement of Article 17 is provided by the case of Mr. Qamar Mansoor PS 83.

On many occasions repeatedly after he had entered his Constituency office, agents of the "Haqiqi" group opened fire with the full support of the Governmental authorities. This was done to achieve the dual purposes mentioned above. In addition to this technique employed by the respondents 1 and 2 enabled the "Haqiqi" croup to function and maintain their office. Simultaneously, many of the political offices of the Petitioner were forcibly occupied by the members of the "Haqiqi" group. These actions had the tacit and overt approval of Respondents No. 1 and 2 and their Law Enforcement Agencies. In this manner the ethos and substance of Article 17 was violated. Also, violated was the jurisprudence enunciated by this Court on this point in the *Benazir Bhutto Case* and that of *Muhammad Nawaz Sharif*. The deprivation of a political party to effectuate and implement the mandate of the people in an Election is palpably in violation of the guarantees provided by this provision of the Constitution.

(d)-That in the Provincial Assembly in Sindh the MQM fielded 28 candidates in the urban centres all of which it won comprehensively. Indeed some of these candidates like Qamer Mansoor in PS 83, secured the highest numbers of votes in the country. Considering that 36 hours previously in the National Assembly polls on October 6, 1993, the turnout was between 2% to 4%, it establishes the categorical strength and superiority of the MQM. *vis-a-vis* the other political parties in these areas of Sindh. Despite this obvious phenomenon Respondents No 1 and 2 prevented this large number of people's representatives from actively participating in the proceedings of the Assembly. The tactics utilised in this respect were varied and diverse. On many Assembly proceeding days Respondent No 2 would prevent any discussion in the Assembly of issues raised by the opposition, in which the MQM formed the nucleus by either adjourning the House or by physically preventing the MQM members from raising the issue. The most shocking episode of this nature occurred on 1 March, 1994, when Ministers of the Peoples Party Government physically attacked MQM members of the Assembly and injured several seriously. According to even news paper reports these attacks resulted in serious head injuries to some, while others were just given a sound beating. Blood was to be found all over the gallery of the Assembly. Arif Siddiqi and Qazi Khalid, Advocate, MPA's, were given severe thrashing with the butts of kalashinkoves which were allowed to be carried into the Assembly Chamber. Newspaper photographs graphically depict some of these tragic scenes. All these high-handed, unlawful and criminal actions carried out at the behest of Respondents No 1 and 2, negate the very essence of representative and democratic Government and massively violates the protections available to the MQM under Article 17 of the Constitution.

(e)-That throughout this period members of the Assembly elected on behalf of the MQM have had to face terrible persecution at the hands of the Respondents-No 1 and 2. There are innumerable criminal cases registered against many such representatives of the people. All these actions of the Government in fabricating these false cases prove the *mala fide* of Respondents No 1 and 2. Indeed so unbelievable is the extent of this malicious design of the said Respondents that Dr. Farooq Sattar, the leader of the Opposition in—the Sindh Assembly, as of the date of filing this petition, has over 80 criminal cases registered against him! Such actions have rendered even participation of MQM legislators in routine proceedings of the Assembly impossible, thereby effectively rendering their elected status as meaningless. Such reprehensible conduct of Respondents No 1 and 2 has deprived the MQM fundamentally and seriously the opportunity to function as a political party as conceived by the Constitution and the Law. *A fortiori*, serious and fundamental breach of Article 17 has occurred.

(f)-That in addition several members of MQM who are important in a political sense, either in the Assembly or otherwise, have been physically attacked or even killed by either Haqiqi terrorists or by "unknown" people who the Petitioner believes were members of the Law Enforcement Agencies. This apprehension and sound suspicion of the Petitioner has been confirmed by no less a person than the world renowned Maulana Abdus Sattar Edhi. After fleeing to London on December 7, he said in an interview with the BBC that the enormous killings in Karachi were the result of the activities of, *inter alia*, the Agencies. In this statement, which has been widely reported by the Pakistan and International press it was candidly remarked by Maulana Edhi that the blame for such killings subsequently is falsely put on either the MQM or religious sectarian groups. This unspeakable state of affairs has been devised to demolish the Petitioner as a political party thereby seriously violating the purpose and scope of the protections of Article 17. The most irreparable personnel loss that has been caused to the MQM in course of such criminal tactics of Respondents No 1 and 2 is the assassination of the MQM Chairman Mr. Azeem Tariq on 1 May, 1993. To this day political murders of this—heinous nature, and there are about over one hundred of these of The top people of the MQM, have not been surprisingly traced thus far, thus proving the callous attitude of the said Respondents in attending to cases of this kind. Thus the purpose of Article 17 allowing a political party like the MQM to conduct its affairs in accordance with the principles and norms of representative Government has been maliciously frustrated by the said Respondents.

(g)-That for greater part of the period since the last General Elections were held various parts of the urban areas of Sindh have remained in virtual condition of curfew. This has been devisedly done to curtail the MQM from either apprising the people of what is occurring or from permitting it to work effectively in a political manner as envisaged by Article 17 of the Constitution. Indeed the helplessness of Respondents No 1 and 2 to maintain normalcy in a city like Karachi or Hyderabad establishes the lack of' political credentials of these Governments. The failure of these Respondents is *per se* evidence of the political fact that nobody or at least in very large numbers accepts their false credentials to form the Government in the Province of Sindh. The inability of Respondents No 1 and 2 to maintain even minimum levels of public security is itself sufficient to prove that these calculated actions maliciously undertaken to render MQM politically ineffective have miserably failed. The failure of the said Respondents to maintain normal civic harmony in the country's largest city and other areas proves that the people have resented and rejected the fact and pretence of the said Respondents that they are "genuinely" the people's representatives of the area. In any case the lack of maintaining conventional and accepted political normalcy and routine law and order situation have rendered the guarantee of the Article 17 redundant as for as the MQM is concerned.

(h)-That the said Respondents have utilised Sate controlled media, particularly the television, to malign and damage politically the MQM. This conduct of the said Respondents is against the law declared by the superior Courts of Pakistan which have held that so far as the television is concerned, being a publicly supported enterprise, it is bound to maintain a balance between the views and policies of the Government and its opponents. The said media particularly the TV has essentially deprived the Petitioner of the substantive guarantees provided in Article 17 of the Constitution.

9-That in addition to periodic but consistent raids of Law Enforcement Agencies at MQM headquarters at "90", Respondents No 1 and 2 utilised the services of the Haqiqi terrorists, at times along with The local Army to physically take over the party's Secretariat at Al-Karam Square, Liaqatabad, Karachi. This building consisting of three blocks and including many rooms and halls was stormed by an assault led by the Army personnel on 19 June, 1992. This was the day when the Army had been called ostensibly to apprehend dacoits in rural Sindh. Since then the entire office paper work, which included thousands of files relating to party affairs were forcibly removed and the premises sealed. The Secretariat housing all the affairs of' the party included file work and papers relating to all the individual constituent units from where the MQM had contested election. MQM Labour Wing papers, Legal Aid Wing papers and files, Medical Aid Committee's files, Accounting and Financial papers, All Pakistan Mohajir Students Organisation, and papers relating to the Establishment and Personnel of the party were thus taken. The sealing of the office, the removal of its entire bureaucratic paper work, not unnaturally resulted in having a crippling effect on the MQM. This kind of havoc cannot be tolerated by any civilised society. More so it destroys the fabric of Constitutionalism and of representative Government. Hence Article 17 has sanguinary been violated by the Respondents and tantamount to a contemptuous dismissal of democracy.

10-That for facts and averments made in this part, it is clear that the respondents No 1 and 2 have actually conspired with malicious intents to damage the MQM in a number of ways so that it is unable to politically function. From the time before the elections to subsequent events narrated above it is established that the State and its principle executive organs at the Federal and Provincial levels have denied relentlessly and unconstitutionally the protections and guarantees available to it under Article 17.

11-That as submitted above, specially in para **(d)** and **(e)** the forced prevention by the State at the instance of Respondents 1 and 2 not to participate in the National Assembly elections rendered the composition of the National Assembly invalid.

PART III

SECTION A

1-That the Constitution of Pakistan guarantees Fundamental Rights including equality of status and of opportunity before the law; also guaranteed are social economical and political justice, and freedom of thought, expression, belief, faith, worship and association (subject to law and public morality).

2-That reliance in this Part will be made on several provisions (other than Article 17) of the Constitution. While some of the protections outlining and emphasising these guarantees are in the PART II of the Constitution under which this Court has jurisdiction to adjudicate on this matter, *a priori*, reference is also necessary to certain fundamental tenets of Pakistan's Organic Law under which a scheme of legal priorities has been outlined to lay the foundations of a democratic, free and representative society which believes and functions under a regime of Constitutionalism. The paramount provision in this context, *inter alia*, is Article 4 of the Constitution. Article 4 of the Constitution deals with the rights of individuals to be dealt with in accordance with law, etc. In particular sub clause 1 of Article 4 says "To enjoy the protection of law and to be treated in accordance with law is the inalienable right of every citizen". Furthermore sub clause 2 of Article 4 provides: "no action detrimental to the life, liberty, body, reputation or property of any person shall be taken except in accordance with law;"

3-That it will be demonstrated most graphically that members of the MQM and millions oft hose who believe in the political ideology of this party have been systematically and routinely deprived of this Constitutional mandate by the Respondents so that their political foot—hold in the province of Sindh becomes firmer. Indeed, since for the last many months, the Government of Pakistan has directly and indirectly created a situation in which about half a dozen to dozen citizens in urban Sindh particularly in the city of Karachi, are being murdered without the apprehension of a single assassin. Yet in a most irresponsible manner Respondent 1 has refused even to acknowledge the unspeakable situation that presently prevails in such areas. Similarly Respondent 2 is utterly oblivious to its duties in this regard. A facade is being maintained for domestic and international consumption that nothing terrible is occurring since these Respondents are aware that a Government which is unable to maintain Law and Order situation has no political or Constitutional "right" to remain in authority and must in accordance with the accepted norms and conventions of parliamentary Government resign and leave office to allow a more responsible Government to come into power.

4-That the alarming lack of Law and Order situation is *per se* so notorious that Pakistan's daily news papers are daily giving horrifying details of the tragedies that prevail in this regard in all areas where the MQM has a demonstrable political and factual majority. This honourable Court can, in accordance with the settled law, take judicial notice of this matter. Some evidence of these brutalities will be adduced with this petition in the form of details of occurrences, their photographic depiction and also a video tape to prove this point; however, recourse is always possible to examine contemporary published public account of how massively the fundamental rights guaranteed by the Constitution with regard to the protection of life, liberty and person are being trampled upon of those who belong to the MQM.

5-That the next guiding principle, light and wisdom from which must be continuously taken while interpreting the deprivation of the Fundamental Rights of the Petitioner is Article 2 and 2A of the Constitution. Not only the teachings of Islam be looked into while interpreting such matters, it is necessary also to utilise the genesis and philosophy of the Objectives Resolution in properly comprehending the Constitution. It is submitted that the denial of Fundamental Rights as explained hereinafter while fully establishing the case of the Petitioner is further made more glaring when looked at from the perspective of these two Articles.

6-That when we actually turn to the primary protection directly contained in the Constitution in the chapter dealing with Fundamental Rights mention is necessary of Article 9. Article 9 of the Constitution deals with security of person and provides as follows:

"No person shall be deprived of life or liberty save in accordance with law".

The above mentioned Article has been grossly violated and few incidents clearly explain the violation:-

(a)-Arrest and brutal murders of two MQM workers by the Police. I—On October 17, 1994, two MQM workers were apprehended and murdered. They were, namely;

1-Hafiz Muhammad Zulfiqar Ali aged 32, S/0 Haji Qamerdin resident of House No. 280-3-B, Saeed Abad, Karachi.

2-Muhammad Hanif resident of Memon Colony, Saeed Abad, Karachi.

According to details, heavy contingent of police conducted raid at the Sector office of MQM at Unit No. 115, Baldia Town, Karachi, at 4 p.m. One MQM worker was arrested while three workers in an attempt to save themselves from unlawful arrest and torture, ran from the spot on a motorbike. Police opened fire on them. Their bike slipped and two of them were arrested while the third one could escape from the spot and rescue himself. The above named two MQM workers were arrested alive and taken to the police station where they were shot dead in cold blood. Later police declared this brutal killing as an encounter and the innocent victims as dacoits. This incident was identical to the Sukkur incident which took place on 3 May, 1994.

ii-On 20 September, 1994, Mr. Muhammad Murtaza aged 27, s/o Mr. Abdul Ghafoor resident of 14/26,5E, Paposh Nagar, Karachi, died in Central jail Karachi, at 7.45 a.m. He was in charge of the Medical Aid Committee of MQM. Mr. Murtaza was arrested from Abbassi Shaheed Hospital Karachi in July 1994. After undergone severe torture by the Army, Police and other Law Enforcement Agencies, he had developed severe chest pain. On 20 September at 12.30 a.m., instead of taking him to hospital he was given injection of Novalgin at 7.15 a.m. by another prisoner who was a non qualified person. At 7.45 a.m. Mr. Murtaza died in the Jail due to lack of proper treatment.

iii-On 14 September, 1994, three MQM workers were murdered by Police due to indiscriminate firing on the mourners who had gathered at the funeral of a MQM worker Amir. They were:-

1 Asad Khan aged 21 years, s/o Abdul Qadir Khan resident of L-83, Sector 1 I-J, North Karachi, Karachi.

2 Javed Mukhtar aged 22 years, s/o Abrar Hussain resident of L-508, Sector 5-C/4. North Karachi, Karachi.

3 Muhammad Arif s/o Muhammad Iqbal resident of L-226, Sector 11-E, UP Society, North Karachi, Karachi.

That the above named and other MQM workers were busy in arranging the funeral prayer of an MQM worker Amir who was murdered by Haqiqi group a day earlier. SHO (Station House Officer) Aslam Hayat and other personnel of area police opened indiscriminate fire upon MQM workers and as a result the above named MQM workers were shot dead on the spot and several other received severe bullet injuries. Later, police claimed these cold blood murders as an "encounter" and the victims as dacoits.

(b) (i) That Respondent No 1 has devisedly utilised the services of the Pakistan Armed Forces in order to achieve its political goals of gaining political ascendancy in Sindh on the one hand while trying to politically annihilate the MQM on the other hand. As described hithertofore the Armed Forces were called in June 1992 ostensibly to apprehend dacoits who were apparently operating in rural Sindh. It is a known fact that these so-called dacoits had the political patronage of important leaders of either the Government of the day or of the present Government and formed a part of the feudal nature of rulership that unfortunately prevails in Pakistan. It is also a known fact that the Armed Forces during this apparent operation sought the permission of the Civil Authorities to apprehend 72 important people in connection with such nefarious activities. Not only Respondent No 1 or Respondent. No 2 have steadfastly refused to do so, the names in this list have also not been officially released thereby showing their complicity in encouraging such criminality. But as events have shown the calling in of the Armed Forces was actually a pretext for curbing dacoity in Sindh since they were actually extensively employed and posted in urban areas of Sindh having an MQM majority to damage it politically.

(ii) That it is respectfully submitted that it is an established fact that no Army in the world is trained to combat consistently over a long period of time domestic civilian unrest aimed at or because of the unpopularity of the incumbent political leadership. It is not necessary to articulate the well known reasons for this phenomenon; however it is well established that the use of force by the country's Armed Forces against its own population can lead to tragic results. No country's history can demonstrate this fact more emphatically than Pakistan, since half of it was lost because of such operations in 1971 when East Pakistan became Bangladesh. Accordingly by accident, design or inadvertence when military operation of this kind is launched against the country's own civilian population it is unavoidable that occurrences may result which not only bring the Armed Forces good name into disrepute amongst the citizens of the country but also creates tragedies which produce irreversible consequences. Thus the continued misuse of the Army by The Respondents No 1 and 2 was not only to satisfy the political needs of the Governments in question it presumable was aimed at harming the prestige, status and the image of the Armed Forces of the Country in the eyes of the Nation.

(iii) That while it is not intended to give complete details of the sufferings of the people of Pakistan who belonged to the MQM during the stay of the Army in the province of the Sindh, few details may still be given to prove and establish that not only the MQM was deprived by such actions to function as a political party, many of its members lost their lives or limbs in violation of Article 9 of the Constitution. Cases which deserve mention are the following:-

(a)-That in Sukkur, Army, Police and Rangers opened fire with automatic weapons upon MQM workers on 3 May 1994, killing the following five persons:-
1. Muhammad Nasir 22, s/o Muhammad Sharif Ansari of Nusrat Colony Sukkur.
2. Saeed Ahmed 19, s/o Abdul Majeed of Nusrat Colony Sukkur.
3. Muhammad Ismael 20, s/o Summo of Nusrat Colony Sukkur.
4. Muhammad Usman 30, s/o Muhammad Islam of Nusrat Colony Sukkur.
5. Muhammad Tahir 26, s/o Abdul Ghaffar of Nusrat Colony, Sukkur.

That the Government of Pakistan had claimed that those five persons were dacoits and were killed during police encounter. Contrary to these claims, consistent testimonies of the residents of the area proved that no encounter happened there. The reality is that these innocent citizens were picked up from their houses by the Law Enforcement Agencies, then blindfolded; hands tied at their backs, inhumanely treated and then shot dead in cold blood. Moreover, their dead bodies were not handed over to their relatives as the Law Enforcement Agencies buried them hurriedly in a nearby graveyard. As a corroborative evidence of this incident, the report published by the Human Rights Commission of Pakistan can be consulted.

This report was based on the data collected by the fact finding team of HRCP. The members of the team surveyed the area of Nusrat Colony, Old Sukkur, collected the facts and then compiled the report.

(b)-On 16 February, 1994, premeditated murder of a MQM worker Tanweer Hassan Khan took place. Tanweer Hassan Khan s/o Ahsan Hassan Khan, 24, of Block; 5-A, House No-323, Paposh Nagar Nazimabad Karachi was shot dead cold bloodedly by the Army while he was chalking on the wall. Tanweer was shot at point blank range by FIT (Field Intelligence Team) personnel and his body was left behind bleeding on the ground till he died. Tanweer Hassan Khan was a degree course student and associated with MQM news section. He was a senior and dedicated worker of MQM.

(c)-On 10 June, 1994, The Law Enforcement Agencies under the protection of the Armed Forces arrested 3 members of the All Pakistan Mohajir Students Organisation (APMSO) without disclosing any reason. They remained missing from the evening of 9 June 1994 for several hours. The arrested students were;

1. Muhammad Ashfaq, age 26, s/o Muhammad Yuosuf, resident of House 34/543, Street No., Bandhani Colony, Liaqatabad, Karachi.
2. Sohail Qaimkhani, age 17, s/o Yasin Khan, House No. 623, Iqbal B Line, Tando Allahyar
3. Asif Ali, Address unknown.

On the morning of 10 June 1994, the dead body of Muhammad Ashfaq was discovered at a street in Nazimabad. His body had received 17 bullet wounds. One bullet recovered is only in the possession of the Armed Forces since it had a special prohibited bore category. Similarly the mutilated body of Sohail was discovered at a street in Landhi, Karachi. Asif Ali, according to eye witnesses was brought to Abbassi Shaheed Hospital by the infamous SHO Bahadur Ali. According to evidence of the eye witnesses Asif Ali's body showed extreme torture having been inflicted upon as a consequence of which he had lost his power of speech.(This case is also reported by the daily "Guardian", London).

(d)-On 25 March, 1994, a young woman, named Naheed Butt, age 22, disclosed that at 1.30 a.m., the Law Enforcement Agencies consisting of the Rangers and accompanied by the Army personnel raided her house in order to search for her brother. When she was unable to divulge, the raiding party strip ped her naked, verbally abused her and hit her on the back; with baton sticks. There after, she was pushed in the bathroom and forced her to even take off her underclothing. This horrifying incident provoked such terror and repulsion that on the 27 of March a

General Strike was observed in Karachi and the Amnesty International has included the mention of this incident in their report of 5 April 1994 bearing number AI Index: ASA 33/WU 01/94.

(e)-Zahid Ali 25, s/o Asif Ali, resident of B 41/9, B Area, Malir Extension Colony, Karachi, was arrested by Law Enforcement Agencies. When his body was later recovered it had wounds which indicated that he was brutally tortured and then shot dead. Details were given in the Guardian of 9 July 1994.

(f)-On 3 May, 1994, cold blooded murder of MQM workers in Karachi, took place. Army, Police and Rangers opened indiscriminate fire with automatic weapons upon MQM workers, killing the following:

1. Muzamil of Block M, North Nazimabad, Karachi.
2. Zafer Iqbal of Khawja Ajmeer Nagri, New Karachi.
3. Muhammad Anwar 25, of New Karachi, Karachi.

(g)-On 5 November, 1992, the Army personnel along with other Law Enforcement Agencies raided the house of a worker of MQM Ahmed Abdul Majid resident of 14-A, Shadman Town, North Karachi, Karachi, and arrested his elder brother Ahmed Abdul Sajid aged 28 years and took him away. The relatives begged the raiding officers to release the said Ahmed Abdul Sajid since he was not even a member of MQM and had come from Sui, Balochistan, only to visit his family. He was an employee in the Sui Gas Company. A few days later, the dead body of Ahmed Abdul Sajid was recovered by Edhi Trust, a Charitable Organisation. This incident was investigated and verified by the Ansar Burni Welfare Trust (International).

7-That the Law Enforcement Agencies of Respondents No 1 and 2 have also consistently violated as a matter common practice the guarantee provided by Article 10 of the Constitution. While doing so the officials and employees of such agencies have *ipso facto* committed several cognisable offences in the guise of maintaining the law and order situation in the province of Sindh. As expected under the circumstances not only the relevant Government authorities have taken no action against the culprits who are their employees, a deaf ear has been turned to the thousands of complaints lodged in this behalf by the sufferers who belonged to MQM. In this context reference is necessary to Article 10 of the Constitution which in its operative parts reads as follows: Article 10 sub clause 1 provides "No person shall be detained in custody without being informed, as soon as may be, of the grounds of such arrest, nor shall he be denied the rights to consult and be defended by a legal practitioner of his choice".

Similarly Article 10 sub clause 2 says:-

"Every person who is arrested and detained in custody shall be produced before a Magistrate within a period of twenty-four hours of such arrest, excluding the time necessary for the journey from the place of arrest to the Court of the nearest Magistrate, and no such person shall be detained in custody beyond the said period without the authority of a Magistrate".

8-That over the last two and a half years, thousands of members and workers of MQM have been denied the protection mentioned above, resulting in:-
a-Illegal arrest of innocent citizens without any warrant.
b-Extra-judicial detention and detention in incommunicado of these politically motivated arrests.
c-Death in custody.
d-Extrajudicial execution.

9-That even a brief glimpse of a few recent cases will demonstrate the rampant violation of Article 10 of the Constitution in the manner aforesaid:-

(a)-On March, 1994, following arrest was made by FIT personnel:-

The arrest of Muhammad Naveed Ahmed s/o Nazeer Ahmed of AH-1/3 Housing Complex, Central Jacob Lines Area, Karachi, Needs mention. He was arrested by the personnel of FIT (Field Intelligence Team). While in custody, he was severely beaten and forced to sign a confession and several other papers. On 2nd April, 1994, he was transferred to the Central Jail. Muhammad Naveed informed the Superintendent of the Jail about the papers which he had signed under duress. He was going to file an application which was prepared for the Court. Sensing his intentions, the FIT personnel began to threaten his family of dire consequences and told them if the application was not stopped all of them would be eliminated. His sister was kidnapped in the process and not released until he yielded to the wishes of the authorities.

(b)-On 21 March, 1994, raids, arrests and plunders by the Rangers and police occurred. The cases that need mention are:-

(i)-The case of Khalid a worker of MQM, resident of Chandi Chowk Paposh Nagar, Nazimabad, Karachi, deserves attention. His house was ransacked and family assets were looted including a VCR, a Television, some gold ornaments and about Rs. 20,000 in cash. The raiding party comprising of Police and Rangers entered the house without any search warrant and threatened his family members not to inform the press what had happened. Plunders of this kind remained a routine occurrence for the MQM supporters.

(ii)-Similarly, Haroon Hashmi of R-816, 15-A-4 Buffer Zone, Karachi a MQM sympathiser became a victim. Police and Rangers raided his house without any search warrant, misbehaved with his family members and robbed cash money, approximately 50,000 rupees, of his family.

(iii)-Jamil Ahmed s/o Jamal Ahmed, a worker of MQM and Ex Councillor of Bazarta Line, Karachi, was arrested during such a raid, kept in confinement while his house was ransacked by the authorities.

(iv)-On 11 May, 1994, several raids at "90", the Central Office and the residence of Mr. Altaf Hussain took place. Initially the Army, Rangers and Police raided the house of Mr. Altaf Hussain leader of the MQM, for the tenth time during the past week preceding this date. Elderly gentlemen and family members were beaten up by the police by rifle butts, torn off their shirts and kept blindfolded. Those arrested are:

1. Muhammad Tasnim.
2. Zafer Ahmed.
3. Alauddin.
4. Hajan from Shah Faisal Colony unit of Karachi.
5. Zakir.
6. Naushad Ahmed.
7. S A Rizvi of New Karachi unit.

The raiding party was led by SDM (Sub Divisional Magistrate) Ms Naheed Shah daughter of Qaim Ali Shah President of Pakistan People's Party Sindh and Ex Chief Minister of Sindh subsequently. The residence of Mr. Altaf Hussain was sealed officially. During the day, these raids were repeatedly conducted with similar results.

(v)-On the same day Mr. Abdul Waheed Arshi, a MQM worker of ward 35 Burns Road, Karachi, was arrested without a warrant during a raid at his residence. Others similarly arrested were: Imran, a MQM sympathiser of Burns Road without a warrant, Yaqoob a sympathiser of MQM unit Burns Road (also without any warrant), one Arif Garki, a MQM worker of ward 85 was also arrested without any warrant, (earlier in June 1992 he had been arrested and kept in illegal detention for several months during which he was badly tortured and his property stolen from his house).

8-That many MQM Members of the Provincial Assembly were arrested from time to time apparently initially without charges. Those who were arrested by the Army on 4 May, 1994, from the residence of Mr. Altaf Hussain, 494/8, Azizabad, Karachi, and initially kept at some unknown place where they were severely tortured. They were eventually transferred to the Central Jail on 13 May, 1994. Their names are as follows:-

1. Dr Farooq Sattar, Member Provincial Assembly and leader of opposition in Sindh.
2. Dr Sagheer Ansari, Member Provincial Assembly Sindh.
3. Mr. Wasim Akhter Member Provincial Assembly Sindh.
4. Mr. Haroon Siddiqi, Member Provincial Assembly Sindh.
5. Mr. S Mohiuddin, Member Provincial Assembly Sindh.
6. Mr. Muhammad Ayub.
7. Mr. Manzoor.
8. Professor A K Shams.
9. Mr. Muhammad Yousuf
10. Mr. Khalid Murtaza

9-That on 9 May, 1994, raids, plunders, kidnappings and harassment by the Law Enforcement—Agencies and the Haqiqi group took place. Names of some victims may now be given:-

(a)-Asad, a worker of MQM and Ex member councillor committee of unit 174, North Nazimabad, Karachi. Army, Rangers and Police entered his house without any search warrant and harassed the household members.

(b)-Bhore Khan, Ex Councillor of MQM North Nazimabad Karachi. His house was raided early in the morning and in his absence his family members were verbally abused.

(c)-Syed Kamran s/o Syed Mohsin a MQM worker of unit 106, R/O 2/74, Big Plot Shah Faisal Colony No-2 Karachi. His house was surrounded and fired upon by terrorists of Haqiqi group.

(d)-Mubarak a worker of MQM and member of working committee of unit 109. He was kidnapped by the "Haqiqi" group and was tortured for whole night till morning and then released.

(e)-Afzal Anwar, member of Provincial Assembly Sindh R/O Nazimabad Karachi. His house was raided at 3.30 in the morning by Army, Rangers and Police. In his absence his family members were taken to the area police station and released after two hours of interrogation. His Charade car and two licensed rifles were also confiscated.

(f)-Farooque s/o Azher a MQM worker. His house was looted and plundered by the terrorists of the "Haqiqi" group and his household goods were set ablaze outside the house. Relatives present in the house were also beaten.

(g)-Bhole, Sagheer and Kamran were MQM workers. "Haqiqi" attacked their house and badly beat up their family members.

(h)-MQM unit office of unit 89 was set ablaze and telephone and stationary were taken away by the terrorists of the "Haqiqi" group.

(i)-On this day MQM unit office of unit 85 was also broken and things were taken away.

10-That on 8 May, 1994, many more incidents of this nature occurred, viz:-

(a)-Asghar Painter, MQM sector incharge of a sector in Hyderabad. Police opened fire and arrested him from Tilak Chari, Hyderabad, on his way back home.

(b)-Ilias, member, sector committee of Hyderabad was arrested from Tilak Chari Hyderabad by Police and was handed over to Army.

(c)-Rahim Nagat, Ex-councillor of MQM of No 11 Latifabad, Hyderabad, was arrested by agents of the Law Enforcement Agency.

(d)-Amir Iqbal, member sector committee APMSO (All Pakistan Mohajir Students Organisation) and his brother Arsalan who came to meet him from Tando Alahyar, were arrested from Hyderabad by a Law Enforcement Agency.

(e)-Irshad Ahmed, member sector committee sector 7 of Hyderabad was arrested from his residence. His mother was beaten up by the personnel of Law Enforcement Agency.

11-That incidents of 5 May, 1994, also deserve attention.

Mr. Khalid Bin Waleed, Ex Councillor of MQM, resident of Noor Apartments, North Nazimabad, Karachi. His relatives gathered at his residence to mourn the fortieth day of his father's death. Army, Rangers and Police raided his house and arrested all men present there while women were verbally abused.

12-That similarly incidents of 4 May, 1994, may be mentioned:-

(a)-An armed attack at MQM Headquarters, "90", was carried out in the morning, at 9.00 a.m. by the "Haqiqi" terrorists. MQM's members of Central Co-ordination Committee barely managed to save their lives.

(b)-That later at 5.30 p.m., the Army raided the MQM Headquarters "90". Many were arrested during this Army raid and simultaneously all the telephones at "90" were disconnected and remained so for days, under the instructions of PPP Federal and Provincial Governments. Those arrested were:-

(i) Following members of the MQM Central Co-ordination Committee:-
1. Mr. Kanwar Khalid Younus Ex Member National Assembly Pakistan.
2. Mr. Farooq Sattar, Ex Mayor Karachi Metropolitan Corporation, Ex. Member National Assembly (Pakistan), present Member Provincial Assembly and Leader of Opposition in Sindh.
3. Mr. Hasan Mussana Alvi.
4. Mr. Yousuf.
5. Professor A K Shams.
6. Mr. Bashir Farooqi.

(ii) Following members of Provincial Assembly of Sindh :-
1. Mr. Wasim Akhter.
2. Mr. Muhammad Haroon Siddiqui.
3. Mr. S M Mohiuddin.
4. Dr Sagheer Ansari.

(iii) Also arrested were many residents of the Azizabad area who had gathered at "90" and were protesting against the actions of Respondents; they were:-
1. Mr. Abdur Rauf 35, s/o Abdul Ghafoor Khan of 233/8 Azizabad, Karachi.
2. Mr. Shamim Ahmed s/o Hafiz Ahmed of 275/8 Azizabad, Karachi.
3. Mr. Ejaz Ahmed, aged 25, s/o Shmim Ahmed, 275/8 Azizabad, Karachi.
4. Mr. Fayyaz Ahmed aged 20, s/o Shamim Ahmed, 275/8 Azizabad, Karachi.
5. Mr. Irshad Ahmed aged 23 years, s/o Shamim Ahmed, 275/8 Azizabad, Karachi.
6. Mr. Asif, aged 22, s/o Abdus Sattar, 291/8 Azizabad, Karachi.
7. Syed Rehan Ali s/o Syed Israr Ali, 293/8 Azizabad, Karachi.
8. Mr. Wali Qureshi, 236/8 Azizabad, Karachi.
9. Mr. Muhammad Rais, 240/8 Azizabad, Karachi.
10. Mr. Rooh-u-Ullah Jami, 259/8 Azizabad, Karachi.
11. Syed Abul Hasan Zaidi s/o Syed Zaidi of 326/8 Azizabad, Karachi.
12. Mr. Riasat Hussain Chisti, 827/8 Azizabad, Karachi.

(c)-On this day raids on the other areas of Karachi were also conducted and following people were arrested, apparently without charges:-

1. Adnan s/o Zaheer of Buffer Zone, Karachi.
2. Mr. Bashir Uzair Alvi, aged 24, s/o Azizuddin Alvi, R-141/9, Dastagir, Karachi.
3. Mr. Dawood was arrested and his 10 motorbikes and a yellow cab were confiscated.
4. Mr. N Ahmed Siddiqui s/o M. Ahmed Siddiqui, 3-B, 7/8 Nazimabad, Karachi.
5. Mr. Shamim Ahmed Khan s/o Mansoor A. Khan, 23-D Shah Faisal Colony, Karachi.
6. Mr. Muhammad Aslam s/o Muhammad Yousuf.
7. Mr. Nadeem Altaf s/o Altaf Azad of Malir, Karachi.

(d)-That plundering was a normal routine of the Law Enforcement Agencies while raiding the houses of the MQM supporters. Illustrations of this kind are:-

1. The house of Riaz, unit incharge of MQM unit 99, was attacked by Pappi, Maqbul, Rashid and Mahfooz, members of the "Haqiqi" group. They beat up the household members, molested the women, the houses were looted and ransacked.
2. The house of Shakoor, a worker of MQM in unit 198, Malir Colony Karachi, was raided by the personnel of the Law Enforcement Agencies. As usual ladies were molested, household members were beaten up and valuables were looted.

(e)-That on 25 April, 1994, arrest of MQM Senators took place. These MQM Senators included, 70 year old Mr. Ishtiaq Azher, lady Senator Nasreen Jalil and Mr. Aftab Ahmed Shaikh, Advocate; they offered their voluntary arrests to the authorities as a protest against continued atrocities inflicted upon Mohajirs and renewed upsurge of terrorist activities of the "Haqiqi" group resulting in killings of many MQM workers. Subsequently, however, all these Senators were booked on false charges at the behest of Respondents No 1 and 2.

13-That the illustrative list given above, though not exhaustive, by any means, eloquently proves that:-

(a)-That members and supporters of MQM were routinely rounded up for months to-.act as a deterrent and to ensure that the party, while being deprived of its workers to operate viably in the country, also lost its membership in order to demolish it as a political entity.

(b)-That the Law Enforcement Agencies were allowed a free hand by the Respondents to enter in the houses and property of the members of the MQM and its supporters so that they be deprived of the sanctity of security of their living and business dwellings.

(c)-That the non production of hundreds and thousands of workers And members of the MQM before magistrates was designed as an action *in trrorem* by the employees of the Respondents 1 and 2 to discourage and prevent them from actively supporting their party.

(d)-That the detaining in illegal confinement of scores and scores of such MQM supporters was again aimed to decapacitate the party from effectively participating in the normal political activities conferred upon it by the Constitution.

(e)-That gross high handedness by the Law Enforcement Agencies of Respondents No 1 and 2 in the manner described above resulted in such massive violation of Articles 9 and 10 of the Constitution that effectively the MQM was prevented from performing its activities as authorised by the Constitution and as authoritatively pronounced by this Court in landmark cases of 1988 and 1993 in which the main petitioners were the two Prime Ministers of this country namely, Ms Benazir Bhutto and Mian Muhammad Nawaz Sharif'.

14-That palpability of falsity of cases against MQM leadership and admission of "mistake" by the Law Enforcement Agencies, has been a discernible phenomenon.

15-That it has been repeatedly falsely claimed by the above named two Respondents that the action taken against the MQM was because its members were acting as "terrorists" or that they were ordinary criminals. Not only such vague and unsubstantiated accusations are self-serving in nature but utterly preposterous. The party believes and wants to function in accordance with law and has been indeed functioning under the Constitution. Indeed the main operation of any political party being its representative character, the MQM has amply demonstrated its high quality performance in winning by large margins the elections in which it has participated. The ridiculous nature of the trumped-up charges against the MQM leadership can be judged by this fact alone that Senator Ishtiaq Azher who is over seventy years old has been accused of kidnapping for ransom! This honourable Court may be pleased to summon this honourable senator of MQM to see his frail and elderly person and to judge how a reputed journalist who is physically so unwell that his hands tremble because of age and sickness, can possibly kidnap anyone as absurdly alleged by the Government. As such it is respectfully submitted that the nature of cases continuously been registered against the MQM leadership and workers represents a malicious policy of the Government to cripple its effective functioning in the politics of the country. *Pari passu,* with this fact is the awareness that law Enforcement Agencies can commit horrendous blunders while acting ostensibly to enforce the law. In the tragic but well known case of Tando Bahawal in which nine ordinary villagers were shot dead in cold blood by the Army personnel, the military authorities themselves, after the matter received wide spread notoriety Court Martialled the concerned officer for acting contrary to law. However, this isolated incident has not been followed by any of the other Law Enforcement Agencies who have routinely otherwise followed to hide their unlawful actions against the population by bogus and self-serving pronouncements. But this proves that even the most disciplined and trained force of the country can commit the kind of mistake in which ordinary citizens end-up dead.

16-That as authoritatively held by this Court in 1993, the Constitution of Pakistan guarantees the citizens and no less, the Nation's political parties the inviolability of dignity of man. Article 14 of the constitution deals with inviolability of dignity of man, etc. Article 14 sub clause 1 reads "The dignity of man and, subject to law, the privacy of home, shall be inviolable". Article 14 sub clause 2 reads "No person shall be subjected to torture for the purpose of extracting evidence".

17-That though the scope and ambit of "dignity" still requires an exhaustive pronouncement by this Court, it is still submitted that at a minimum it mandates that the citizens and the political parties would be accorded by the State and the Government both at the Federal and Provincial levels, the normal courtesies and privileges, which civilised behaviour warrants the world over. The details given above of specific instances are also tantamount to a gross violation of Article 14. No civilised modern country whose Government as now represented by Respondents No 1 and 2 (which never stops in proclaiming itself as "democratic") can possibly systematically humiliate hundreds and thousands of its citizens simply because they belong to a certain political party. The membership of MQM and its leadership have been the consistent victim of State enforced brutalities and humiliation which is in violation of the aforesaid constitutional mandate.

18-That there are numerous concrete cases fully exemplifying the above sufferings of the MQM as a political party and its leadership and its membership at large. A few tragic and notorious cases of this nature can be briefly mentioned:-

(a)-The most recent case of this nature is the occurrence of 29 November, 1994, at Korangi, Karachi. In the garb of arresting some alleged criminals about whom nothing was divulged, in an area of about four square miles, the Law Enforcement

Agencies cordoned off a number of villages inhabited by the followers of MQM and forcibly gathered over 5000 people which consisted of all old people, all young men and even children over the age of 12. After lining up all the male people of the large locality in a shameful manner (naked and hands tied at their backs) like herds of cattle, the State officials entered the poor dwellings and huts of this poor community. They dishonoured the women as they pleased and indulged in large scale stealing of jewellery of women that remained in-doors terrified and speechless. The area was sealed in such a way that nothing, not even an Ambulance, was allowed to enter or leave the area. This one incident alone explains the biased and hateful treatment of Mohajirs by the local Army, Rangers and other Law Enforcement Agencies. In this incident, on November 29, 94, a pregnant lady resident of sector 33-D, Korangi, Karachi had labour pains at 4.00 A.M. Her husband Muhammad Imran requested the raiding party to allow him to take his wife to the hospital. The officials blatantly refused and did not give permission. She delivered a still baby. Thereafter, despite the cry and humble request of the parents, they were not allowed funeral for over twelve hours.

(b)-Other incidents of this kind involved similar raids on MQM followers in various colonies in which they lived. The most hated occurrence of this kind in the past occurred on 30 September 1988, during the first tenure of Government of the present regime. This is the Hyderabad massacre in which, under a ruthless and inhuman conspiracy hardened and known criminals and dacoits were provided weapons. They were provided transport by the Government authorities and allowed to enter the city in the evening and directed to proceed to the congested part of the city and in half an hour indiscriminate shooting spree, more than two hundred MQM supporters were shot dead. This was done in a medieval hunting manner which is both shocking and abhorrent to the civilized mankind. Behaviour of this kind not only violates several Articles of the Constitution occurring in Part II thereof dealing with Fundamental Rights, it infringes sub clause 1 of Article 14 of the Constitution. Since the Nazi atrocities in which the human race was degraded by being killed or herded together for massacres or humiliation, the aforementioned instances provide the most harrowing and obnoxious illustration of meting out gross indignity to mankind by a Government which claims to be civilised, Islamic and democratic.

(c)-That in all these instances in which large sections of the population were put in the formation of herds, the aim was to either extract confessions or to obtain forced evidence against members of the MQM who were already in custody or those that the authorities wished to imprison to adversely effect the political functioning of the MQM. Numerous attempts by the MQM as a party or by individual people who belonged to the MQM to register police complaints against such unlawful activities, proved futile. Nevertheless these actions of Respondents No 1 and 2 violate Article 14 sub clause 2 of the Constitution in the manner aforesaid. The Respondent Governments have exhibited the most manifest contempt for the concept of dignity of man and are thus guilty of violating these cherished rights of the Petitioner.

(d)-That other instances involving schematically the same nature of events are borne out by further instances of this kind. For the past few weeks local Army, Rangers, Police and other Law Enforcement Agencies under the State patronage have adopted a new method of humiliating and of physically and verbally abusing the innocent Mohajirs. They imposed undeclared curfew, sealed off some areas, broke into the houses of innocent Mohajirs on the pretext of "searches". During "search" they humiliated physically and verbally the female members of the house. The male members were usually dragged down to the streets, their clothes torn and made to undress. They were also forced to stand in the scorching sun heat for hours. Few instances and their details are given below:

(i) On 19 September, 1994, in the Lines area which is a centrally located area in Karachi was completely sealed for over 48 hours and activities of above nature carried out.

(ii) On 21 and 22 September 1994, Sector 5-D, New Karachi, was cordoned off for over 30 hours. On the same day Nasir Colony, Korangi, Karachi, was cordoned off for over 24 hours and similar search operation conducted.

(iii) On 26 September 1994, Nata Khan Goth and the adjacent areas of Shah Faisal Colony, Karachi, were sealed completely for such searches.

(iv) On 13 October 1994, C area of Liaqatabad, Karachi, was sealed between 11.00 am. to 1.00 a.m. and searches of this kind performed.

(v) On 15 October 1994, the area of Hasrat Mohani Colony in Pak Colony, Karachi was sealed for over 24 hours for conducting such searches.

(vi) Maskan apartments and Alah Noor apartments in Blocks 7, and 5 of Gulshan-e-Iqbal, Karachi, were cordoned off and house to house search was conducted in the same manner; also Paposh Nagar and Ashraf Colony in Nazimabad, Karachi, were completely sealed. Even a single ambulance was not allowed in the area and an elderly man died because he could not be taken in hospital while such searches were in progress.

(vii) On 20 October 1994, similarly the Nasir Colony in Korangi, Karachi, was sealed at 5.00 a.m., and the search continued for over 48 hours.

(viii) On 18-21 October 1994, Sectors l-D And l-S of Malir, Karachi, were cordoned for over four days. During search more than four hundred Mohajirs including children and elderly persons were arrested and brought to an Army play ground. The members of the Haqiqi identified the workers of MQM who were beaten up.

(ix) On 23 October 1994, Sahafi Colony (Journalist Colony), Karachi, was sealed from 3.00 a.m., to 7.00 p.m. All the male members between 12 years and 70 years of age were forced to come out of their houses and the female members were abused and molested during the search operations.

19-That since the commencement of the Army Operation "Clean-Up" on 19 June 1992, Army, police and other Law Enforcement Agencies have been adopting other methods to crush MQM. For this purpose they have aided the activities of Haqiqi group to kidnap, torture and kill MQM workers, its sympathisers and supporters. Thus thousands of MQM workers and sympathisers have had to go into hiding for the safety of their lives and are still away from their families for months. Still thousands of MQM workers have been arrested; other kidnapped, tortured, killed and many rendered disabled and destitute, jobless and homeless. In a number of cases the only bread-winner of the families have died. Despite All these atrocities inflicted upon Mohajirs, they have remained united under the flag of MQM. Now under the guise of house to house "search" (allegedly for finding individuals or weapons) the Mohajirs are subjected to such a deplorable attitude that they feel the most humiliated people on the earth because the perpetrators of their brutality are their own countrymen. These actions taken by the Government of Pakistan, are in total contravention with the Constitution of Pakistan, Part II, dealing with. Fundamental Rights.

20-That in addition to violation of the previous Articles of the Constitution, it is clear that many unlawful actions of Respondents No 1 and 2 have also violated Article 15 of the Constitution which guarantees freedom of movement Article 15 of the constitution deals with freedom of movement, etc. Article 15/1 reads as "Every citizen shall have the right to remain in, and, subject to any reasonable restriction imposed by the law in the public interest, enter and move freely throughout Pakistan and to reside and settle in any part thereof".

21-That by the continuos cordoning off, various areas of the city of Karachi particularly, in the aforesaid manner, Respondents No 1 and 2 through the Law

Enforcement Agencies at their command, prevented free movement of the MQM workers thus effectively preventing their political and social operations. All these actions have failed to subjugate the people of Karachi particularly, which by and large are MQM supporters; it is to be particularly noticed that the Prime Minister and indeed the President have now publicly acknowledged the need to have parleys about achieving harmony in Karachi by inviting and involving the MQM. This is a belated and a disguised attempt by the ruling regime to maintain its ruling status and hegemony in the Province of Sindh. But it p roves the crucial significance of the MQM and that even presently, Respondents continue parleys with it. Had the MQM not been denied its right to move freely in the areas of their political influence, matters would not have deteriorated as they have.

22-That in 1992 and again in 1994, when the founder and the supreme leader of the MQM wished to address public gatherings in places other than Sindh, the Federal authorities conspicuously denied such opportunity by refusing him permission to address these public gatherings. This also violates Article 19 of the Constitution which guarantees freedom of speech. It provides:

"Every citizen shall have the right to freedom of speech and expression, and there shall be freedom of the press."

23-That by denying the acknowledged leader of MQM to make these public addresses and by preventing MQM membership and leaders to move freely in the country Respondents No 1 and 2 have violated Fundamental Rights of the Petitioner contained Articles 15 and 19 of the Constitution. In particular the Respondents have been at pains to prevent Mr. Altaf Hussain from making a political entry in the Punjab.

24-That conceptually allied to a free exercise of the rights is the callous treatment given to the stranded Pakistanis on whose behalf the MQM has been forcefully advocating for repatriation. In particular it should be borne in mind that the previous Federal Government under Mr. Nawaz Sharif had arranged for the repatriation of a few hundred stranded Pakistanis during 1993. The present regime has not only totally stopped this process but has declared that it will not allow them to settle wherever they want since it apprehends that they will opt to go to Karachi thus increasing the strength of MQM. This seriously damages the MQM and the concept of free movement of the citizens in the country.

25-That about 250 000 Pakistanis are languishing in Bangladesh since 1971 and are living there in subhuman conditions in 66 Red Cross Camps. Their repatriation to Pakistan is the responsibility of Government of Pakistan. Successive

Governments in Pakistan have made promises several times but the reality is that they are still waiting for their repatriation to Pakistan. They are deprived of the basic necessities of life and fundamental rights such as proper food, clothing, housing, education, proper sanitation, medical relief and participation in the National activities.

26-That unnecessary delay in their return to Pakistan, particularly now at the behest of the Respondent No 1, is in contravention with the article 25 and 15 of the Constitution of Pakistan and International Law as well. Repatriation of these stranded Pakistanis is the Constitutional duty of the Government and failing the fulfilment of this duty, the Government of Pakistan is perpetually violating a number of Fundamental Rights of the petitioner and of its party members and workers.

27-That the Respondents 1 and 2 have also violated Article 16 of the Constitution by preventing continuously since the involvement of the Army authorities in June 1992, the right of the workers, members and sympathisers of the MQM to assemble in accordance with the age old conventions of democracy. Petitioner's Right to discuss and disseminate matters and issues relating to national, political, economic and social spheres of the lives of the people has been denied. This has been done either by enforcing an undeclared curfew, or by preventing access to places of public congregation or by the use of strong arm tactics by deployment of personnel of either the "Haqiqi" group or the Law Enforcement Agencies. Indeed this ceaseless activities of the Respondents has totally demolished the foundations of a democratic system which depends on the free flow of ideas and suggestions in the politically conscious segments of the society.

28-That the Respondents have also violated Article 19 of the Constitution which says:-

Freedom of speech, etc.—"Every citizen shall have the right to freedom of speech and expression, and there shall be freedom of the press, subject to any reasonable restrictions imposed by law in the interest of the glory of Islam or the integrity, security or defence of Pakistan or any part thereof, friendly relations with foreign States public order, decency or morality, or in relation to contempt of Court, 13 [Commission of] incitement to an offence".

29-That since June 1992 the Respondents aforesaid have intentionally conspired to put a clog on the freedom of speech in such a way that MQM is unable to put its views across to the public. As already described in this petition elsewhere workers of the Petitioner have been indeed killed while placing posters or while chalking the walls which is a basic means of reaching the public in Pakistan. One of the well known Karachi's newspaper, namely, "Amn", which is a MQM sympathiser has been the prime target of this policy. For example its respected editor Mr. Ajmal Dehlvi was arrested on 6 September 1992 and taken to Police Station, Civil Lines. There he was told by the D S P and the S D M that they had been ordered by their "superiors" to keep him as a "state guest". This was disclosed when Mr. Ajmal Dehlvi asked them to show him a copy of an FIR in pursuance of which he had been arrested. During the course of this session over 200 journalists came to the Civil Lines Police Station from a Defence of Pakistan Day function when they learnt what had occurred. For one day Mr. Dehlvi was kept at the Police Station under arrest after which he was released as no F I R existed against him and the Respondents were apprehensive of adverse public reaction from the local journalist community.

30-That similarly, another standard tool utilised by the Respondents to curtail freedom of' speech is by withholding State sponsored advertisements. A striking example of this kind of victimisation and violation of Article 19 is provided by the case of the daily evening news paper "Parcham". As a sympathiser of MQM it has been penalised not being given a single advertisement since the last two and half years.

31-That the next Fundamental Right violated of the MQM as a political party is by penalising its workers, followers and members by denying them access and admission to educational institutions on the basis of their merit. In this context Article 22 of the Constitution which deals with the safeguard as to educational institutions in respect of religion, etc. provides in sub clause 3(b):-

"no citizen shall be denied admission to any educational institution receiving aid from public revenues on the ground only of race, religion, caste or place of birth."

32-That a "Quota System" was imposed in 1971 by the first Pakistan Peoples Party regime for entry into colleges. It was based on a distinction between rural and urban population. The proclaimed idea behind this urban and rural quota was to provide equal opportunity in education, to the people of rural areas for higher education. The execution and the way of implementation of this system did not conform with the pretence of its proclamation.

33-That the rural and urban areas exist in all the four provinces of Pakistan. The quota system was only executed in Sindh province. The *rasion d'etre* of this formula was in truth to accommodate people with less merit in rural Sindh at the expanse of the urban population in which well over 90% population belongs to MQM. Thus irrespective of the constitutionality of *quotas*, in this instance it was specifically done to bolster up the people of rural Sindh from the constituencies of which the nucleus of the Leadership of the ruling party of the time came and which has formed presently the Federal Government and that of the Province of Sindh. Unfortunately, the ruling party has not reconciled with the fact that while even today it asserts to being the dominant party from the Province of Sindh it is not in fact so. The Province of Sindh has a population just over three crores, that is over 30 million out of which the followers and workers of the MQM chiefly in the metropolitan areas of Karachi, Hyderabad and Sukkur constitute about 17 million. Thus as a matter of fact it is the MQM which constitutes the majority party in the Province of Sindh. However by gerrymandering of constituencies or by patently unequal distribution of numbers in different constituencies between rural and urban Sindh, the MQM despite completely sweeping the polls in the areas of its majority, is not able to win the number of seats in the Sindh Assembly or in the National Assembly which its population should in principle get. Thus there is a continuous desire in the present ruling party.(the Pakistan Peoples Party) which has formed the Government of the Federation in 1973, in 1988 and again in 1993 to falsely claim to represent the Province of Sindh presumably because a considerable number of its loyalists are indigenous people of Sindh. The people of Pakistan as proclaimed by the Quaid-e-Azam constitutes the single Muslim Nation. There is no room for proclamation which aim at emphasising the parochial affiliation or background of the people of a certain Province. As such the clearly acceptable criteria for representing any Province is Majority. As the MQM has numerical majority in the Province of Sindh, it has legal right in any representative Government to be the nominee of the people of this province.

34-That accordingly three Peoples Party Governments have deprived the majority of the population of Sindh, their Constitutional educational opportunities to educate their children and youth on the basis of their merit. Thus Article 22 has been violated by the Respondents No 1 and 2 in order to irreparably damage the MQM and the future of the children of its followers.

35-That the question that therefore, naturally arises for consideration is that:-

a—If this system was introduced to provide equal opportunity to the people of the rural areas then why this system was only executed in the Province of Sindh?

or conversely, b—Why this criterion for the people of urban and rural areas was not applied in other provinces?

36-That in the Sindh province of Pakistan there is a distinct demarcation on linguistic basis; that is the Mohajirs are predominant in the urban areas while the rural areas are generally populated by the Sindhis. In the other provinces of Pakistan this kind of demarcation does not exist.

37-That the *mala fide* intentions behind imposition of this quota system and its execution in Sindh province only, were to subdue the Mohajirs, and to deprive them of their fundamental rights of education. This clearly proves that this quota system was objectively and ostensibly aimed to subjugate, discriminate and deprive the followers and supporters of MQM of their fundamental rights of education. As Article 22 has thus been violated in a pernicious manner it has drastically effected the prospects of the MQM which are otherwise available to it and its followers under the Constitution.

38-That similarly in services and of equality before the law the MQM has been targeted and discriminated against by the Respondents No 1 and 2. Article 25 of the Constitution deals with the equality of the citizens. It says:-"All citizens are equal before law and are entitled to equal protection of law."

39-That the Census figures of 1961, 1972 and 1981 were so doctored that the population of urban areas of Sindh, where the predominant incumbents are Mohajirs, was shown 50% less than that of the actual population. Besides quota system and other Legislative measures which were adopted to subdue the Mohajirs of their actual representation and legitimate rights in the Federal and Provincial services, professional institutes and representation in the national and provincial assemblies, the distorted population figures have left baneful tremendous effect in the development of MQM.

40-That the population of Karachi city has exceeded 15 million people. The present interior minister Mr. Naseerullah Babar of the Peoples Party Government has recently commented that the population of the city of Karachi is more than 12 million. That works out to be 10% of the total population of the country. This figure suggests that the National Assembly seats for only Karachi division should be 10% of the total strength and which work out to be 21.7 seats approximately. Contrary to this realty only 13 constituencies of National Assembly exist in Karachi city, This reflects great disparity as regards the population of Mohajirs and their representation in the National Assembly. Likewise the constituencies of the Provincial Assembly of Sindh for Karachi city should be 46 in number to correspond with the actual population.

41-That to deprive the citizens of their representation to their number and their right of being represented in the National and Provincial Assemblies and Senate of Pakistan on such basis alone is a right conferred by the Constitution of Pakistan to every citizen.

42-That another Article of the Constitution which deals with singular matters is Article 27. It deals with safeguard against discrimination in services. Article 27 sub clause 1 reads as follows:-

"No citizen otherwise qualified for appointment in the service of Pakistan shall be discriminated against in respect of any such appointment on the ground only of race, religion, caste, sex, residence or place of birth."

43-That in Federal and Provincial services the urban quota is 7.6% and 40% respectively and the present strength of Mohajirs is 1% and 15% only. These figures do not satisfy even the presently allocated quota that needs to be enhanced to compensate the disparity. Disparity and discrimination can be well understood by comparing the strength the Mohajirs in the Federal, Provincial and semi-governmental services.

44-That this gross difference clearly explains the biased and unjust attitude of the successive regimes and of the present Government in particular. Thus both Articles 25 and 27 stand violated. These extremely adverse actions of the Respondents No 1 and 2 have enormously damaged the MQM as a political party and denuded its supporters and members of economic integrity and have also in the process denied to a large segment of the Pakistani population which lives in the urban areas of Sindh, their lawful and legitimate rights of equality before the law and to earn their livelihood as guaranteed by the Constitution.

45-That in the perspective of the submissions made in this petition (i.e. para 40 and 41 above) the respondents have in effect put a ban on the activities of the Petitioner which it is entitled to exercise under the Constitution. It is clear that under an engineered format initially the then Government was forced to leave Office despite enjoying 2/3rd majority, than under the garb of neutral imported Cent ral Government authority, elections were held which have produced a result which we are now witnessing., Under this scheme the Petitioner was deprived from holding all elected offices, from that of the Municipality of Karachi to that of the National Assembly.

SECTION B

1-That given at the outset of this PART of the petition was an enumerated list of the Fundamental Rights on which reliance is placed to invoke the original jurisdiction of' this Court under Article 184 Sub Clause 3. While "political justice" does not find mention as such in Part II of the Constitution, this Court has nevertheless made observations in leading recent cases that by the incorporation of the Objective Resolutions in the Constitution which contains this concept, *per se* it has now assumed the status of directly enumerated Fundamental Rights. Be that as it may it is undeniable that while the conceptual and lexicographic contours of this right still awaits an exhaustive examination, in the light of existing *dicta* this right manifestly embraces a commitment by the Constitution that political activity of recognised parties will be respected and allowed to continue unhampered.

2-That as held by this Court, therefore, that political parties compete to form government, signifies that not only the ruling party of the time has this right and privilege to operate with full vigour every other party has similar prerogative. Indeed this is the *sine qua non* of parliamentary government which is protected and projected for enforcement in accordance with its recognised norms by the Constitution of the country. The MQM, in view of the facts narrated above has been ruthlessly denied such a right for the last two and half years leading to inflicting irreparable damage to it in the body politics of this country. Indeed since available pronouncements of this Court in the jurisprudence enunciated on this topic emphasise that denial of this nature will be tantamount to a violation of Article 17, it is submitted that Respondents 1 and 2 have conspired and acted maliciously to deprive the Petitioner the enjoyment of this right particular right as well.

3-That available observations of this Court also indicate that the expression "political justice" also incorporates diversified facets of principles of democracy as enunciated by Islam, it is submitted that the compendium of denial of Fundamental Rights in the manner aforesaid deserve the severest condemnation and a determination that the Petitioner has been maliciously prevented from operating as a political party of high profile in provincial and national politics of Pakistan. This is a sinister schematic formula maliciously acted upon by the ruling regime not only to damage the MQM but to irreparably harm the national interest and integrity of the country.

4-That reluctantly but firmly the petitioner respectfully submits that the relentless and wilful desire of the present ruling Federal Government comprising mainly the Pakistan Peoples Party which has demonstrated since the 1971 crisis that resulted in the dismemberment of the country, that it is determined to oust all contenders for power by the use of non-political means as well, that the actions impugned herein were calculated to politically damage the MQM. When the aforementioned military operation was begun on 19 June 1992, the authority of the Federation vested in a Government of the Muslim League with which Petitioner was a partner. It signifies that the real Establishment of the country that might be, decided to impose certain political conclusions as a *fiat accompli* in the country by trying to achieve the ouster of the MQM from provincial and National politics. This assertion of the Petitioner is based upon its own knowledge and information of the Affairs of State of the relevant time.

5-That in the historical context in which Pakistan was created it is crucial to remember that the then Prime Minister of Sindh, Sir Ghulam Hussain Hidayatullah before the partition said in the meeting of The Council of All India Muslim League on the 9 June 1947 under the chairmanship of the Quaid-e-Azam Muhammad Ali Jinnah, at Imperial Hotel, New Delhi that in the new country of Pakistan as a matter of principle Muslims from all over India would come to inhabit the new State. The new separate Nation of the Muslims of the Indian Sub-Continent would be sovereign and would be providing a heaven of refuge to the Muslims. This particular address of the then Prime Minister of Sindh provides eloquent historical testimony that the immigrants while free to settle anywhere in the new State were particularly being welcomed in the then province of Sindh. It is noteworthy to emphasise that as such the creation of Pakistan was in large measure due to the political decisions of the then Sindhi Government (see **The Transfer of Power, 1942-47, Volume II, pp 244-246, published by Her Majesty's Office, London 1970**). That similarly the policy declaration of the British Government made by Earl Mountbatten in pursuance of the commitment made by the future Governments of India and Pakistan was to the effect:-

"The two Governments declared that "It is their intention to safeguard the legitimate interests of all citizens, irrespective of religion, cast or sex. In the exercise of their-normal civic rights all citizens will be regarded as equal and both the Governments will assure to all people within the territory the exercise of liberties such as freedom of speech, the right to form associations, the right to worship in their own way and the protection of Their language and culture.

Both Governments further undertake that there shall be no discrimination against those who before August 15 had been political-opponents". "(Op. cit. Volume XII, pp 781-782).

6-That millions of followers of the MQM have a right to demand as a matter of political justice that the promise and commitment made to the Muslims of India to migrate to the new State of Pakistan to enjoy and participate fully in National polity made by the Fathers of the Constitution which is binding on all State institutions. However in the manner aforesaid it is apparent that Respondents No 1 and 2 are determined to deny the petitioner all such political privileges and liberties in order to gain undue advantage in State affairs and to deny the same to the MQM.

7-That in this context the famous first address of the Quaid-e-Azam to the Constituent Assembly of Pakistan on the 10 August, 1947, it is also of everlasting guiding dynamics. The Quaid-e-Azam (Muhammad Ali Jinnah) said :-

"You may belong to any religion, or cast or creed, that has nothing to do with the business of state (hear, applause).... We are starting in the days when there is no discrimination, no distinction between one community and another. We are starting with this fundamental principle that we are all citizens and equal citizens of one new State (loud applause)".

8-That despite the ethos of such principle and historic Legacy millions of followers of the MQM are being treated even below the category of being second class in their own country and are denied by force of State Agencies their due share and role in the affairs of State. This needs immediate redress if Pakistan is to be preserved as a sovereign democratic State as conceived of in 1947.

PART IV

1-That like in all civilised countries, the Constitution of Pakistan protects lawful conduct of earning a means of livelihood. Article 18 of the Constitution provides:-
"Freedom of trade, business or profession. Subject to such qualifications, if any, as may be prescribed by the law, every citizen shall have the right to enter upon any lawful profession or occupation, and to conduct any lawful trade or business: Provide that nothing in this Article shall prevent:-

(a) the regulation of any trade, or profession by a licensing system; or
(b) the regulation of trade, commerce or industry in the interest of free competition therein; or

(e) the carrying on, by the Federal Government or a Provincial Government, or by a corporation controlled by any such Government of any trade, business, industry or service, to the exclusion complete or partial of other persons".

2-That the philosophy of this Article of the Constitution is that State will not interfere in the lawful business or trade of the citizens so that they can sustain themselves economically. The MQM, its leadership, rank and file and supporters have been consistently made the target of victimisation with the aim of deprivation of economic and financial sustenance. There are also many instances of shocking nature exhibiting targeting of the MQM supporters in this manner. All local public offices of Respondents 1 and 2 adopt a stance and posture to greatly discourage MQM inclined business houses from remaining in operation. In a third world country like Pakistan, where bureaucratic control and red tape can effectively close down any economic enterprise, such a policy has clearly effectively demolished the very being of the MQM as an organisation. A few notorious cases of this category may be mentioned in this context which also exhibit the pattern of economic victimisation of the Petitioner and its supporters.

3-That for example MQM ex-councillor Mr. Khalid Bin Waleed whose family was running small business in the form of a factory, managed by his brothers in Karachi, was effectively shutdown after the "Operation Clean-Up" began in June 1992. The Law Enforcement Agencies alone or with the Haqiqi group would either prevent the entry of the owners in the factory or else they would come periodically and demand *bhatta*. Since neither of these tactics could be acceptable to the owners, this business was closed down. Another MPA of MQM Kamran Jaferi whose family owned a general merchant store was also shut down because repeatedly the representatives of Respondent No 2 in the garb of checking licenses etc., harassed the owners. This is a standard technique which has been utilised against scores of MQM activists in order to deter them from working or supporting the party. For example MQM MPA Babar Khan Ghori owned a marriage hall cum Garden in North Nazimabad, Karachi. The Respondents in order to terrorise or win over the said MPA tried to persuade him to desert the MQM. On his refusal to do so, Respondent No 2 sealed his premises which remains so closed until now. Another notorious case is that of Ms Shenaz Saigol, who operated a family construction business. Her husband Mushtaq Saigol had been an Advisor in the Sindh Government between 1990 and 1992. The Respondents by diversified means completely wrecked her business because of their family support for the MQM. She was even arrested and tortured along with some of the members of the family. She eventually obtained relief from personal arrest from the Sindh High Court, but the family business stands shattered.

4-That these examples have only been given to buttress the submission made above. The truth of the matter is that in more ways than one the Respondents tried relentlessly to cause grave and irreparable financial damage to MQM and its supporters so that the party becomes less effective. Hence the guarantee provided by Article 18 has been seriously violated by the Respondents.

PART V

PERSISTENT GENOCIDE

1-That both under the Pakistan Constitutional law and International law, large scale killings by or on behest of the State, of through its connivance, of a particular group class or ethnic minority is utterly prohibited. Those who perpetrate this heinous crime are themselves guilty of the international crime of Genocide. Under the Constitution of Pakistan Article 9 guarantees safet y of person. *Prima facie* the prohibition against unlawful killing of one individual includes that of many people as well. In the international legal field, the Nuremberg jurisprudence, which led to the ultimate framing of the Genocide Convention, 1948, mass killings of people with a view to their elimination from the confines of any society is proscribed and punishable as an international crime. Pakistan is a signatory to the above Convention and indeed invoked it in the 1971 crisis dealing with Pakistani Prisoners of War then held by India, before the International Court of Justice.

2-That it is regretfully and with painful anguish submitted that Respondents No 1 and 2 and their agents have consistently under a devised plan acted with malice aforethought to achieve the "cleansing" of Sindh by **(a)** terrorising the Mohajir population to move away from Karachi, and thus leave for other places to provide a numerical majority to the indigenous people of Sindh and **(b)** to exterminate and kill the top several layers of leadership of MQM.

3-That since the summer of 1992, as described in various parts of this petition, the MQM has lost through systematic murders dozens of its important members. These killings have been perpetrated by the Law Enforcement. Agencies working for or with the approval of Respondents No 1 and 2 and their sponsored and protected group of the Haqiqi.

4-That the rampant killings in Karachi alone have become a phenomenon of daily reporting by the news papers of the country, international media, and sometime even the official media is forced to admit such massacres. It is a fact of Pakistan's political life that not only the leading politicians of the country, but even the President, the Prime Minister, and the leader of the Opposition have publicly acknowledged that the law and order situation in Karachi has reached alarming proportions. Some leaders of public opinion in the country have equated that the Situation is so bad that we are approaching the strife state of affairs which prevailed in Beirut during the civil war in Lebanon. Thus sadly it will be requested that the Court take judicial notice of this situation as perceptions and perspectives about it permeate the entirety of the evaluatory matter of this petition.

5-That ostensibly it has been made public that the Army personnel effectively in control in important places in interior and Southern Sindh like Karachi are being withdrawn since November 30, 1994. However, irrespective of the fact that such a move has not been officially announced or denied to have occurred, killings in Karachi continue with great speed daily. For example on December 4, 1994, Mr. Salahuddin, the eminent journalist and editor of Takbeer was ruthlessly killed with bullets while he was returning from his office in the evening. It is well known that he was a prominent and fearless human rights advocate and critical of the present Government and regime in power. On the 7 December, 1991, world renowned humanitarian social worker Maulana Abdus Sattar Edhi was compelled to flee from Karachi since he feared for his life at the hand of the Government Agencies, who according to him would subsequently falsely put the blame for his death on the Petitioner or perhaps sectarian religious groups. There is no local bias in presentation of this interview of Maulana Edhi, since it was given to the BBC in London upon arrival and broadcasted internationally. Hence this is a compelling and conclusive objective testimony that not only the Respondents are behind daily and routine killings in Karachi, they are also aiming to create chaos and anarchy locally so as to create an atmosphere in which further bloodshed can conceivably occur and mostly that of the MQM.

6-That official accounts of murders of such category as reported in the daily press for the month of November alone are given to be about 200 causalities in Karachi alone. In these official figures, which are grossly understated for obvious reasons, there were many martyrs belonging to the MQM or its supporters. A tabulated list of some of such persons appears below:-

(i)-On 29 November, 1994, Haqiqi Group murdered two young Mohajirs Arif Ali and Naveed Hussain. According to details on 29 November 1994, at 11.00 P.M., Haqiqi agents armed with sophisticated weapons attacked a video film shop at Nazimabad, Karachi. The terrorists kidnapped Arif Ali aged 20 S/0 Hameed Khan resident of 1-J, Muslim League Quarters, Nazimabad No. 1, Karachi, and his friend Naveed Hussain aged 28 years, s/o Muqeed Hussain resident of house No. 1/4 I-J, Muslim League Quarters, Nazimabad No. 1, Karachi. Next morning at 10.00 A.M., their bodies were recovered from a street near Humdard Dawakhana at Gol Market, Nazimabad, Karachi. Their bodies bore the marks of severe torture. Both the young men were supporters of MQM and Arif Ali was brother of Asif Ali who is an active worker of MQM unit 184.

(ii)-On 26 November, 1994, Javed Ilahi aged 28 years s/o Sirajul Hasan resident of C-3/586, Saeedabad, Baldia Town, Karachi, was murdered by the indiscriminate firing of Haqiqi agents. He was a worker of MQM Sector Baldia town. On 26 November 1994, he went to New Karachi, for some work. On the New Karachi Road, terrorists opened indiscriminate fire which resulted in his death.

(iii)-On 23 November, 1994, murder of two sympathisers of MQM took place. Abid Khan aged 25 years s/o Muhammad Idrees resident of Malir, Karachi, and Muhammad Nabi aged 55 years s/o Ali Hasan resident of Malir, Karachi, were sympathisers of MQM. They both were motor cycle mechanics. On 23 November, terrorists in the guise of repairing their motor cycles, took them to a vacant plot, and after torture, murdered them callously.

(iv)-On 23 November, 1994, terrorists fired a burst of Kalashinkove upon Israr Ahmed and murdered him. Israr Ahmed aged 26 years s/o Muhammad Anwer resident of L-679, 48/B, Korangi No. 2, Karachi, was a sympathizer of MQM unit 75. On 23 November, he was going on his Suzuki car. At 1.30 P.M., some terrorists alighted him from his car and told him to run away. When he ran they opened fire upon him and he fell down. Later terrorists fired burst of Kalashinkov upon him and he died on the spot. Israr Ahmed was nephew of Muhammad Farooq who is unit secretary of MQM unit 81.

(v)-On 21 November, 1994, Mr. Abdul Rahim father of Nasir, a worker of MQM, was brutally murdered by Haqiqi agents. Abdul Rahim Khan aged 55 years, s/o Abdul Hameed Khan resident of House No: D-33, Street No. 17, Area 36-G, Sharif Colony, Landhi No. 6, Karachi, was father of an active worker of MQM Abdul Nasir. After the commencement of the Army Operation "Clean-Up", they had shifted to a temporary address at House No. 390, Sector 1-J Korangi No. 5, Karachi, due to the constant threat of dire consequences by the Haqiqi group. On 21 November 1994, agents of Haqiqi group namely Zubair alias Kala and other broke into the house of Abdul Rahim from the backyard. They were: armed with latest weapons including Kalashinkoves and G-3 rifles. They locked the female members of the house in a room. They took Abdul Rahim in the kitchen and forced him to sign his personal cheque book and then tied him on a chair. Then they opened burst of Kalashinkove and shot him dead on the spot. They started firing and set ablaze the house and escaped from the spot. Neighbours rescued the remaining family members from burning. After this incident the terrorists kept on marauding, aided and abetted, in the area and did not allow the relatives to recover the body for three hours. The deceased left six sons and nine daughters.

(vi)-That on 20 November, 1994, a ruthless murder of MQM worker Muhammad Arshad and his uncle Ghulam Mohiuddin was committed by the Haqiqi group. Muhammad Arshad Siddiqui aged 30 years s/o Ajmaeri Khan resident of House No: L-677, Sector 5-C, North Karachi, was an active worker of MQM Sector 5-C-1, North Karachi. On 20 November 1994, he went to visit his uncle Mr. Ghulam Mohiuddin aged 45 years s/o Waheeduddin resident of House No: 31/12, Jinnah Square, Malir, Karachi. Agents of the Haqiqi group broke into the house of Mr. Ghulam Mohiuddin. They were armed with automatic weapons including Kalashinkoves and G-3 Rifles. They opened fire upon the members of the family. Mr. Arshad and Ghulam Mohiuddin were shot dead on the spot. Mrs Ghulam Mohiuddin and her daughter were severely injured.

(vii) On 20 November, 1994, MQM sympathiser Abdul Waheed was compelled to commit suicide. Abdul Waheed s/o Abdul Hakeem resident of house No: 828, Sector 1-D, Orangi Town, Karachi, was brother of Abdur Rauf who is an active member of MQM. He was an employee of Pakistan Steel Mills. He was dismissed from employment during the on-going Army Operation "Clean-Up". He was the only bread winner of his family consisting of ten members including his old parents, wife and daughters. He had been trying for reinstatement of his services but could not succeed due to the biased attitude of the Government. On 20 November 1994, he went to see the Chairman of Pakistan Steel Mills Mr. Sajjad Hussain and appealed him for reinstatement. The Chairman is an appointee of Respondent No 1 on the basis of his political affiliations with PPP. The Chairman asked him to bring a recommendation of a PPP office bearer but he replied that he had no connection with any PPP leader. Waheed explained his miserable condition and intensity of his frustration that he had no choice except to commit suicide if he was not reinstated. The Chairman humiliated him and told him to get out of his room. Due to this humiliation, Waheed, in frustration and disappointment, jumped from the fifth floor, his skull broke into pieces, and he died on the spot. It is pertinent to mention here that after the commencement of the Army Operation "Clean-Up" against MQM in June 1992, over 6500 Mohajir workers were expelled from Pakistan Steel Mills.

(viii) On 19 November, 1994, MQM worker Naseer was brutally murdered by the Haqiqi group. Syed Naseer aged 23 years, s/o Syed Farooq resident of House No: 10/47, Block 5-E, Nazimabad, Karachi, was a worker of MQM. He and his family members were receiving threats to Leave MQM or face the dire consequences by Haqiqi agents for quite some time. Three days earlier he was kidnapped by the agents of the Haqiqi group. On 19 November, his body was recovered from Gujar Nala. The wounds on his body suggest that he was brutally tortured and then shot dead.

(ix) On 19 November 1994, Haqiqi agents alighted Zamir Ahmed from a wagon and shot him dead. Zamir Ahmed Aged 30 years s/o Amir Ahmed resident of House No: 410, Sector 51/B, Korangi, Karachi, was a worker of MQM. On 20 November 1994, Haqiqi agents Fahim alias Lamba, Irshad and other alighted him from his wagon at bus stop of Korangi no. 5-1/2. They opened fire upon him which resulted in his death on the spot.

(x) On 18 November, 1994, brutal murder of Irfan a sympathiser of MQM took place by the Haqiqi group. Irfan s/o Ismael resident of House No: 601/602, Sector 1A, Orangi Town, Karachi, was a Sympathiser of MQM unit 131. Haqiqi agents murdered him in front of his house.

(xi) On 16 November, 1994, Nadeem Ahmed Khan aged 23 years s/o late Nisar Ahmed Khan resident of House No: 49, Sector 35-B, Korangi No 4, Karachi, was a worker of MQM, was attacked by the Haqiqi agents with lethal weapons, while he was sitting in front of his house. 'The terrorists opened fire and shot him dead on the spot.

(xii) On the same day, another MQM worker Muhammad Imran aged 18 years s/o Muhammad Yasin resident of House No: 10, Sector L, Korangi, Karachi, was shot; he was also present with Nadeem. He received severe bullet injuries.

(xii) On 6 November, 1994, a MQM worker of Unit 79, Mirza Naveed Baig s/o Mirza Rasheed Baig resident of House No. 507, Sector B-51, Korangi No. 6, Karachi, was sitting in front of the house of Aleem who is a Joint Unit Incharge of MQM unit 79. Haqiqi agents, driving a yellow cab and motorcycles, came and started indiscriminate fire upon them. He received bullet wounds and died on the spot. The other workers namely Feroze Ur Rehman s/o Jilani, Ahmed Sharif s/o Qadir Sharif and Naeem received bullet injuries. They were hospitalised in Jinnah Post Graduate Medical Centre. On the day of incident heavy contingent of Army and other Law Enforcement Agencies were patrolling in the area and they fully knew what was happening.

(xiii) On 3 November, 1994, murder of a MQM sympat hiser, Nazakat s/o Liaqat aged 18 years, resident of 4.A-24/1, Landhi No. 4, Karachi, took place. On 3

November, at 9.00 a.m., Haqiqi agents alighted him from a coach and kidnapped him. In the night his body was recovered from Edhi Centre (a Charitable organisation).

(xiv) On the same day, another sympathiser of MQM, Muhammad Rashid s/o Muhammad Majeed aged 29 years, resident of A 4 A-23/2, Landhi, Karachi, was murdered. In the morning of 3 November, he was kidnapped by Haqiqi agents. The same day his body was recovered at Edhi Centre at Sohrab Goth, Karachi.

7-That in the month of October, 1994, the news paper reported that over 150 people were killed in Karachi alone and among those most belonged to the MQM. Few details of such causalities are given below:-

(a) On 30 October, 1994, a worker of MQM, Muhammad Naeem aged 28 years, resident of Unit No. 94, Musarat Colony, Malir City, Near Ibne Hasan Clinic was kidnapped and murdered by Haqiqi agents. In the afternoon of 30 October, Haqiqi agents kidnapped him from Liaqat Market at Malir, Karachi. Later his body was recovered at 10.30 p.m. from Mehran Goth a remote an area of Malir, Karachi. His body bore the wounds of torture and bullets.

(b) On 27 October, 1994, Muhammad Bilal aged 23 years, s/o Sanaullah resident of House No. 235, Sector H, Korangi No. 5-1/2, Karachi, a worker of MQM, was kidnapped by Haqiqi agents from a bus stop at 6.00 p.m. Next morning his body was recovered from Darul Ulum, K area, Korangi. The wounds on his body indicated that he had undergone severe torture. According to witnesses, Haqiqi agents namely Nasir alias Chingari, Raees alias Mulla and Wasim alias Kala had kidnapped him from the bus stop.

(c) On 24 October, 1994, Israr Ahmed, aged 24 years, s/o Iftikhar Ahmed resident of House No. 561, area 3-A, Unit 85, Landhi, Karachi, a worker of MQM was kidnapped and murdered. According to witnesses, agents of the Haqiqi group namely Naeem alias Chotu, Zahid alias Dacoit and Rashid kidnapped him two days earlier. On 26 October, his body was recovered from a Suzuki car.

(d) On 23 October, 1994, Barkat Khan aged 35 Years, s/o Munawar Khan resident of Roshanabad, Block B, near Muhammadi Mosque, Shah Faisal Colony No. 5, Karachi, an active worker of MQM Unit 109 Shah Faisal Colony, was kidnapped and brutally murdered by Haqiqi group. "Haqiqi" agents kidnapped him on the evening of 23 October. Next morning mutilated body of Barkat was recovered from a Soap Factory near Malir River The wounds on his body indicated that he was brutally tortured and then murdered in cold blood. According to witnesses Barkat was kidnapped by the Haqiqi agents namely Tahir, Amir alias Bhora, Fahim Bhora, Shahid Anwar, Mumtaz Mulla and others.

(e) On 17 October, 1994, two workers of MQM were arrested alive and later killed in custody of Law Enforcement Agencies. These MQM workers namely, (1)-Hafiz Muhammad Zulfiqar Ali aged 32, s/o Haji Qamerdin resident of House No. 280-3-B, Saeed Abad, Karachi. (2)-Muhammad Hanif resident of Memon Colony, Saeed Abad, Karachi. According to details, heavy contingent of police conducted a raid at the Sector office of MQM at Unit No. 115, Baldia Town, Karachi, at 4 p.m. One MQM worker was arrested while three workers in an attempt to save themselves from unlawful arrest, ran from the spot on a motor-bike. Police opened fire on them. Their bike slipped and two of them were arrested while the third one could escape from the spot. The above named two MQM workers were arrested alive and taken to the police station where they were shot dead in cold blood. Later police declared this brutal killing as an encounter and the innocent victims as dacoits. This incidence was identical to the Sukkur incident which took place on 3 May, 1994, in which five innocent MQM workers were brutally killed by the police and other Law Enforcement Agencies and the killing was also claimed as an "encounter". This incident was investigated by the Human Rights Commission of Pakistan and a report was published in which it was declared that it was an illegal arrest and murder by the Law Enforcement Agencies and a gross human rights violation.

(f)-On 17 October, 1994, three workers of MQM were killed by Haqiqi agents These MQM workers were namely, 1-Sagheer Ahmed aged 26, s/o late Ehteshamuddin resident of Shah Faisal Colony, Karachi. 2-Afaq Ahmed aged 27, s/o Ashfaq Ahmed resident of Shah Faisal Colony, Karachi. 3-Khursheed Hussain aged 17, s/o Javed Hussain resident of Shah Faisal Colony, Karachi. The above named MQM workers were kidnapped from their houses at Shah Faisal Colony, Karachi, by Haqiqi agents on 16 October 1994. Next day the dead bodies recovered from Malir River at Shah Faisal Colony, were blind folded and their hands tied at their backs. The bodies were taken to Jinnah Post Graduate Medical Centre. Their bodies bore the marks that they were brutally tortured and then shot dead in cold blood. Police refused to register their case and the culprits are still at large.

(g)-On 9 October, 1994, an active worker of MQM Malir Unit, was brutally murdered by Haqiqi agents. Muhammad Nadeem aged 19 years, s/o Abdus Salam resident B/69, Shed No 2, Malir, Karachi. On 9 October, four Haqiqi agents came at his residence. At that time he was standing in front of his house. Haqiqi agents fired upon him. He received bullet injuries on his face, head and chest and died on the spot.

(h)-On the same day another incidence took place in the Government Degree Science College at Korangi No. 6, Karachi when the "Haqiqi" agents attacked the said college and verbally and physically abused the girls students, beat them up and cut their flesh with blades.

8-That targeted and separate killings of MQM supporters, workers and Leadership have to be seen in the context of the initial onslaught on the Petitioner when the Army Operation began in June 1992. By affording cover to the Haqiqi group the local Army personnel along with the police agencies of Respondents 1 and 2 set fire to numerous houses of the MQM supporters and workers leading to the burning alive of several hundred families in separate incidents. The Petitioner calculates that thus far since June 1992, upto now in a 30 months period over twenty thousand civilians, mostly of the MQM, have been killed in this manner. The Respondents are thus guilty of violating many laws, National and International, including Article 9 of the Constitution.

9-That the Respondents' officials and agents who have been a part of this killing campaign are guilty of Genocide rendering the Governments answerable to International Law as well.

PART VI

MR ALTAF HUSSAIN'S STAND ON SEVERAL ISSUES

1-That as analysed in this petition, the Mohajirs found in the person of Mr. Altaf Hussain, their supreme leader and reposed confidence in the dynamism of this man who became the mover of the *Tehrik* through which a national movement of middle class led democracy is to be established in the country. It is now necessary, for a proper adjudication of this matter, to briefly refer to the stand taken by Mr. Altaf Hussain in the context of several issues necessarily involved and connected with the facts of this case. Two and a half years of oppression by the Respondents has failed to reduce the affection, respect and admiration for this leader in the hearts of millions of followers of the Petitioner. It establishes that leadership of genuine eminence cannot be tarnished by even tyranny or brutality. Mr. Altaf Hussain remains to be the true leader of the MQM and occupies a unique position in the political Leadership in Pakistan. In January 1990, when the COP (Combined Opposition Parties) was formed Mr. Altaf Hussain alone had the distinction of addressing perhaps the biggest political meeting in the history of

Pakistan when he spoke to a gathering of over 5 million people at the Mazar-e-Quaid, in Karachi, and every one paid the highest tributes to him by giving him a standing ovation for over half an hour.

2-That it is manifest that the rise of the MQM was so phenomenal and spectacular that it utterly astonished the pundits of local politics. In a matter of months Mr. Altaf Hussain was able to obtain the allegiance of millions of admirers and supporters to the great political chagrin of many. When within a very short time the MQM became a part of the Government both in Sindh and in Islamabad, it was logical that it brought fear into the thinking and psyche of other political parties and the Establishment since it was foreclosing the entry of many Waderas and Jagirdars into the corridors of power. Particularly incensed was the Pakistan Peoples Party which had continuously asserted, but falsely that it solely represented the Province of Sindh. The ascent of MQM brought a pall of doom in its leadership which since 1971 had been acting through official State instrumentality to diminish and minimise the Mohajir community in the Province of Sindh.

3-That the Establishment, therefore, moved in a panic when Operation Clean-Up of the Army was launched on 19 June 1992. It is well known and established political wisdom, that force cannot re-channel political thinking or affiliation or affection of the public few genuine leadership. This is fully borne out by the events already analysed in this petition. The Army Operation of 1992, which apparently had no Constitutional cover in the cities such as Karachi was explained as being an operat ion against criminals, car lifters and gangsters. Yet the majority of the attention of the Armed Forces in Sindh was asked by the Respondents to be entirely aimed at the political leadership of the MQM as hundreds of them were arrested and detained without lawful authority not only by the local police but by the Army as well who had no such authority under the Constitutional law of the land.

4-That in this context the Respondents patronage of the so-called Haqiqi group was described to be merely the affording of "protection" to one of the two groups of MQM. Many direct unlawful actions of the Haqiqi group against MQM were explained as an "infighting" between the two factions of the MQM. So farcical and ridiculous is this assertion that were this true then in 1993 General Elections, the MQM greatly handicapped and on a day's notice swept the polls while the Haqiqi miserably failed to obtain even a few hundred of votes in any constituency.

5-That another false argument raised by those who initiated the June 1992 operation and by the present Respondents is that the MQM had operated "persecution houses" and terrorised millions of people in places like Karachi. This is a preposterous and a false allegation. Were this true then when the June 1992 operation began people in Karachi should have welcomed and garlanded the liberators and the Respondents. Nothing of the kind happened. The truth of the matter, moreover, is that when in 1993 General elections were held, it was the MQM which led in achieving comprehensive electoral victory. Had it been a terrorism inclined political party, the people of Sindh, particularly of urban areas should have rejected it. However, the MQM was embraced with a glowing victory at the polls. This was achieved despite the multifarious handicaps that existed against it in the environment of the time. It is axiomatic that people's affection can not turn to those who perpetrate tyranny. As such this is a living proof, that people who danced with joy when the MQM decided to contest the elections on October 7, 1993, remained 100% with this party. Thus the allegation against the MQM of indulging in unlawful terrorist activities are utter lies and falsely made by its opponents and are utterly rejected by the Petitioner.

6-That the Petitioner also believes as does its leader, Mr. Altaf Hussain, that all public issues be debated in accordance with civilised behaviour. Mr. Altaf Hussain is also an ardent believer and advocate of the ideology of representative Government and that democracy can only be successfully operated in a healthy manner by the middle and poor classes of the country. Conversely, he has always advocated that the Jagirdars, Waderas and Sardars, who enjoy feudal wealth, operate feudal estates, and inflict upon the poor masses a feudal style of politics have no place in a democratic Pakistan.

No wonder the elite in the Establishment and the major political parties of the country, particularly those in Sindh haven no hand of friendship for the MQM since this party will bring to an end the hegemony in National affairs of the former. Mr. Altaf Hussain believes in genuine democracy in which feudalism has no place. He wants the supremacy of Rule of Law under which the poor and the rest are governed by one law of the land and there are no special laws for the privileged few, as currently prevail, in a system controlled by Jagirdarism, Waderaism and Sardarism. It is unconscionable that 2% of rich control 98% of the wealth of the nation. It is equally shocking that the same 2% rule the country, no matter what party comes in power, while 98% of the people have to watch the outcome of their destiny from a distance always convinced that they have no role to perform in the leadership of the country. Mr. Altaf Hussain wants to change this, and did so indeed through the MQM in a manner which is truly democratic.

7-That at diverse places in this petition adverse analysis to the image of the Army may be erroneously perceived. As the four letters appended with this petition by Mr. Altaf Hussain show, he considers highly the role and functions of the Armed Forces in Pakistan. Indeed he has directly appealed to the Chief of the Army Staff and the patriotic Generals of the land that this institution may not be allowed to be used by the malicious schemes of conniving with corrupt politicians and the bureaucracy which really constitutes the core of country's Establishment. Events and incidents described in this petition reveal in eloquent terms that from June 1992 upto now a number of Army personnel were deployed and utilized in Sindh by Respondent No 1 to strengthen its own political control and that of Respondent No 2 specially in the urban areas of Sindh wherein it had no effective say or civic respect. As such we have to keep in mind the tragic circumstances of Bangladesh crisis when corrupt political manoeuvring dismembered the country and severely damaged the image of the Army.

8-That political matters should be solved by political people by the deployment of political methods. Use of force is not one of such methods needs no emphasis. Hence there is no doubt that the Pakistan Armed Forces, who command great respect in the masses, would themselves like to remain out of the political controversies of the country. This is indeed echoed in numerous recent statements of the present Chief of the Army Staff. Hence the matters alluded to in this petition in which the Local Army personnel acted in a manner which was prejudicial to the political well-being and integrity of the MQM was the result of a sinister conspiracy hatched by the elite and the Establishment of the country (which has maliciously succeeded in ruling this country for the greater part of its history) by treacherously inducing the former for working for their goals.

9-That the history of this country bespeaks of crises and tragedies in which the most fundamental and far reaching decisions of the nation were taken by Sardars and Waderas in their drawing rooms oblivious of what they were doing to the country. The poor country and the Nation have been ceaselessly held hostage in the greedy hands of avaricious and corrupt politicians whose vested interests in the existing system have prevented the emergence of a genuine people's rule in the country. Mr. Altaf Hussain's dynamic political attack on the current system while being supported by the poor masses and the middle classes naturally spells doom for the country entrenched present corrupt political system. The MQM stands for vigorous and a united Pakistan with strong and highly trained professional Army as well as for the right of all the poor and middle class Pakistanis. It was indeed his pronouncement that the Mohajir Qoumi Movement was to be transformed into the "Muttaheda Qoumi Movement" on the 14 August 1992 in Lahore which shook the citadels of political powers of the country. In order to prevent him from engulfing the entire country in the pursuit of pure people's rule, these "powers that might be" moved against him and the political party that was about to move in a countrywide *Tehrik* along these lines. As explained above, the MQM has no groups or factions, since it remains a single unified representative voice of the oppressed against the oppressors.

10-That another malicious tirade levelled against the MQM was the so-called "discovery" of a fabricated map proclaiming allegedly the Stale of "Jinnah Pur". Mr. Altaf Hussain categorically repudiates this preposterous accusation. Indeed the Army authorities themselves denied that the alleged "discovery" was ever made and announced that the Petitioner and Mr. Altaf Hussain had never prepared any such scheme or my map for this purpose. Mr. Altaf Hussain strongly believes in a united Pakistan which is prosperous and truly democratic. He strongly condemns any secessionist thinking and abhors movements such as those that that want to create Sindhu Desh. Indeed it is necessary at this time to particularly acknowledge that the Army authorities acted with honour when they disowned the alleged discovery of such a map which had been in fact fabricated.

11-That, moreover, Mr. Altaf Hussain believes in an egalitarian society in which while the affluent and the rich can keep their riches, the poor are not discriminated against because of their lower economic capabilities. He believes in a society which tolerates dissent and in which the law of the land is the same for every citizen. He further believes that if given the chance the MQM will model a society in Pakistan on the pattern of modern industrialised democracies such as that of the United States, Europe and Japan. He is not n fundamentalist, and like the Quaid-e-Azam desires that followers of all religions have complete freedom of faith and they are to be considered as Pakistanis because they are citizens of this country.

12-That in support of these stands that Mr. Altaf Hussain believes in a few of his detailed addresses and open letters are being appended with this petition. Also included are materials in the form of video tapes, audio tapes and photographs along with Vol. Six to substantiate the averments of this petition.

13-That to show the complete unrepresentative character of the Government in the Province of Sindh and elsewhere it should be noted that no local body elections have been held Karachi and Hyderabad particularly nor are likely to be held.

14-That the social welfare related work of the Petitioner is similar in nature to that of the Edhi Foundation. The Petitioner has operated its Khidmat-e-Khalq Committee many other Centres successfully to assist the needy, disabled and sick. In this cont ext dispensaries, blood bank and educational scholarships are also provided. No political party in Pakistan matches the humanitarian work of the Petitioner.

NATIONALISM AND ITS SIGNIFICANCE

Nationalism has been the subject of hundreds of analyses and dozens of theories. Political scientists draw a sharp distinction between the concepts of *state* and *nation*. State refers to government and other institutions which run the country. Nation, by contrast, is a psychological characteristic, what individuals identify with. There are nation-states in which almost everyone accepts the state as theirs and makes it the primary home of their political identity and loyalty. That would certainly be true of most people in the United States or France, but is less true in countries where people might think of themselves as Scots more than British, Quebecois more than Canadian, or Walloon more than Belgian or Urdu-speaking (Mohajir) than Pakistani. There are also countries with important Diasporas or groups of people who live outside the countries' borders but would rather not do so. In my opinion, the greatest example of Yugoslavia's disintegration into now six separate states show that identity is indeed an important factor which can never be ignored. This is for this reason, I am a great advocate of disintegration of Pakistan on the same lines, that is, as I say that if Yugoslavia could disintegrate, why not Pakistan?

Nationalism and the state are surprisingly new phenomena given the importance they play in international relations today. If this is about State, then it is quite clear that Pakistan today is a failed state which has withered away. A wide array of anti-state actors is currently engaged in varying degrees of violence and subversion in an extended swathe of territory. A cursory look at the map indicates that the North West Frontier Province (Pakhtoonistan), Federally Administered Tribal Areas (FATA), and Balochistan are witnessing large-scale violence and insurgency. Violence in parts of the Sindh, Punjab and Gilgit-Baltistan has also brought these areas under the security scanner. Islamabad's writ is and has been challenged vigorously and violently or otherwise in wide geographical areas, and on a multiplicity of issues. The tragedy of Lal Masjid is a living proof. Well over half of the territory presently under Pakistan's control, including Gilgit-Baltistan and Azad Jammu & Kashmir, has passed outside the realm of governance of Pakistan's military dictatorship and hence there is no concept of any type of civil rule in those areas. For the sake of understanding the ground realities, following charts will show the facts and figures about Pakistan's inevitable political demise:

Terrorism-related Fatalities in Pakistan, 2007

	Civilians	Security Force Personnel	Terrorists/Insurgents	Total
January	26	16	29	71
February	35	4	8	47
March	28	21	261	310
April	176	18	83	277
May	57	10	14	81
June	31	12	40	83
July	144	143	191	478
August	56	63	117	236
September	101	67	144	312
October	282	101	154	537
November	293	94	341	728
December	293	48	97	438
Total	1523	597	1479	3599

Comparative Levels of Violence in Pakistan, 2003-2007

Year	Civilians	Security Force Personnel	Terrorist	Total
2003	140	24	25	189
2004	435	184	244	863
2005	430	81	137	648
2006	608	325	538	1471
2007	1523	597	1479	3599

Source: Institute for Conflict Management Database

Sectarian Violence

Compared to 2006, when approximately 201 persons were killed and 349 others injured in 38 incidents of sectarian violence, there has been a substantial increase in the fatality index in 2007 when 441 people died and 630 were wounded in 341 incidents.

Sectarian Violence in Pakistan, 2007

Month	Incidents	Killed	Injured
January	3	5	21
February	0	0	0
March	9	8	1
April	72	121	119
May	2	3	1
June	0	0	0
July	0	0	0
August	2	2	0
September	0	0	0
October	0	0	0
November	118	181	314
December	135	121	174
Total	341	441	630

Source: Institute for Conflict Management database

Most of the fatalities in sectarian violence occurred in the Kurram Agency, which has emerged as the new sectarian battleground. In fact more than 300 people have been killed in the Agency just since November 2007. The main Tull and Parachinar Highway has been closed since the last week of November 2007, leading to an acute shortages of edible items and medicines in Kurram Agency. In an indication of the worsening situation, Afghan officials said on January 3, 2008, that about 900 families most of them Sunnis, had fled across the border in the preceding two weeks, to the provinces of Khost and Paktia.

Despite the occasional reverses, the Lashkar-e-Jhangvi, the main Wahabi terrorist/militant group which believes in truthfulness of first three hypocrite Caliphs of Islam, has retained a substantial capacity to strike in the area, and, more significantly, has emerged as a key provider of logistical support and personnel to

Al-Qaeda and the Taliban in Pakistan. This is still a mystry as to how such Wahabi terrorist groups get their funding and financial support. Indeed, it is not possible that they are getting help directly from the skies. The other Wahabi terrorist group, the Sipah-e-Sahaba Pakistan which was formed by late military dictator called General Ziaul Haq lay low during 2007. They have not, however, altered their organizational structures and objectives and, though their cadres remain underground, they continue to function. It is my firm belief that Lashkar-e-Jhangvi and Sipah-e-Sahaba Pakistan are financed, supported and strengthened by none other than Pakistan's intelligence agencies which have funds worth billions of dollars at their disposal. These funds have come primarily from drug trade via ISI and filtered down US assistance in the name of War on Terror.

The foundations of sectarian terror share their ideological bases with Islamist extremist groupings engaged in a wide range of international terrorist incidents and movements, and it is evident that the operational capacities of both these are yet to be significantly eroded. The crackdown targeting sectarian groups has failed to produce the desired impact, and continuing sectarian violence across Pakistan suggests that the underground networks and support structures of sectarian groups, particularly those of the Sipah-e-Sahaba Pakistan and Lashkar-e-Jhangvi remain unimpaired, and may, indeed, have achieved greater complexity and resilience through their linkages with other terrorist organizations.

Suicide Attacks

There were 56 suicide attacks in 2007 as against seven in year 2006. 729 persons, including 552 civilians and 177 Security Forces personnel, were killed and 1,677 persons injured by 58 suicide bombers involved in these incidents in 2007. The magnitude of Pakistan's failure to exist as an independent country is best illustrated by the fact that, between March 22, 2002 (the first suicide attack) and end-2006, there were 22 suicide attacks; in 2007 alone, there were 56 such attacks. In 2007, the organized suicide squads unceasingly targeted Army convoys and check-posts, police stations and training units, government officials, restaurants and mosques. While 27 of the 56 suicide attacks occurred in Pakhtoonistan (NWFP), there were 13 in FATA and five attacks in the national capital, Islamabad. While there were three instances in 2007 when Pakhtoonistan (NWFP) witnessed two suicide attacks on a single day, the province also witnessed the first suicide attack by a woman when, on December 4, 2007, a female suicide bomber blew herself up in a high security zone in the provincial capital, Peshawar. Except for the suicide bomber, who was said to be in her mid-30s, no other casualty was reported in the blast. The intensity of suicide attacks in Pakistan is such that there were eight instances during 2007 when there were multiple suicide attacks across the various provinces on a single day. Even Benazir Bhutto, daughter of Zulfiqar Ali Bhutto also died in a suicide attack in Rawalpindi in December 2007 which put the last nail in Pakistan's coffin.

Evidence that the Pakistani footprint of terror continues to torment Afghanistan was available in abundance. For instance, more than 80 per cent of suicide bombers in Afghanistan are recruited and trained in Pakistan, the United Nations said in a report in September 2007. The United Nations Assistance Mission to Afghanistan, in its report "Suicide Attacks in Afghanistan (2001-2007)", stated that "The tribal areas of Pakistan remain an important source of human and material assistance for suicide attacks in Afghanistan." According to the report: "Little is known about the identity and motivation of suicide bombers in Afghanistan. They appear to be young (sometimes children), poor, uneducated, easily influenced by recruiters and draw heavily from *madaris* [religious schools] across the border in Pakistan."

Socio-Economic Disaster

Pakistan's economic downfall under Pervez Musharraf has been dominated by increasing macro-imbalances, high levels of poverty, and poor human development indicators. A record current account deficit, stagnant exports, an increasing fiscal deficit, social indicators that are still amongst the worst in Asia, an energy shortage and rising inflation with artificially-controlled prices are just a few of the challenges faced by Pakistan's economy.

Syed Fazl-e-Haider, a Quetta-based development analyst, projects, "Foreign direct investment and portfolio flows are likely to decline, negatively affecting Pakistan's external liquidity position, given its large current account deficit of about 4.8 per cent of gross domestic product. The country may encounter increasing difficulty in refinancing its external and domestic debt if lenders risk aversion toward Pakistan increases. In addition, fiscal slippages may arise, pushing deficits beyond the government's target of 4 per cent of GDP, jeopardizing the currently favorable debt trajectory."

Many of the significant indicators of social and living standards in Pakistan have reportedly gone from bad to worse in the last five years. According to the Pakistan Social and Living Standards Measurement (PSLM) survey 2005-06, the total enrolment in Government schools has been on a steady decline since 2001-02 when it stood at 74 per cent. The PSLM survey 2004-05 reported "decrease in the share of primary enrolment that is in Government schools. The overall share has

declined from 72 per cent in 2004-05 to 65 per cent in 2005-06." Full immuniza-
tion of children has declined from 77 per cent in 2004-05 to 71 per cent in 2005-
06. The survey reveals that more than 30 per cent population did not have toilet
facility while more than 41 per cent people did not have any sanitation system. In
Pakistan, World Bank estimates indicate that only 57 per cent of girls and women
can read and write and in rural areas only 22 per cent of girls have completed primary level schooling, as compared to 47 per cent of boys.

Balochistan has the smallest number of educational institutions, the lowest literacy rate among both males and females, the lowest ranking in the Gender Parity
Index and the smallest presence of private educational institutes in the country,
according to the National Economic Survey (NWS). About six per cent of the
schools in Balochistan do not have buildings, nine per cent lack electricity, 12
per cent are devoid of clean drinking water and 11 per cent are without proper
latrines. The province also has the smallest number of educational institutions i.e.
10,381 against the national number of 216,490, out of which 106,435 are located
in the Punjab only which is the province of 90% military dictators, 46,862 in
Sindh and 36,029 in Pakhtoonistan (NWFP). According to the NES, "out of the
total number of institutions, 48 per cent are to be found in the Punjab, 22 per cent
in Sindh, 17 per cent in NWFP (Pakhtoonistan) and 5 per cent in Balochistan."
Accounting for approximately 44 per cent of Pakistan's landmass, Balochistan is
the largest province with the lowest literacy rate. This shows that Pakistan does
not deserve to remain in its present geographical form where such imbalances have
only proved that Pakistan is not a country but a colony which came into existence
accidentally because of negligence by top political leaders of United India who
could not resist the negative approach that emerged during 1940s.

Sindh and Punjab have, among the four provinces, shown the highest increase in
literacy rates between the fiscal years 2001-02 and 2005-06, according to a report
released by the State Bank of Pakistan (SBP). Punjab currently has the highest
literacy rate, 56 per cent (47 per cent in 2002), followed by Sindh at 55 per cent
(46 per cent in 2002). Pakhtoonistan (NWFP) follows with a literacy rate of 46
per cent (38 per cent in 2002). A growth rate of two per cent was recorded in
Balochistan, which showed a literacy rate of 38 per cent at the end of the 2005-06
fiscal year. Pakistan has the highest mortality rate for infants (70 per 1,000) and
children under the age of five (101 per 1,000) in South Asia, according to a SBP
report.

Around 89 of Pakistan's 112 Districts are facing problems of food insecurity,
including malnutrition, under-nutrition, hunger, diseases and poverty, according

to a World Food Programme study. The study, the first of its kind in Pakistan, was done to identify food insecure segments in urban areas of Pakistan. The study declares 39 Districts extremely vulnerable, 31 very vulnerable and 19 vulnerable to food insecurity. Among the Districts with food security it places 15 districts under the category of normal and eight under the sufficient category. The question arises about the billions of dollars collected by Pervez Musharraf and his corrupt team of army generals from USA in the name of War on Terror. Where these billions of dollars have gone while the people are still hungry and have nothing to survive on?

Almost all state institutions are now vulnerable against the activities of terrorist groups causing violence in Pakistan. Consequently, the misuse of these institutions is presently at peak. Abusing and disempowering state institutions, Pervez Musharraf manipulated his way into another Presidency in an illegitimate manner though he was forced out of his uniform. Pakistan's destiny as a nation remains captive to President Musharraf's uncertain destiny, irrespective of how the newly elected baby National Assembly comprising of PPP-PML(N)-ANP reacts to Pervez Musharraf's dictates. Pakistan should, therefore, be disintegrated before it is too late. Pervez Musharraf's much-propagated "enlightened moderation" has entirely failed just like "Two-Nation Thoery", if at all it was intended to be implemented. If Pakistan is not divided immediately into 6 parts within next few years, it will be a great disaster for people living under Pakistan army's military siege as well as the whole world.

Nationalism is important in two ways. The first is relatively simple and is best seen in the patriotism of most people in the United States, the United Kingdom, or France. In those countries, almost everyone believes that the state is legitimate and therefore supports it often without question. In countries that still have problems of governance, nationalism is something beyond understanding by common people living in such countries.

Misunderstanding of true nationalism may pave way for wars. As far as interstate war is concerned, there is no more obvious example than World War II. Japan, Italy, and especially Germany were all led by leaders who stressed unmet nationalist goals and grievances in the years leading up to the outbreak of fighting in 1939. While psychologists and historians still debate exactly how this took place, there is little doubt that the intense emotions felt by leaders and followers alike contributed to the atrocities committed by people from all three of these countries.

The term "nationalism" is generally used to describe two phenomena: (1) the attitude that the members of a nation have when they care about their national identity and (2) the actions that the members of a nation take when seeking to achieve (or sustain) self-determination. (1) raises questions about the concept of nation (or national identity), which is often defined in terms of common origin, ethnicity, or cultural ties, and while an individual's membership in a nation is often regarded as involuntary, it is sometimes regarded as voluntary. (2) raises questions about whether self-determination must be understood as involving having full statehood with complete authority over domestic and international affairs, or whether something less is required. It is traditional, therefore, to distinguish nations from states—whereas a nation often consists of an ethnic or cultural community, a state is a political entity with a high degree of sovereignty. While many states are nations in some sense, there are many nations which are not fully sovereign states.—*Internet Encyclopedia of Philosophy*

Nationalism develops from the idea that the nation, in contrast to the nation-state, is formed of the indigenous people to an area. It is the longest-lasting and most sensible form of government, for it groups together people who have culture, heritage and language in common. The modern nation-state imposes political boundaries on an area, moves people into it, and declares it a "nation," but without this lack of inherent consensus such states become marketplaces instead of living cultural entities. Pakistan is an example of such an artificial cultural entity or say modern day 'colony' where certain nations have been assembled by force or by an act of conspiracy to remain intact on the basis of a false theory propagated as "Two-Nation Thoery".

Nationalism was the most successful political force of the 19th century. It emerged from two main sources: the Romantic exaltation of "feeling" and "identity" and the Liberal requirement that a legitimate state be based on a "people" rather than, for example, a dynasty, God, or imperial domination. Both Romantic "identity nationalism" and Liberal "civic nationalism" were essentially middle class movements.—*Modern History Sourcebook*

Malcolm X advocated black nationalism—an ideology that encouraged African Americans to live separate from white society. He was critical of the desire of many civil rights leaders for racial integration, arguing that whites would never accept African Americans as equals. He also believed that integration represented a rejection of black culture and an adoption of white values and white culture. "The white man has brainwashed the so-called Negro to the point of believing white supremacy so much so that today some Negroes think that they are not making progress or that they don't have anything unless they have a white man's neighborhood, a seat in the white man's school, or a position in a white man's job." In my opinion, if I apply theory of Malcolm X to current Pakistani cultural fabric, the role of Punjabi nation is similar to that of a White man while other nations like Pathans, Balochis, Sindhis, Siraekis, Urdu-speaking people are treated like black men (or negroes). The actual concept of Malcolm X was to explain the superior vs inferior conflict. He tried to prove that White man is regarded as 'superior' and the black man is considered as 'inferior'. Regardless of the circumstances which prevailed during the times of Malcolm X, I am 100% correct in my analysis that in the present undivided Pakistan is clearly divided in terms of 'haves' and 'havenots'. Punjab represent 'haves' because of its military dictatorship and control on country's assets while Pathans, Balochis, Sindhis, Siraekis and Urdu-speaking people represent 'havenots'. USA survived on the basis of autonomy given to all its States. On the contrary, Pakistan failed to give any autonomy to various nations who had assembled in 1947 (voluntarily or non-voluntarily) under its umbrella. The Bengalis were the first ones to leave the vicious domination of Punjab back in 1971 by forming their own country called Bangladesh. Time has come that Pathans, Balochis, Sindhis, Siraekis and Urdu-speaking people should also follow suit by winning their respective independence. This is exactly what this book is about.

Coming to the concept of Pan-nationalism, or world nationalism, it is related to the idea that each ethnic-cultural group (joined by language, heritage and culture) deserves its own nation. Pan-nationalism suggests that no nationalist can afford to work only for his or her own tribe, but must realize that all tribes are joined in the same quest: to bring about a nationalist order on earth. Our enemy is not each other. Our enemy is the system of "modern society" that exploits us. Our goal is to re-structure modern society to keep its good aspects (technology) and weed out its destructive aspects. This is achieved by putting culture before commerce in every nation on earth, and our method of reaching this is Pan-Nationalism.

A typically-overlooked but crucial focus of integration is ideological, something that has been little in evidence since the end of the Cold War conflict between capitalism and Leninism-Stalinism-Máoism (which was often mischaracterized as a conflict between democracy and tyranny, or between capitalism and communism-socialism). The democratic states occasionally use liberal democracy as one of several organizing parameters in their institutions, but not consistently. The European Union, the Organization of American States, the Organization for Economic Cooperation and Development, and the Commonwealth are examples of groupings that have employed liberal democracy internally as a guide. But the Commonwealth has at most suspended a member, like Zimbabwe, for violation of principles of liberal democracy, which weakens the case for including parliamentary democracy as one of the legacies that the members are supposed to have in common. The commitment of the OAS to democracy is recent and largely coincident with the democratization of the hemisphere. There are at present only one clear non-democracy, Cuba, and one probable non-democracy, Haïti, in the hemisphere; the Castro government is excluded from the OAS, and the weakness of democracy in Haïti is a matter of concern. But the support of the US for the most recent putsch in Venezuela has certainly undermined the centrality of democracy in the hemisphere. The OECD is composed entirely of democracies, but economics is more a factor in their selection. The EU began and in some ways still functions as an economic association, but its leaders have seen democracy as an important element of the free-market economies that they were working to integrate, and have included Spain, Portugal, and Greece, for instance, only when they were democratic, and are applying the same standard to eastward expansion. The recent (temporary) suspension of Austria, when the far-right Freedom Party was included in government, demonstrated that the EU was willing to take the issue further; though Austria's partners spoke of problems of "democracy" in Austria, they clearly meant not democracy but liberalism. And indeed, liberal democracy is an example of what is now viewed as a shared value of the EU, making it more than simply a common market. The EU has explicitly endorsed the promotion of liberal democracy internally and externally as an appropriate matter for the union.

But the most important global organizations for integration, the UN and the WTO, do not consider democracy at all. The UN is theoretically geographically comprehensive, and the WTO is theoretically meant to be so. But each has, for different reasons, excluded states and specifically democracies. This, in turn, has made some of these organizations' goals much more difficult to achieve. The UN works for international political cooperation, peace, and the rule of law. But tens of its members do not even practice democracy and the rule of law internally, and many others of its members fail to promote them geopolitically. The WTO has been hampered by the global lack of agreement on the appropriate weight of democracy, human rights, and economic justice in economic and trade decisions. If WTO is a democratic organization, why Russia is resisted to become its member?

While there is something to be said for a comprehensive organization like the UN, absent of course the political machinations that ignore certain geopolitical realities, on the whole the democracies of the world would do better by their own values and for their own interests to replace both the UN and the WTO, as well as NATO, the OECD, and the Commonwealth, with a new commonwealth, organized explicitly around liberal democracy. Within this organization, all democracies and only democracies would be admitted, each would commit to ever-increasing political liberalism, and their principal international relationships would be within the group.

Politically, international law would be redefined. Full diplomatic recognition would be accorded to democracies. No principle of state sovereignty would exist; states would derive their legitimacy from their actions, and from the electoral will of their citizenries. Mutual defense would be inherent in the formation of the commonwealth. In addition, the members would agree to be bound by the principle of respect for liberal democracy, internally and externally, so that there would be the presumption of internal and external action in support of liberal democracy. This action would be presumed to extend as far, if necessary, as military intervention.

Economically, this association of democracies would be the ideal arrangement to avoid the political disagreements on the relative weight of trade and justice, and the moral problems of abetting dictatorship and corruption. At least within the commonwealth, it could be agreed that trade was indeed a good thing, and if genuinely free, as opposed to favorable towards the most developed members, would avoid further that moral question. The ultimate goal would be a single economy for the commonwealth—a single market, common currency, and unified laws governing commerce. Included in that would be common protection of air, water, and wilderness, through laws and regulations, and through land-reserve programs crossing state borders.

Integration of the right sort is a good thing; of the wrong sort, by definition, not a good thing. And while there is certain to be an entropic complication of the world, for the most part the trend, from both deliberate and inadvertent human action, is towards a more integrated world. The world will ultimately be united politically, economically, and culturally, at least as much as any society is today. Our choices should be made to bring about a world society that reflects the best that modern societies have to offer, and while some elements are arbitrary, of equal value, and should be preserved in as much diversity as possible, other elements are clearly not of equal value. To the extent that liberalism and democracy are not deemed expendable by those whose societies have them, and are the objects of striving and great sacrifice by those whose societies do not, we should build those into our institutions of integration from the beginning, the better to make them an inseparable part of our future world.

When considering integration, there is perhaps one clear differentiation between global and regional—integration that is not based on geographical proximity, and integration that is. The latter category may be shrinking, but only slowly, and it begins as the more important, as even now the effects of distance are great. It is possible in specialized discussion to analyze particular forms of integration and disintegration, whether global or regional, but if this proves convenient it also proves imperfect, for at least in one way the world is already integrated: everything will ultimately affect everything else.

When considering integration and disintegration that is geographically based, the world breaks down surprisingly well by a number of criteria, with the regions showing strong connections in language, culture, politics, history, race, religion, economy, and physical geography. The extent of any one of these characteristics is often enough to define the regions; and there is a fair degree of uniformity across the categories. Some of these regions are fairly-well integrated and aligned on these criteria, some are quite diverse, and some places and cultures belong to more than one such region such as Turkey, Moldova, Mongolia, the Caucasus, and the México-US border region. But taken as a whole, the existence of these regions and their overlapping determinants strongly indicates that the determinants work together, that integration is, so to speak, integrated, that it takes place simultaneously and synergistically across all spheres of activity. In European integration study, this is known as 'spillover'—one form of integration leading to or even requiring another.

In the case of Europe, that was deliberate. The project began with integration of the coal and steel industries in six European states, with the key states being France and Germany. It was these two at the center of so much of Europe's warfare. The economic integration of the industrial foundations of military strength, particularly of Germany's military strength, under a supranational body would remove the independent ability of Germany or any other state to arm itself and attack, as well as provide for an immediate economic cost to war—a state would be attacking its own economy by attacking another's. The end goal was political integration, and while that has not fully come about, it has definitely progressed, and will progress further. In order to achieve economic integration, which by now is much deeper than merely coal and steel, the European Union states have been forced to cooperate politically to a great extent, pooling their sovereignty as it is described. In fact, the member-states have surrendered a great deal of sovereignty to this supranational body, because only so could economic integration work. The common market, the level playing field, the elimination of internal barriers: all imply a common legal framework, and this is what the European Union has developed. And living within a single market, with free movement of persons, under a common legal framework, erodes cultural distinctions and even national identities. Some differences will always remain; but some distinctions that individuals draw are based solely on unfamiliarity.

But Europe is not sui generis. The processes at work in Europe are happening in other regions, of various sizes and compositions, and ultimately in the world as a whole. The world is in the process of sorting itself out, of determining which differences matter and which differences do not, and finding that even the differences that matter are diminishing over time. If world integration is inevitable, then it is only so because humans, cumulatively, are making the choices that will integrate the world. If we better understand the process and our own contributions to it, we will be in a better position to guide the process towards a deliberate outcome. We can, and should, take responsibility for the world we are creating.

The starting point for a consideration of integration and disintegration in the world must be a consideration of the actual state of the world, particularly as it differs from perceived or attributed reality. The usual picture of the world—a map—presents a series of geographical areas clearly delineated, within each of which is taken to operate a single sovereign government, an independent economy, and a populace that identifies nationalistically with that area. That these states are somewhat mythical is not a new insight, but it is an insight that needs to be stated and examined anew.

As a matter of political sovereignty, here defined as impunity de facto, there are nearly, and perhaps greatly in excess of, two hundred fifty sovereign states in the world, as opposed to the one hundred ninety-two recognized by the United Nations and most of its members. One non-member, Taiwan, is a stable, prosperous, and now democratic state which formerly was recognized, is still recognized by a number of states, and is in any case tacitly acknowledged to be a state by all the world, including China. Of the five dozen or so unrecognized states, they fall largely into three categories: entities nominally affiliated with another state but with tacit sovereignty; contesting entities in conflict with and sundered from another state; and zones of mixed sovereignty, in which control is shared by more than one power. There are also numerous cases where the areas of control between sovereignties differ in recognition and reality. If the many unrecognized divisions in the world are perpetuated, it will only be apparent disintegration; and if they are ended, it will be genuine integration, or at least reintegration.

—Greenland and the Faroe Islands

These autonomous regions, nominally under the control of Denmark, exert a great deal of local control and possess the recognized right to secede, which they have failed to exercise primarily for economic reasons, id est, subsidies from Denmark. But, by local choice, each is excluded from the European Union.

—Mount Athos

This religious enclave, roughly analogous to the Vatican, is an autonomous protector-ate of Greece. The Holy Mount is a self-governed part of the Greek state, subject to the Ministry of Foreign Affairs in its political aspect and to the Ecumenical Patriarch of Constantinopole as regards its religious aspect. It has been divided into twenty self-governed territories. Each territory consists of a cardinal monastery and some other monastic establishments that surround it (cloisters, cells, cottages, seats, hermitages). All the monasteries are communes (of a convent nature) which means that there is com-mon liturgy, prayer, housing, nourishing and work among the monks. The Superior of the monastery, being elected by the monks for life, is responsible for the affairs of the monastery. The Superiors of the monasteries are members of the Holy Assembly and exercise legislative authority. Moreover, every year the monastery elects its representa-tive to the Holy Community which exercises administrative authority, while the Holy Supervision exercises executive authority and consists of 4 members, elected by the 5 hierarchically preceding monasteries.

—Colombia

Two major guerrilla groups, the Fuerzas Armadas Revolucionarias de Colombia and the Ejército de Liberación Nacional, and one major paramilitary group, the Autodefensas Unidas de Colombia, share control with the recognized government, which controls less than half of the recognized territory.

—Sendero Luminoso (Shining Path)

This revolt against Perú has waxed and waned under various governments; under the present, less authoritarian, government, it is gaining in strength.

—Mafia Italy

While the mafia acts with a degree of impunity in most of its locations, in its homeland it controls definite territory and exists in a state of war with the Italian government.

—Transdniestria

This Slavic-inhabited territory east of the Dniester River is officially an autonomous region of Moldova, but effectively independent.

—Chechnya

All of Chechnya was for several years controlled by a democratic separatist government; at present, Russia controls most Chechen territory, but the remainder is still independent.

—South Ossetia

Nominally a part of Georgia, it has fought for independence, and presumably some form of reunion with North Ossetia, in Russia.

—Abkhazia

Also nominally a part of Georgia, it has not only secured sovereignty but maintained a democracy; and it has been a major source of tension between Georgia and Russia, who accuse each other of support for their insurgents.

—South Lebanon

While the recognized Lebanese state is controlled by its own Lebanese Government, the southern part of the country is greatly influenced by Hizbullah, apparently with Syria's consent.

—Casamance

A part of the southern territory of Sénégal lying opposite the Gambia from Dakar, Casamance is under insurrectionist control.

—Djibouti

The two ethnolinguistic groups in Djibouti, the Somalis (Issas) and A'fars, have in fact divided the recognized state between them, with the former holding international recognition.

—Congo

The Democratic Republic of the Congo, also Congo-Kinshasa or Zaïre, has for long been divided into three sovereignties. The recognized portion, the west and south of the country, includes Kinshasa. There are also segments controlled by the Rassemblement Congolais pour la Démocratie, once backed by Rwanda, and the Mouvement de

Libération du Congo, once backed by Uganda. The RCD is the more powerful, based in Goma but also controlling Kisangani and the center west of the Congo. The MLC controls the north, and has in fact functioned as a state even in international affairs, intervening in the neighboring Central African Republic in favor of the now-ousted elected government. The three states and the civil opposition in Congo-Kinshasa have signed and partially implemented an accord to reunify Congo, but are stalled on the issue of military integration.

—**Uganda**

The one-party state of Uganda is facing an insurgency by the Lords Resistance Army, which controls territory in the north and has existed for seventeen years.

—**Burundi**

While at the presidential level a transition under a peace plan has taken place from a Tutsi to a Hutu, the minority Tutsi still dominate the state, and a Hutu insurrection persists.

—**Cabinda**

The Angolan exclave has effective independence, though under military dispute.

—**Nzwani**

This island of the Comoros is represented in the central government, but its status in the federation is uncertain, and its ability to separate itself much clearer.

—**Tajikistan**

Remnants of a previous insurgency remain in local control as warlords, in opposition to the central government.

—**Afghanistan**

A central administration exists, supported to a greater extent by international forces like NATO and aid, but most of the provinces are controlled by TALIBAN

—**India**

Numerous separatist insurrections exist, especially in the northeast and also the south. The central government follows various strategies in dealing with them.

—Sri Lanka

The Tamil minority in the north and east of the island has long demanded either independence or autonomy from the Sinhala majority, from whom they differ in dialect and religion, and have successfully controlled parts of the Tamil areas. The Tamil insurgent group, the Liberation Tigers of Tamil Eelam, has indicated it is willing to accept autonomy instead of full sovereignty, and is negotiating (off and on) with the parliamentary half of Sri Lanka's mixed government (the president, of a different party, seems more interested in a military solution).

—Burma

Numerous minority groups have been in rebellion against the central, mostly military, governments since independence from Britain; one of these, the Wa, has a tacit understanding of independence with the recognized government.

—Acheh

This province has never acceded to Indonesian rule, and has seen a long insurrection, with furious counterattacks from Jakarta, including one taking place at present. This appears to be going in favor of Indonesia.

—Mindanao

The southernmost island of the Philippines has a large Muslim population, as distinct from the Roman Catholic majority of the rest of the Philippines, and several insurrectionist groups have fought successfully for local control. Some autonomy has also been granted in Mindanao as a way of defusing these insurrections.

—Bougainville

The island is culturally and geographically part of the Solomon Islands, but recognized as part of Papua New Guinea, with which it is in conflict.

—Solomon Islands

While central-government control and democracy have largely been restored, a faction of Guadalcanal islanders remains in defiance of the government; the current Australian-led intervention will probably reunify the state.

Mixed entities

—The United Nations itself

The UN controls a small amount of land, a bureaucracy, and a budget through the joint decisions of its members, particularly the members of the Security Council and most particularly its permanent members, the United States, Russia, China, Britain, and France.

—The European Union

This is a voluntary, but internally-binding, confederation of states. Members, and their joint institutions, make collective decisions on a broad range of political matters.

—Arab Palestine

The occupied territories are recognized as a state by a number of other states, particularly Arab states. It has a definite amount of control, but is in other ways subordinate to Israel.

—Monaco

Control of the state is divided between a local democratic administration, a local hereditary monarchy, and the French state.

Special cases

—The Western Sahara

While not generally recognized as independent, it is also not recognized as a part of Morocco, though most of it actually is. The rest is controlled by an insurrectionist group, Polisario.

—Cyprus

The island was roughly (but only roughly) divided north and south between the minority Türks and the majority Greeks. A 1974 coup by Greek nationalists intent on union with Greece (then under military government) prompted an invasion by Turkey. The northern portion of the island is recognized by itself and Turkey alone as a sovereign state, but is in fact an autonomous region of Turkey, with which it is also culturally and economically integrated. Greek Cyprus has been admitted to the EU at Greek insistence, and will be taken to represent the entire island, as it is in international institutions. While the Turkish Cypriot government is democratic, there is some indication of growing support in the north for unification with Greek Cyprus, presumably for the economic benefits of EU membership and above all the end of the effective sanctions on Cypriot Türks. Just recently, serious efforts have been made and the divided city of Nicosia has become one again as an indication of one Cyprus state very soon.

—Nagorno-Karabakh

While officially an autonomous region of Azerbaijan, this Armenian-dominated territory is in fact an autonomous region of Armenia, and treated as such by Armenia and by the inhabitants. The current president of Armenia, Robert Kocharyan, was elevated to the premiership of Armenia while serving as president of Nagorno-Karabakh.

—Kurdistan

Two separate states in so-called Iraqi Kurdistan have existed, partially under Western military protection, since the uprising following the 1991 Persian Gulf War. They remain sovereign; but under immense international pressure, both states have surrendered their claims to independence, and as Iraq is rebuilt, they will come under further pressure to accept autonomy and submit themselves to Baghdad. They have already joined the interim governing council, and during the war they captured and then turned over two key cities, Kirkuk and Mosul, the former of which, with its oil reserves, could have made a Kurdish state more viable.

Global prospects for further political disintegration, or in a few cases integration, depend on a rationalization of the nation-state system. The nations and states of the world are far from alignment. The nation, the primary group identification for the individual, is usually based on common cultural or ethnic factors and a common evolutionary connection. While a few nations, notably the United States, have been defined by political boundaries, more often this form of nationality and nationalism is an imposition by a ruling class or a dominant majority, to augment its own power through the diversion of allegiance from cultural or ethnic nationalism. This is never more than partially successful, and always in conflict with the preexisting national identities.

Political realignment can be expected mostly as a result of attempts to harmonize state borders with national borders. The principle of self-determination demands that we support such efforts, even if done by force, for the opposite is to allow self-determination to be suppressed by force. It needn't be pointed out that there is a consensus *across the ruling classes* against self-determination; self-determination weakens those already in power. The reality is a conflict between the assertion of a legitimate right and the assertion of an illegitimate right based on force and the status quo, cloaked in arguments about stability, sovereignty, territorial integrity, and charges of terrorism and 'splittism'.

LANGUAGE

Language is both an object of integration and a facilitator of integration. But first it must be recognized that language, like geography, does not truly consist of clean lines around self-contained entities. While it is often recognized that the lay distinction between a 'language' and a 'dialect' is political, there is an assumption that linguists, at least, can make a technical distinction, and this may be true. The usual criterion, mutual intelligibility, applies on a continuum. Even unrelated dialects have intelligibility through borrowing, either one from another, or each from a third source.

Language is the use of symbols. A symbol is a sign whose association between perceptual paradigm and another concept is one of convention. (The first convention must be established by coincidence, where two interpreters—human minds, in this case—form the same association based on some common experience. That first convention can then serve as the basis for further conventions.) A logic is a system for deriving new symbols from existing ones, by combining or altering them according to certain conventional rules. The set of all symbols and logics understood by an interpreter is that interpreter's idiolect. The intersection of two or more idiolects is a dialect. It is the linguistic joint product of a group, and such a joint product exists for every possible combination of language users, with the dialect for some groups (a close family, say) being quite large, that for other groups presumably being an empty set. It would be possible to consider fixed dialect groups, linguistic communities, linking persons by chains of intersecting idiolects, but such could conceivably have no common dialect, if two extremes on the continuum have no dialect between themselves. In this analysis, only 'dialect' is used, in place of both 'language' and 'dialect'.

Urdu, which is the main language of residents of Karachi (Pakistan), was created around the 1600's in Central Asia. The word 'Urdu' comes from the Turkish word 'ordu' meaning 'camp' or 'army'. It was used as a unifying communication tool between the Muslim soldiers during their conquest of Ancient India (including Countries east until Myanmar) and Eastern Persia. These soldiers were of Persian, Arab, or Turkish descent. The majority of the soldiers, however, were of Persian origin. This directly affected the language to be used between them. The language of the government and that which dominated earlier on was Farsi, but eventually changed to Urdu to accommodate the other races. Despite the fact, Urdu vocabulary contains approximately 70% Farsi and the rest being a mix of Arabic and Turkish. The grammar takes some elements from Farsi and Arabic but also has elements that are unique and different from all three of its mother tongues.

In current times, however, many Urdu speakers have adopted many English and Hindi terms following the effects of globalization. It is the power of this language which will make formation of Republic of Jinnahpur a great success.

Linguistic evolution has primarily been through the process of division, a result of geographical isolation and lack of cultural interchange. Language change has always been a given. As populations were sundered, their dialects continued to change, and without the possibility of innovations passing between the populations, the dialects changed in separate ways and lost mutual intelligibility. Now, the process has actually begun reversing. Modern technology and the progressive integration of communications and infrastructure have made possible broadcast to large geographical areas, interpersonal communication by phone, satellite, and of course the internet, and the ready transportation of persons through the shortening of travel times. The process of dialect division is now over, exchanged for one of assimilation. This will happen around a broadcast standard, driven by culturally-dominant dialects and subdialects. Those dialects today that are still mutually intelligible will eventually collapse, through the tightening of paradigms and the expansion of symbol- and logic-sets.

There are and for some time will continue to be at least three linguistic tiers for the world. The primary form of communication is of course the local or vernacular dialect. In most of the world there is also a regional lingua franca, typically the dialect of the colonial power. The global dialect, as it stands and as it is likely to remain, is basically English. This is a historical accident, resulting from the advent of mass communication and cultural assimilation at a time when two successive states in the leading geopolitical position have been Anglophone. In particular, Britain and then the United States were the world's leading industrial, commercial, and naval powers, and have projected their power around the world, securing the functioning of a global system conducive to their economic and strategic interests. This was done in English; and because mass communication requires a global dialect, English has that position. By the time the United States loses its preeminence, English will probably be secure in its position, in the same way that European dialects have been maintained in former colonies despite the withdrawal of the sponsoring power.

But the English vocabulary is drawn from three major sources, and has a history of importing and coining words which suggests that the common dialect will be only distantly related to the Anglo-Saxon from which it evolved. The existence of a global dialect, and its use in global institutions and as a bearer of global culture, will lead to its adoption by more and more communities as a local dialect, until it is in fact a common dialect. And though it will continue to evolve, it will do so on a global basis, and remain a common dialect.

On expectation of assimilation, there are a number of dialect groups that must be considered as one for the future, where mutual intelligibility is strong enough that intergroup communication is still possible. This will definitely include: Kinyarwanda and Kirundi; Czech and Slovak; Kazak, Karakalpak, and Kyrgyz; Hindi and Urdu; Farsi, Dari, and Tajiki; Malinke, Bambara, and Dyula; Thai and Lao; Sotho, Pedi, and Tswana; Portuguese and Galician; Zulu and Ndebele; Bulgarian and Macedonian; Baltic-Finnic (Finnish, Estonian, and Karelian); Scandinavian (Danish, Norwegian, New Norwegian, Swedish, and Scanian); Sukuma, Nyamwezi, and Sumbwa; Swahili and Comorien; Karamojong and Turkana; several sets of colloquial Arabic dialects; and the East Slavic dialects. It may well include: Portuguese and Spanish; most of the Türkic dialects; and the South Slavic dialects.

RELIGION

While there is certainly some geographical component to religious integration, it is also a globalizing phenomenon. Like all aspects of cultural integration, it benefits from modern communications. The ability of the Wahabi Islam to remain unified and coordinated in the Saudi Kingdom was dependent, for most of the kingdom's existence, on the speed of kingdom's interpretation of Islam; in the modern modern Muslim world, it is nearly as easy for the Wahabi religious cleric to call or e-mail a cleric in Indonesia as one in Egypt. And as with language evolution, religious evolution now happens globally, rather than regionally.

There is also the possibility of division and schism among sects. It is probable that one or more of the denominations, even major denominations, will rupture over the issue of homosexuality. This has already been foreshadowed in the international Anglican church, where liberalization in England itself, and in North America, has caused a backlash in more conservative countries. The Southern Baptist church in the US has seen the beginnings of a similar split. Ironically, the world's largest church, Roman Catholicism, which has historically been the product of several major Christian schisms, notably those separating it from the Orthodox, Protestant (Lutheran and Calvinist), and Anglican traditions, is probably immune to further schism. Catholics are aware of their church's conservatism and will either reform it slowly and collectively, or leave individually. On the other hand, religion is perhaps most vulnerable to the principle of entropy. Given the size of new religions, it is impossible to detect the emergence of all of them, or to track the emergence of new religions in history for comparison; but each creation of a new religion introduces new distinction into the world, and there are as many possibilities as there are persons, an ever-increasing number.

Schism and proliferation are not the only possibilities. While it must be recognized that syncretism is ultimately just another avenue to schism, there have been successful mergers of denominations, such as the Unitarians and Universalists, and merger of smaller denominations in the US with mainline Protestant churches, as well as the formation of 'communions', as with the US Lutheran and Episcopalian (Anglican) churches, or 'covenants', as with the Methodist and Anglican churches in other parts of the Commonwealth. In time, as sects evolve, and evolve, moreover, from the same external pressures, they will evolve towards common points. As doctrine shifts and rites become more generic, sectarian differences will be minimized, and will finally be resolved through executive action. In this way there may be further consolidation among Protestant denominations. Beyond that, ecumenism within Christianity, Islam, and Buddhism may lead to greater understanding, doctrinal or liturgical harmonization, and a kind of reciprocity of recognition. Christians have produced a degree of entente. Muslims have gone further, creating the Organization of the Islamic Conference. In both cases, identification with the overall religion is often quite strong, sometimes trumping the sect identification. It is also possible that the ecumenical non-descript monotheism indicated, for example, in the term 'Judeo-Christian' and in the rhetoric of many political leaders and some religious leaders will lead to a non-denominational reality.

Religious integration is not necessarily a good thing in all cases. The emergence (or at least the recognition of the emergence) of Al-Qaida has shown that a globalized religious ideology can be more dangerous than a parochial one (though one could argue that the ideology itself in this case is parochial). Al-Qaida's vision of a revived Caliphate, a single theocratic state for the entire Ummah, or Muslim world, is an excellent example of an integrationist effort that has serious oppressive potential, seeking to impose the most extreme version of Islamic fundamentalism, which exists in only a few places, throughout the Islamic sphere. But then the last so-called Caliphate, under the Ottoman sultan, was hardly all-powerful, and the Al-Qaida ideology glosses over the distinctions between Sunni and Shia, Arab and non-Arab—successfully, to an extent, but only among its limited followers.

ECONOMY

The strongest global integrative force is economics, specifically trade. The aptly-named Washington Consensus in favor of a particular version of capitalism may not actually be a consensus (except in the Giscard sense), but it does have present dominance. Its ideal is a world of universal private ownership and the unfettered acquisition, production, and exchange of resources, goods, services, and capital. A number of organizations exist for the direct promotion of this. The Group of Seven, the seven industrialized states with the largest economies, gathers regularly at the ministerial level to discuss the management of the world's economy; and there is no question of the basic assumptions or of the fact that these seven finance ministers can, in fact, control the world's economy, as much as anyone can. As an outgrowth of this power and mindset, the International Monetary Fund, which once administered the world's currency union de facto, is now a lead institution in propagating the macroeconomic, financial, and monetary policies of the Washington Consensus. Annual meetings of the World Economic Forum (often referenced by the name of its usual meeting place, Davos Switzerland) have encouraged a common thinking among the world's politically- and economically-powerful individuals. The Organization for Economic Cooperation and Development is essentially an extended version of the G-7—industrialized democracies with a high GDP per capita. It includes (with overlap) all the states of the EU, NAFTA, and NATO, as well as Japan, South Korea, Australia, New Zealand, Slovakia, and Switzerland. And while the World Bank (a group of institutions around the International Bank for Reconstruction and Development) is not oriented by mission towards spreading the Consensus, nor by size of loans able to control the nature of economies in the developing world, its imprimatur, as that of the IMF, is so important to other lenders that in fact the Bank can control what developing states do, and it is now widely felt to be an instrument of the Consensus, demanding structural economic reforms as a condition for its own loans and those that follow it. While there is a basis to this perception, there are staff throughout the Bank and the Fund, including at the highest levels, who recognize the limitations of the full capitalist model.

Theoretically, a free trade area eliminates internal tariffs, a customs union eliminates internal tariffs and sets a common external tariff, and a common market eliminates all internal barriers to the movement of persons, goods, services, and capital. The World Trade Organization, an outgrowth of one of the original Bretton Woods institutions, the General Agreement on Tariffs and Trade, may eventually establish a nominal common market for the world; but even the United States does not actually have an internal common market, and the distances between locations will never cease to be a factor in the movement of either persons or goods. The WTO has been officially notified of the following customs unions: the Eurasian Economic Community; the European Union along with Andorrà, Turkey, Greek Cyprus, and Malta; the Czech and Slovak Republics; Mercosur;

the Caribbean Community; and the Central American Common Market. Many more free trade agreements have been registered, and an increasing number of service agreements (that is, free trade in services rather than goods). These regional agreements, and the aspiringly-global WTO, are removing legal barriers to economic integration, and this process will continue. And even bureaucratic impediments are being removed: through the World Customs Organization, a so-called Harmonized System for customs administration has extended to virtually all (98%) of merchandise trade. But there is also a significant amount of posturing and false pronouncement; free trade and common markets are nowhere achieved cleanly, or finally, or irrevocably.

But legal obstacles to economic integration may be among the last to fall. Economic integration is being driven by two other factors, physical and cultural integration. As communications, travel, and shipping become cheaper, faster, and more accessible, provision of goods and services on a global scale becomes an attractive possibility. As humans are exposed through technology to each other and to modern material culture, including technology itself, their desires assimilate. While some cultural protectionists, in for instance Canada or France, concern themselves with US dominance of mass culture such as film, they ignore the facts that, in the modern world, US producers of cultural products are playing to a global audience, that the US market is itself open to products from other cultures, and that there is a demand in global markets for the globalized culture, in some cases dissociating it from its US base and in some cases celebrating that base. The same phenomenon can be seen in other products, especially automobiles and electronics.

Cartels, most famously the Organization of Petroleum Exporting Countries, have recognized both the requirements and the benefits of economic globalization. OPEC has striven for a global monopoly in oil—regional monopolies are meaningless in a globalized economy. At the same time, a cartel has a natural interest in matching its intended universality of production with a universality of distribution. Lacking both competitors and barriers, profits for essential goods are virtually limitless. But a similar incentive applies short of the establishment of a cartel or a monopoly. Taking advantage of so-called economies of scale, companies have expanded, formed joint ventures, and merged in the global marketplace. This is most advanced in regions, like Europe, where the state-based economies are already integrating; the same process takes place globally as well.

New aid crisis in Pakistan

According to a press report, former Pakistan's military government had been preventing aid groups from helping more than 80,000 people—many of them acutely malnourished children—who had been displaced by a widening civil war in remote southern Balochistan, say international aid workers and diplomats.

UNICEF and Pakistan provincial health officials, who surveyed the area in July and August, report that 59,000 of those suffering were women and children and that 28 percent of the children under 5 were "acutely malnourished." Six percent of the children were so underfed that they would die without immediate medical attention. "I would say this now qualifies as a 'crimes against humanity' situation," says one foreign observer who had interviewed delegates from the region. For six months, aid agencies and diplomats have been pressing Pakistan authorities to permit them to distribute aid packages, which include emergency rations, tents, and medicine. The UN won't deliver aid without permission from the host nation, says Robert van Dijk, the top UNICEF officer for Pakistan. He and other aid workers say provincial officials have continued to assist his local staff in monitoring conditions in southern Balochistan, but more senior provincial and federal officials have simply refused his requests or derailed efforts with endless bureaucratic hurdles. "We have tried everything to get our aid there," says Mr. van Dijk. "I even know of aid groups that tried to deliver relief without permits, but they got turned back on the road." Meanwhile, reports from the region indicate the situation has grown even more wretched with the onset of winter.

Pakistani authorities have dismissed the UNICEF report as overblown, saying the majority of people in Balochistan were already dirt-poor and nomadic, and that most of those displaced by fighting returned home after an important rebel leader was killed in August. "This report is untrue," said Maj. Gen. Shaukut Sultan, a spokesman for the military and very close puppet of President Pervez Musharraf. "Almost all of those people have gone back." Van Dijk agrees that some did return home in September, but says a recent UN assessment showed that other villagers have since been displaced. "When we went back there recently, we found the same numbers of people," he says, "and even worse conditions—among the worst I've ever seen."

A story which appeared in THE WASHINGTON POST, painted the true picture of food and energy crisis in Pakistan in the following words:

"The line for cooking oil was nearly a block long, just a few miles from the Parliament building. Saida Bibi, fistful of rupees in hand, elbowed her way to the front of the angry crowd shoving its way into the government food shop. She had waited in the line seven times for seven hours over the course of a week and left empty-handed every time. But with the price of cooking oil at most markets nearly double what it was at government-subsidized food shops, she couldn't afford to do anything but wait. "I'm a poor woman. I cannot purchase this from the open market for 140 rupees a kilogram," Bibi said. "They should do something for us. First, it was a flour crisis. Then it was cooking oil prices. What are we supposed to do next?"

With consumer prices for basic goods hitting new highs in Pakistan, anxieties about the country's economy are also on the rise. After seeing five years of strong gains under the government of President Pervez Musharraf, officials are scaling back expectations for growth in the face of wrenching food and energy shortages. The crisis has taken a severe toll on Musharraf politically—public frustration with rising prices helped the opposition win big in parliamentary elections last month. Now those parties, the Pakistan People's Party and a faction of the Pakistan Muslim League led by Nawaz Sharif, must confront the unpleasant task of managing the crisis. Economists here say a surge of foreign investment and export growth are needed.

The economic downturn has hit poor Pakistanis hardest. But at the same time, the middle class, which has prospered under Musharraf's government, is feeling the pinch, particularly in the country's all-important flour industry.

Qasim Ali Khan, who owns a flour mill in the northwest frontier town of Charsadda, said wheat shortages have put a dozen mill owners out of business in his district alone. He blames Musharraf's government for the crisis. "There is a lot of wheat in our country. The government gave all the surplus wheat to foreign countries," he said. "If there is a problem with wheat, it's in Islamabad, not the northwest. The government has robbed us."

Sakib Sherani, chief economist for ABN Amro Bank Pakistan, blames years of "bad administration and bad governance" for the situation. He said overblown government projections of a bumper wheat crop are just one example of the Musharraf government's missteps. Smugglers are increasingly taking wheat from Pakistan to Afghanistan, where it is in even shorter supply. "There's a very clear incentive to smuggle wheat at this stage," Sherani said. "If you can get four or five times the price across the Afghan border, why not try it?"

As for energy crisis, from Karachi to Islamabad, meanwhile, the rattle of backup diesel generators has become the theme song of nearly every commercial enterprise that can afford one. That tune is unlikely to change while demand for power continues to outpace supply from the country's overburdened energy infrastructure. "For the next two to three years this will be a serious problem. It will be very dramatic for the economy because factories will have to shut down. It is certainly affecting business," said Kaiser Bengali, an independent economist based in Karachi. "It has become a shortage economy here. Everything is short."

Power shortages have crippled many factories and textile manufacturers across the country and shut down dozens of mills, exacerbating the problem of flour shortages.

Riazula Khan, owner of the Khan Flour Mill on the outskirts of the garrison city of Rawalpindi, said electricity prices for his family-owned mill have nearly doubled in the last year. A recent supply of government-subsidized wheat has offset some of the mill's overhead, Khan said. But the mill has been plagued by constant power outages in the last year. Over two days last month, the power went out 28 times, he said. "We are not getting any profits for our business because everything has increased," Khan said. "The price of electricity has gone up, the price of labor has gone up, the price of transport has gone up."

PAKISTAN'S POVERTY REPORT

Poverty rates in Pakistan began climbing in the 1990s after a sharp decline in the 1980s. Generally, rural poverty increased at a much faster rate than urban poverty and income inequality in the 1990s was greater than at any time in the country's history. Pakistan's rising poverty can be explained by successive governments' inability to translate economic growth into reduction of poverty and sustainable development prospects for the poor. The country has maintained an average GDP growth rate of six percent per year since the late 1940s.

Poverty can be defined as a lack of sufficient food or income. Or we can use the broader definition of a lack of access to opportunities. Either way, a quarter to a half of all Pakistanis live in poverty. Pakistan's income poverty has increased from 25% in 1985 to 30% in 1995. This 30 percent figure is a sharp increase from 20 percent in 1990. In practical terms, it means that between 1990 and 1995, as many as 18 million people may have been added to the ranks of the absolute poor in Pakistan.

During the 1980s, the proportion of absolute poor of the total population was estimated to have gone down from 38 percent in 1980 to 20 percent in 1990. In other words, the number of absolute poor decreased by at least 10 million, from

34 million in 1980 to 24 million in 1990. This diminishing poverty between 1980 and 1990 was not because of government policy or initiative. Rather, it was the result of a number of developments in the private sector.

The most important factor in poverty's decline in that ten-year period was the influx of remittances from Pakistani workers in the Middle East. These remittances made up 10 percent of the country's GNP at their peak and benefited about 25 million Pakistanis, mostly from the lower middle class.

A second factor was the Green Revolution of the 1970s. This reform helped increase the productivity of small and middle-sized farms and did not just benefit large farms.

The third factor in Pakistan's poverty decline during the 1980s was the rise of small industrial enterprises borne out of a more liberal import policy for steel and other raw materials.

However, the situation has deteriorated considerably since 1990. Pakistan's GDP growth rate slowed to 4.4 percent per year between 1990 and 1995. In addition, the remittances from the Middle East have dwindled to a mere 4.6 percent— roughly $2 billion—of the country's GDP. As well, there has been a significant slowdown in small-scale industrial growth and small-farm production. Rising inflation has also translated into a heavier burden of indirect taxes. And Pakistan's notoriously widespread corruption and endless political confrontations have taken their toll on the poor.

Other structural reasons for poverty in Pakistan include unequal income and asset (especially land) distribution, inadequate investment in providing basic social services to all Pakistanis and the country's powerful feudal structure which aims to hinder the benefits of growth to the ordinary Pakistani, instead concentrating such benefits among the country's small elite consisting of rural landlords, army generals, bureaucrats, feudals, industrialists from Punjab and certain close puppets of the military dictators.

According to Qurratulain Akhtar (link: http://qurratulain.wordpress.com/2006/09/02/poverty-in-pakistan), poverty cannot be described. It can only be felt. One knows more about poverty when he is hungry and cannot purchase food, he and his children want new clothes but they can't purchase it because of low income, he's sick and doesn't have money to have medicine, he wants to send his children to school but can't bear educational expenditures. The world Development Reports define poverty as "pronounced deprivation in well being'. Poverty can be measured by following three methods, i.e. Head Count Ratio, Basic Needs Approach, and Poverty of Opportunity.

According to Head Count Ratio, the persons who fall below the poverty line as determined in the country are regarded as poor. In Pakistan, for instance, the persons who earn income which cannot meet the daily intake of about 2350 calories per person are considered to fall below the poverty line. Basic Need's Approach suggests the measurement of 'poverty' with reference to income distribution. According to this approach if the persons of a fixed income group cannot purchase basic needs, i.e. food, clothing, housing, education and basic health facilities, they are considered to fall below the poverty line. The third approach which is 'poverty of opportunity', if due to fall in income, health or education the human sufferings increase the people are considered to have fallen below the poverty line.

Case of Pakistan

Poverty has many dimensions in Pakistan. People have not only low incomes but they also are suffering from lack of access over basic needs. The major challenge of today is poverty reduction. In Pakistan, Poverty Reduction Strategy was launched by the government in 2001 in response to the rising trend in poverty during 1990s. It consisted of the following five elements:-

(a) Accelerating economic growth and maintaining macroeconomic stability.

(b) Investing in human capital.

(c) Augmenting targeted interventions.

(d) Expanding social safety nets.

(e) Improving governance.

The net outcome of interactions among these five elements would be the expected reduction in transitory and chronic poverty on a sustained basis. The reduction in poverty and improvement in social indicators and living conditions of the society are being monitored frequently through large—scale household surveys in order to gauge their progress in meeting the targets set by Pakistan for achieving the seven UN Millennium Development Goals by 2015.

In recent years the role of remittances in reducing poverty has been widely acknowledged. Remittances allow families to maintain or increase expenditure on basic consumption, housing, education, and small-business formation. Total remittances inflows since 2001-02 and until 2005-06 have amounted over $ 19 billion or Rs.1129 billion. Such a massive inflow of remittances particularly towards the rural or semi-urban areas of Pakistan must have helped loosen the budget constraints of their recipients, allowing them to increase consumption of both durables and non-durables, on human capital accumulation (through both education and health care), and on real estate. To the extent that the poorer sections of society depend on remittances for their basic consumption needs, increased flow of remittances would be associated with reduction in poverty.

Although, growth is necessary but it is not sufficient to make any significant dent to poverty. Realizing this fact the government had launched a directed program under the title of Poverty Related and Social Sector Program some five years ago. Over the last five years the government has spent Rs.1332 billion on poverty-related and social sector program to cater to the needs of poor and vulnerable sections of the society. Such a huge spending on targeted program is bound to make a significant dent to poverty. The Household Integrated Economic Survey (HIES)—a component of Pakistan Social and Living Standards Measurement (PSLM) Survey provides important data on household income, consumption expenditure and consumption patterns at national and provincial level with rural-urban breakdown. The information pertaining to income and expenditure of the households are used to estimate poverty. The HIES is specifically designed to monitor poverty status of population by collecting information on consumption expenditure at the household level. With a representative sample size of 14706 households, it covered 5808 and 8898 households in the urban and rural areas of the country, respectively. The Survey was started in July 2004 and the entire field operations were completed in June 2005. The poverty line is based on 2350 calories per adult equivalent per day. It is also comparable with poverty line of 2000-01 as it was also based on 2350 calories and calculated from Pakistan Integrated Household Survey (PIHS). The poverty line of 2004-05 is adjusted by the inflation rate during the period 2001-2005.

The latest estimate of inflation—adjusted poverty Line is Rs.878.64 per adult equivalent per month   up from Rs.723.40 in 2001. Headcount ratio, i.e., percentage of population living below the poverty line has fallen from 34.46 percent in 2001 to 23.9 percent in 2004-05, a decline of 10.6 percentage points. In absolute numbers the count of poor persons has fallen from 49.23 million in 2001 to 36.45 million in 2004-05. The percentage of population living below the poverty line in rural areas has declined from 39.26 percent to 28.10 percent while those in urban areas, has declined from 22.69 percent 14.9 percent. In other words, rural poverty has declined by 11.16 percentage points and urban poverty is reduced by 7.79 percentage points.

Consumption inequality increased marginally during the period. These findings are consistent with the developments on economic scene that have taken place in Pakistan since 2000-01. A strong growth in economy, rise in per capita income, a large inflow of remittances and massive spending on poverty-related and social sector programs were expected to reduce poverty in Pakistan. It is important to note that the methodology and the estimates of poverty have been endorsed by the development partners such as the World Bank, the Asian Development Bank, the United Nations Development Program (UNDP) and the Department for International Development (DFID), UK. The service of world renowned poverty expert, Professor Nanak Kakwani was hired by the UNDP to independently look into the methodology as well as poverty estimates. He also authenticated both the methodology and estimates. In order to maintain consistency across years, it is essential that we apply the same agreed upon methodology over the years, irrespective of its weaknesses and strengths.

After that social safety nets have been neglected, there's no proper pronouncement by government in this regard. And finally 'improvement in Governance', which has been left untouched. For a long time, whenever senior government personnel visits a major city like Karachi, all the traffic on the roads is diverted in the streets and all the work being done is stopped in order to ensure the security of the official. By this way those who earn on daily wages, have to suffer loss in daily wages. I quoted this example because when rulers are so 'insecure' in their own homeland how can they improve the governance or develop their country or how can they ensure the safety of the whole country?

Concisely, in spite of all efforts of government poverty still stands as an iron wall for Pakistan's economy. And to break this iron wall we are in need to apply all five poverty reduction strategies at utmost level.

According to a recent press report published in the daily DAWN:

How many poor people are there in Pakistan? After trying to find a convincing answer to this question in the last five years, the government has finally come out with a figure of poor people on the basis of a survey report of the year 2001 that was considered 'flawed and inaccurate'. But to government's misfortune, no one is ready to believe official headcount of poor, even though the data and information on poverty carry endorsement of Pakistan's donors.

According to the government headcount, endorsed by the donors, without which officials feel credibility remains doubtful, the number of poor people in Pakistan had come down to 36.45 million in 2004-05 from 49.23 million in 2001. In the year 2001, the percentage of poor in Pakistan was 34.46 per cent more than one-third of the entire population, which has now come down to 23.9 per cent which is less than a quarter. But even with the endorsement from the donors, many people in Pakistan are not ready to believe the government headcount and there are many questions being raised.

The first question is about making the findings of a survey report basis of the claim of fall in the number of poor people in Pakistan that was doubtful and flawed for the government and still remains a defective document. The Pakistan Household Integrated Household Survey (PIHS) 2000-01 was carried out as a normal, routine and periodical exercise. The Economic Survey 2001-02 informed the public of completion of survey exercise and that the findings and report would soon be made public. It was never made public and was suppressed.

The information and data collected in the PHIS was processed in April 2002. But all the findings were concealed. Sometimes in the year 2002, a World Bank mission led by an Indian lady economist Tara Vishwanath visited Pakistan and carried out a study. During the course of the study, Shaukat Aziz, then finance minister, had a meting with Ms Tara Vishwanath. It was an unpleasant meeting in which there was a sharp difference in poverty perception between the Pakistan government and the visiting World Bank mission. The World Bank then published a comprehensive document entitled "Pakistan: Poverty Assessment, Vulnerabilities, Social Gaps and Rural Dynamics".

The official figures on poverty were announced in a meeting of the Pakistan Development Forum in 2003. It was stated that poverty increased by six per cent during 1996-97 to 1999 when Nawaz Sharif was Prime Minister. The increase in poverty was only 1.5 per cent in 1999-01 when President Musharraf and his team were running the government.

Poverty ratio was then calculated at about 34 per cent. But in the recent announcement, the government considers 34 per cent poverty ratio in 2001 flawed and inaccurate and has put it at 36pc. It gives the government a credit of bringing down poverty level from 36 per cent to about 24pc in just five years. All this achievement is being claimed on the basis of a survey report that was declared flawed and inaccurate when it was framed and even now after all processing its credibility has been put into doubt, as the ratio of poor has been increased from 34 to 36 per cent.

Strangely, the government's recent report on poverty does not give a province-wise breakdown. Each and every province and district have distinct economic, geographic features and population complexion. Why is the government shy of informing poverty incidence in urban and rural Sindh and other parts of the country?

One of the factors contributed to bringing down the poverty level in the country is the inflow of about Rs1.1 trillion remittances during five years. Such a massive inflow of remittances, particularly towards the rural or semi-urban areas of Pakistan must have helped loosen the budget constraint of their recipients, allowing them to increase consumption of both durables and non-durables, on human capital accumulation (through education and healthcare) and on real estate. The conclusion is that poor sections of population depend on remittances.

The question is how many parts of the country receive remittances. Do remittances flow in Jacobabad, Nawabshah, Larkana, Dadu, Sibi, Kalat, etc? Is the poverty level in these districts of Sindh and Balochistan same as that of rural areas of Punjab, NWFP and Kashmir where remittances are flowing in? The third question is how the government can claim an improvement in employment when agriculture growth is abysmally low. Agriculture engages about 43 per cent of labour force. A drop in agriculture is bound to have rendered many thousands jobless as is evident from a jump in urban migration.

Social scientists and economists see growing poverty a big challenge for the country and growing disparities in income as a big threat to stability. In my opinion, instead of concentrating on improvement of Pakistan's overall poverty situation, it is better that Pakistan should be divided into different independent parts in order to make them self-sustainable by exploring their individual resources.

FAILURE OF
TWO-NATION THEORY

The single most important event in Pakistan's history is its first disintegration in 1971 which caused the formation of Bangladesh. Yet, the sentiment sponsored by the then Pakistan's intelligence agencies in connivance with the Military Establishment behind Pakistani nationhood remained the socalled two-nation theory. The interest groups that comprise the Pakistani state are still entirely reliant on this bogus theory to justify the security paradigm that underlies decision-making and allocation of resources. And yet, the single most important event in Pakistan's history has todate remained strangely peripheral and misunderstood, misrepresented as it is by the elite. To understand the concept of Pakistanhood that has been propagated over its 60-year history was actually to understand the political economy of this bogus country.

All state structures that are fundamentally undemocratic rely on means of social control, whether they are coercive or subtle. This social control is usually founded on a basic idea, on a singular ideology that dominates all aspects of life. In Pakistan's case, this ideology in its essence asserts that Muslims are unable to co-exist with Hindus is indeed a great intellectual flaw to believe in. The socalled religious scholars do not tell people that at the time of the holy prophet of Islam Hazrat Muhammad SAW, Jews and Christians were living along with Muslims and there was nothing said by the holy prophet SAW to create any borders between Muslims and Jews/Christians. As such, in the case of Pakistan which was created as a home for the Muslims of the subcontinent, Pakistan today teeters on the brink of political bankruptcy and hence in the top list of failed states of this age just because of leaving the path shown by the holy prophet Hazrat Muhammad SAW. Pakistan today is described by a ravaged economy, all-consuming societal ills, and a political culture that resembles a modern-day monarchy controlled directly or indirectly by military establishment combined with domination by a particular province called Punjab which has a share of 99% in Pakistani army.

The assumption that Muslims were inherently a single nation separate from the nation of Hindus in India, was proven false by the events of 1971, when it became apparent that the Bengali identity was dearer to those who lived in East Pakistan than the Muslim identity. Today, there still are more Muslims in India than in Pakistan. And, have we forgotten that there are still over a hundred thousand Biharis in refugee camps in Bangladesh that the Pakistani state refuses to accept? Well, this refusal is because of cruel Punjabi military dictators who have been ruling Pakistan since long. Still, the two-nation theory continues to inform Pakistan's polity in a profound way, by providing the energy for its Kashmir preoccupation. Kashmir continues to irk because it symbolises a failure to fulfil the two-nation dream. The fallacy of the two-nation theory has been proven time and again, its contradictions undermining its credibility, but the tragedy for Pakistan is that the theory continues to be employed by the military dictatorship and political elite to perpetuate a system that has clearly failed to cater to even the basic needs of its citizens. The fact that the majority of Pakistanis still subscribe to this theory underlines how powerful a means of social control it is. However, this theory shall soon disappear if the single largest political force of Urdu-speaking nation called MQM should understand reasons of failure of two-nation theory and accordingly create awareness among its members in particular and the entire urdu-speaking nation in general.

At the time of partition in 1947, the Pakistani military was a marginal actor. Neither was the religious clergy a major player in the politics of the new nation; in fact, the Jamaat-e-Islami had been opposed to the break up of India. The Hindu intelligentsia and entrepreneurial class from entire regions, including the Siraiki belt and Sindh, had packed up and crossed the new border to India. At that stage then, it was the big landlords, feudals and puppets of English masters that had emerged as the most influential lobby within the Pakistan movement which manipulated the ill-gotten political power. The rest was an unnatural amalgamation of different interest groups aspiring to state power. And from the outset, the Kashmir dispute defined the national psyche.

Mohammad Ali Jinnah is often quoted as having said that religion should not interfere in the affairs of the state. He is said to have asserted on numerous occasions that Pakistan would be a secular state, albeit with a Muslim majority. However, he also made it very clear that Kashmir was Pakistan's "jugular" and the new nation was incomplete without it. Jawaharlal Nehru was similarly uncompromising, promising on the one hand to give Kashmiris the right to decide their own future, and on the other, initiating the militarization of the area by sending thousands of troops to fortify its frontiers. At the very outset, the leaders of the freedom movement made the Kashmir issue contentious, and this has since weighed heavily on the entire region. A mentality that Kashmir must be made part of the country has dominated the public discourse in Pakistan, and as such, has given the military rulers as well as the hypocrites hiding inside Pakistan's religious parties an easy excuse to propagate their destructive ideologies. Meanwhile in India, the establishment continues to mandate gross violations of human rights in Kashmir, claiming it is a secular, democratic state at the same time.

The inordinate amounts of money spent on defence, the extraordinary and unnatural rise of the religious right in the last 30 years, and the degeneration of political parties in Pakistan all have something to do with the security paradigm of the state. Essentially, it is the threat perception from a bigger and stronger India (and therefore, the argument goes, the ten times as many Hindus on that side of the border who thirst for Muslim blood) that gives license to the military establishment in Pakistan to accord special privileges to itself in the name of protecting Pakistan and its Muslim population. The rise of the religious right (and the proliferation of jehadi elements) and the thwarting of the political process are, then, outcomes of the inordinate power that the Pakistan's military establishment exercises. These trends have been reinforced by the whims of the United States both during the Cold War, and now.

Pakistan had reached a critical point when General Zia-ul Haq took over the country in 1977. A year later, the Soviet Union invaded Afghanistan and as the definitive conflict of the Cold War shaped up, Pakistan emerged as western capitalism's point man on the Subcontinent. It is now common knowledge that the US supported the Afghan mujahideen and the many splinter jehadi groups that have since become the US's primary enemy in the "war on terror". Nevertheless, then it was the Islamisation of the country that made it possible for General Zia to propagate the notion of jehad against communist Russia in order to get cheap fighting force ready to fight in the name of Allah.

This process of Islamisation had actually begun with Zulfikar Ali Bhutto. Having come to power on the slogan of Islamic socialism, Bhutto proceeded to oversee the writing of the 1973 constitution in which Ahmadis were declared non-Muslims. In 1974, the socalled "peaceful" nuclear test carried out by India provided impetus for a new wave of hysteria in Pakistan. Bhutto launched the Pakistani nuclear programme, with the slogan ghaas khaenge ("we will eat grass" if we have to but we will make the bomb) to emphasise his commitment to the creation of an Islamic bomb. Once the need to combat the perceived Indian threat was re-established as the primary policy concern of the state, it was less important for Mr Bhutto to make good his populist election promises of roti, kapra, makan (food, clothing and shelter) than it was to stand toe to toe with India.

In many ways, Bhutto's tenure was dominated by efforts to banish the disaster of 1971 from Pakistan's collective memory. The nationalist movement had proved that not only did the Bengalis not have any allegiance to the Kashmir cause but that they also disputed the special privileges accorded to an army that was almost exclusively based in the western wing. Indeed, Sheikh Mujibur Rahman consistently and accurately alleged that East Pakistan's export earnings from jute were being used to fund the army and an industrial complex in West Pakistan rather than to cater to the needs of the eastern wing.

So the security paradigm emerged with renewed vigour after General Zia came to power, courtesy the Afghan war. Along with it came the shocks that split the nation along religious, sectarian, and ethnic lines. The promulgation of "Islamic" laws such as the Hudood Ordinance which openly discriminate against women in cases of sexual abuse, persecution and murder of religious scholars from Shia sect and the explosion of sectarian conflict, all took place during the Zia era. The de-politicisation of society was accompanied by the politicisation of the intelligence agencies. Political parties remained sidelined for almost a decade. By the time elections took place in 1988 by virtue of Zia-ul Haq's mysterious death, state and society had been transformed.

The fallout of 12 years of unstable democracy was an intensification of the influence of the security apparatus in the affairs of the state. It is now common knowledge that Pakistan-based jehadis were at the forefront of the militarised resistance in Kashmir. As such, therefore, Kashmir policy dominated national politics through the 1990s and the military establishment in the post-Zia era has never released its stranglehold on power to any meaningful extent. Development expenditure fell from a high of 7.6 percent of GDP in 1991-92 to 2.8 percent in 2000-01. Meanwhile, ex-penditure on defence and debt servicing was equivalent to 88 percent of total tax revenue in 1991 and increased to over 90 percent of total tax revenue in 2000. Now, in 2008, the economic situation of Pakistan is more worse after yet another 8-year long rule of military dictatorship and puppet political parties like Muslim League (Q) which was established by Pakistan's Inter-Services Intelligence (ISI) to provide legal and political support to Pervez Musharraf.

The stronghold that the military establishment has on resource allocation is at least partly due to the fact that it has such a massive influence on the political process. The intelligence agencies that had been made all-powerful during the covert US operation in Afghanistan in the Cold War era have maintained their grip on Pakistani politics. Meanwhile parochial sectarian, ethnic and jehadi groups have injected a new terror into Pakistani society. Unfortunately, these forces are not accountable to anyone—they have no institutional history, and whether they flourish or wither away is a decision over which the Pakistani public has no control.

While the aftermath of 9-11 has inadvertently led to the exposure of this nexus, it has not changed the way the Pakistani state is structured or the essential power dynamics that exist within Pakistani society. In fact, the military's domination has been cemented during Pervez Musharraf's unending tenure so far. All civilian agencies in the country were headed by retired or serving army officials. Two out of four provincial governors were retired generals. Three federal ministers were retired army men. However, after the February 18's general elections in Pakistan, the situation has changed a bit. Firstly because of the new Army Chief Kiyani who has tried to prove that he is better than Musharraf as he ordered return of military personnel serving in civilian capacities to return to their army positions and secondly because a new socalled democratic setup has been put in place.

Many political parties have been co-opted into this socalled democratic system, which is a reflection not only of the degeneration of politics in the country, but also of the fact that political parties do not expect to ever exercise authority independent of the army's wishes. Ultimately, the established political elite is aware that challenging the military's consumption of a disproportionate share of the budget, or the fact that army men are given special privileges, offices, and rights, will only lead to its own demise. Of course there is the small matter of political parties being unrepresentative and self-interested. Groups with vested interests such as the landed elite, an industrial class which derives its competitive edge through state-sanctioned cronyism, and the civil bureaucracy, have all at one time or the other allied themselves with the military establishment to serve their own needs and wants.

The security paradigm and the accompanying forms of social control that allow the military to continue its domination of state and society are intact. Textbooks used in schools propagate untruths about the atrocities of the independence movement; they also promote intolerance toward religious minorities. State-run television and radio spew out long propaganda programmes highlighting India's evil designs and the need for combat-ready armed forces and modern weapons to repel Indian aggression. PTV often shows a short programme called Kashmir File after its 9 pm Khabarnama, showcasing graphic footage of Kashmiris being abused by Indian soldiers, calling for their freedom from oppression. Other private TV Channels like GEO and ARY do not even talk about Kashmir because of their viewership in India and Kashmir.

Nevertheless, cracks are emerging. The military establishment has been forced to re-evaluate its role in facilitating conflicts on its western and north-eastern borders.

Nation-states peripheral to the global system such as Pakistan have almost completely surrendered sovereignty in crucial affairs, and so perhaps even a US-imposed change could negate the original US-created extremist threat. But US interests do not include forcing a fundamental reorientation of Pakistan's state ideology. The US military-industrial complex reaps many profits from Pakistan's hunger for military technology and infrastructure, and very much wants to maintain its market share in South Asia.

There is no chance for any genuine change in Pakistan which could be based on public recognition within Pakistan that the prevailing state ideology is untenable. As the last budget was released, Pakistani policy-makers are once again hard put to explain away the low growth and the poor level of poverty-related expenditure. They point to a 14 percent increase in defence spending over the past year by way of excuse. They will continue to do so until the global hegemon, international financial institutions or some other influential actor challenges their policies and the wisdom of the imperatives that guide them. The Pakistani people can hardly afford to entrust their destinies and the destiny of their political culture to a verifiably fickle international community.

ANOTHER PERSPECTIVE

Pakistan is an idea that has miserably failed comprehensively. The lawlessness of successive Governments whether military or otherwise, the consistent violence, the contempt for civilised norms of domestic and international conduct, the constant regression to primitive forms of mass mobilisation, are all delayed and protracted manifestations of the fundamental and complete failure of the idea of Pakistan.

This failure was evident in the very first years after the birth of the country out of the falsehood of the 'two-nation theory' and the bloody slaughters of Partition. Within six year of Independence, the poet Faiz Ahmed 'Faiz' wrote, in his poignant and evocative Subh-e-Azadi (The Dawn of Freedom): "This tainted light, this gloom-smothered dawn/This is not the dawn we had hoped for ... The despondent night still lies heavy upon us/The moment of deliverance from bondage is yet to come ..." Faiz spent years in Pakistani jails and in exile, excluded and marginalised by successive regimes, till his death in 1984. The tragic destiny of one of the greatest lights of modern Urdu literature is symbolic of all the good that may have survived the catastrophic creation of Pakistan in the crucible of communal hatred.

After years of exploiting and abusing the Islamic identity and the idea of jihad to fulfil his personal ambitions, and eventually to create the world's first Islamist ideological state, Jinnah declared, on August 11, 1947, "You may belong to any religion, caste or creed, that has nothing to do with the business of the state ... in due course of time Hindus will cease to be Hindus and Muslims will cease to be Muslims—not in a religious sense for that is the personal faith of an individual—but in a political sense as citizens of one state ..."

Whatever the personal beliefs or proclivities of leaders in Pakistan, their practices have invariably played upon and reinforced extremism, producing a politics dominated by obscurantism, on the one hand, and authoritarianism, on the other. Indeed, the 'ideology of Pakistan' precludes the possibility of a secular democratic politics—as any such movement would easily be construed as an attack on Islam itself. The purported 'threat to Islam' has been the essence of political mobilisation from pre-Partition days to the present, and there is, given the present social, political and strategic architecture of Pakistan, no possibility of its dilution in the foreseeable future. Indeed, Pakistan's intervention in Kashmir has exponentially deepened these proclivities, as Jean-Luc Racine notes, putting "incompleteness and exteriority at the heart of its national vision".

The depth to which these elements have become rooted in the institutional, political and social structures in Pakistan is seldom understood by outsiders, who think they can tweak the system here and there—a little madarsa reform, a few hundred million in 'development' aid—and secure the transformation of Pakistan's historical pathologies into a modern and functioning democracy. Unfortunately, the reality of Pakistan is that it cannot lend itself to incremental reform. For the past nearly six years, the West has pumped in billions of dollars in the hope that it can purchase reform and moderation in this country, but these years have seen nothing but a continuous expansion of both obscurantist and authoritarian tendencies.

The Pakistani identity is based on irreducible opposites, an adversarial ideology that initially saw the Hindu as the enemy, but that has thereafter added a multiplicity of 'hostile others'—Ahmedias, Shias, internal regional minorities, the West—in its expanding circle of strife. Much of the violence in the South Asian region—and indeed, a large proportion of Islamist terrorism across the world—finds its roots in this psyche, rather than in any concrete and coherent strategic objectives or interests. Unless the institutional basis of this ideology, the power structure and sections of society that have historically profited from it, are dismantled, Pakistan's pathologies will continue to compound themselves, only occasionally tempered by objective external circumstances and a loss of capacities.

Pakistan's leaders have long committed the country to a course that can only have disastrous consequences for the nation, and unfortunate consequences for the region. Snared in a self-perpetuating dynamic, Pakistan itself cannot generate the means to escape this predicament. Unless strong and sustained external interventions, coherently directed at re-engineering the geography of Pakistan, and at demolishing the ideological state, are not evolved, Pakistan will continue to grow as a threat for the whole world.

Such a strategy is not directed against the people of Pakistan living in its provinces who are the first and most helpless victims of the prevailing conditions. To understand what is being suggested, it is useful to take the analogy of another ideological state—the Soviet Union—which, at one time, sought to export its ideology across the world through movements of mass mobilisation and violence. The collapse of the Soviet Union was engineered through a slow strategy of internal erosion and unsustainable defence competition with the West. But when that collapse came, the unyielding hostility and suspicion between the so-called Eastern Bloc and the West simply evaporated, as did one of the principal sources of international tension since the Second World War.

Pakistan is no Soviet Union but yes Pakistan can be another Yugoslavia as far as its disintegration is concerned. The threat of global terror that currently emanates from Pakistani soil is disruptive and disturbing, but it wanes into insignificance against the threat of 'mutually assured destruction' with which the polarised Soviet and Western blocs confronted the world. 'Re-engineering' Pakistan has now become an inevitable task. Has someone also called it "Balkanization"? Indeed yes.

URDU-SPEAKING PEOPLE OF KARACHI: ARE THEY A NATION OR COMMUNITY?

The Urdu-speaking people settled in Karachi have a rich history, a unique heritage and an identity cutting across religious beliefs. Having said so, it is needed to be considered whether Urdu-speaking people can be called a separate Nation or a separate Community. Let us first define what we mean by Nation or Community as also discussed by me in another chapter on "Nationalism".

The Oxford Dictionary defines Nation as "Distinct race of people having common descent, language, history or political institutions". Community on the other hand has been defined as "Identity of character; organised political, municipal or social body, body of men living in same locality, body of men having religion, profession etc in common; the public, monastic, socialistic or other body". By definition the former implies a larger group of people for which religion is not a determining factor. The latter implies a smaller and a local or regional identity in which religion or profession can also be determining factors. We may now view the concept of nationhood as it has evolved in history. Human beings have been graduating from small groupings to larger groupings. Starting from the family, to the tribe, to the community, to the Nation and now to an era of globalization and inter-dependence, in which nationalism is melting down to acquire an international character.

The definition of Nation in the dictionary appears incomplete on two counts. Geography has not been taken into account nor the desire of the people to live together as a Nation. We can amplify this by giving examples. President Nasser in conjunction with his counterpart in Syria conceived the idea of a bigger Nation State on the basis of common ethnic and religious identity. A United Arab Republic was formed comprising Egypt and Syria but the experiment did not succeed for geographical reasons. The two countries reverted back to their separate national identity. The other example is of Pakistan. It once broke up in 1971 not only because of linguistic differences but also due to lack of geographical connection. Even now, Pakistan can be further disintegrated because people living in Karachi have nothing to do with the War-on-Terror being fought between the NATO forces and the radical Taliban forces in the North Western border of presently undivided Pakistan. Geographically speaking, Karachi has no connection with this socalled War-on-Terror.

The other attribute of nationhood not included in the definition of a Nation is the desire of the people wanting to live together as one political entity. This is best illustrated from the example of the USA. It was the desire of the migrants from different countries in Europe to live together as a Nation, despite their historical, ethnic, cultural and linguistic disparities, which became the basis for the emergence of the mightiest Nation of the World today. In the case of Pakistan, the Bengali Muslims decided to live on their own and hence got their independence in 1971.

It is pertinent that religion has not been mentioned in the dictionary definition of Nation and rightly so. There have only been two Nation States formed on the basis of religion in the history of mankind. These are Israel for Jews and Pakistan for Muslims. Both these examples have not been very happy ones. Israel is a running sore disturbing peace and enmity in the Middle East. As for Pakistan, religion could not keep its two wings together. The formation of Bangladesh proclaimed it loud and clear, that religion is not the binding force to prevent the break up of a political entity. It also demonstrated the failure of the Two-Nation theory.

The most eloquent vision of Indian nationhood has been given by Dr. Muhammad Iqbal (famous poet from Sialkot) in his immortal poem which read as

"Sare Jahan Se Acha Hindustan Hamara, Ham Bulbule Hai Iske Yeh Gulistan Hamara"

and his reference to the Indian ancient civilization

"Yunan-u-Misr-u-Rooma Sab Mit Gaye Jahan Se, Baqi Magar Hai Ab Tak Naamo Nishan Hamara

Kuch Baat Hai Ki Hasti Mitati Nahi Hamari, Sadiyoon Raha Hai Dushman Daure Zaman Hamara"

What is it which has made the Indian nation survive and be the only surviving ancient civilization of the world? It has been of its pluralistic outlook, composite culture and ideals of love and brotherhood. All this is best epitomized in the concept of Kashmiriyat forged by Indians in Kashmir, which is not only India's cherished heritage but a beacon for rest of the humanity. On the contrary, Pakistan has emerged as a failed state. Pakistan's disintegration has become inevitable in view of growing terrorist threat to the whole world from its soil.

YUGOSLAVIA VS PAKISTAN IN THE CONTEXT OF DISINTEGRATION

The disintegration of the Socialist Federal Republic of Yugoslavia (SFRY) was part of the process of atomization within the Eastern and Central European socialist states brought about by the collapse of the socialist bloc, a crucial aspect of which was the suicidal disappearance of the Soviet Union. Similarly, Pakistan's disintegration can be part of the process of its denuclearization in view of the threat that the radical Islamist forces sponsored and funded by Pakistan's own military establishment may capture the nuclear arsenal of Pakistan and put the whole world into jeopardy.

In 1991, when the process of Yugoslavia's disintegration began, the SFRY had a socialist development model with its own characteristics, based on economic self-management. It was a state made up of various republics and a central federal government. Pakistan is also in some way similar to this type of mechanism for the sole reason that presently undivided Pakistan has 4 provinces which have been structured on the basis of ethnicity. Punjabis live in Punjab, Sindhis live in Sindh, Pakhtoons live in NWFP (Pakhtoonistan) and Balochis live in Balochistan while Urdu-speaking nation live in Karachi (the proposed Republic of Jinnahpur) which is currently part of Sindh province as a glaring conspiracy since the inception of Pakistan.

With its own economic development, SFRY had its own levels of productivity, public health, education and social welfare that were on a par with many other developed European countries. Same case is with presently undivided Pakistan.

However, Yugoslavia's political role within the Non-Aligned Movement and its close relationship with the Third World nations kept it in the sights of the West Germany and the United States in particular which were interested in dispensing with the last vestiges of socialism in Central Europe. On the contrary, Pakistan is still enjoying its independence because of certain political miracles which enabled

145

this fraudulent country to exist beyond its natural life although Pakistan did taste some disintegration back in 1971. For the Western world, radical Islam is also a threat similar to Socialism. Hence, in view of this fact, there should be honest efforts to be applied by the Western world to ensure that Pakistan is also disintegrated in order to combat the spread of radical Islamization in the region.

In the case of former Yugoslavia, an area of geopolitical influence for Germany, historically interested in having a more active role in this part of the Balkans, it also came to be a central element within the U.S. concept of a unipolar world governed by Washington. In that context, the socialist bloc's collapse and the disintegration of the Soviet Union formed a perfect pretext for foreign appetites finding any justification whatsoever. By exacerbating millennia-long ethnic, religious and nationalist problems, they initially focused on Bosnia and Herzegovina and now the entire Federal Republic of Yugoslavia has been fully disintegrated in its true perspective with the formation of an Independent Kosovo recently. If this can happen to Yugoslavia, why not to Pakistan?

The Downfall of East Pakistan

In December 1970 Pakistan held general elections, its first since independence. The Awami League, headed by East Pakistan's popular Bengali leader Mujibur Rahman (Sheikh Mujib; 1920-75), won a majority of seats in the new assembly, but West Pakistan's chief martial law administrator and president, General Agha Mohammad Yahya Khan, refused to honour the democratic choice of his nation's majority. At the end of March 1971, after failed negotiations in which Mujib demanded virtual independence for East Pakistan, Yahya Khan ordered a military massacre in Dhaka (Dacca). Though Mujib was arrested and flown to prison in West Pakistan, he called upon his followers in the east to rise up and proclaim their independence as Bangladesh ("Land of the Bengalis"). No fewer than 10 million refugees fled East Pakistan across the border to India in the ensuing eight months of martial rule and sporadic firing by West Pakistan's army. Soon after the monsoon stopped, India's army moved up to the Bangladesh border and by early December advanced virtually unopposed to Dhaka, which was surrendered in mid-December 1971. Mujib, released by President Bhutto, who had taken over from the disgraced Yahya Khan, flew home to a hero's welcome and in January 1972 became the first prime minister of the People's Republic of Bangladesh.

India's stunning victory over Pakistan in the Bangladesh war was achieved in part because of Soviet military support and diplomatic assurances. The Treaty of Peace, Friendship, and Cooperation, signed in 1971 by India with the Soviet Union, gave India the arms it used in the war. With the birth of Bangladesh, India's position in South Asia became dominant, and its foreign policy, which remained officially nonaligned, tilted toward the Soviet Union.

The origins of the third Indo-Pakistani conflict (1971) were different from the previous conflicts. The Pakistani failure to accommodate demands for autonomy in East Pakistan in 1970 led to secessionist demands in 1971 (see The Rise of Indira Gandhi, ch. 1). In March 1971, Pakistan's armed forces launched a fierce campaign to suppress the resistance movement that had emerged but encountered unexpected mass defections among East Pakistani soldiers and police. The Pakistani forces regrouped and reasserted their authority over most of East Pakistan by May.

As a result of these military actions, thousands of East Pakistanis died at the hands of the Pakistani army. Resistance fighters and nearly 10 million refugees fled to sanctuary in West Bengal, the adjacent Indian state. By midsummer, the Indian leadership, in the absence of a political solution to the East Pakistan crisis, had fashioned a strategy designed to assist the establishment of the independent nation of Bangladesh. As part of this strategy, in August 1971, India signed a twenty-year Treaty of Peace, Friendship, and Cooperation with the Soviet Union. One of the treaty's clauses implied that each nation was expected to come to the assistance of the other in the event of a threat to national security such as that occurring in the 1965 war with Pakistan. Simultaneously, India organized, trained, and provided sanctuary to the Mukti Bahini (meaning Liberation Force in Bengali), the East Pakistani armed resistance fighters.

Unable to deter India's activities in the eastern sector, on December 3, 1971, Pakistan launched an air attack in the western sector on a number of Indian airfields, including Ambala in Haryana, Amritsar in Punjab, and Udhampur in Jammu and Kashmir. The attacks did not succeed in inflicting substantial damage. The Indian air force retaliated the next day and quickly achieved air superiority. On the ground, the strategy in the eastern sector marked a significant departure from previous Indian battle plans and tactics, which had emphasized set-piece battles and slow advances. The strategy adopted was a swift, three-pronged assault of nine infantry divisions with attached armored units and close air support that rapidly converged on Dhaka, the capital of East Pakistan. Lieutenant General Sagat Singh, who commanded the eighth, twenty-third, and fifty-seventh divisions, led the Indian thrust into East Pakistan. As these forces attacked Pakistani formations, the Indian air force rapidly destroyed the small air contingent in East Pakistan and put the Dhaka airfield out of commission. In the meantime, the

Indian navy effectively blockaded East Pakistan. Dhaka fell to combined Indian and Mukti Bahini forces on December 16, bringing a quick end to the war.

Action in the western sector was divided into four segments, from the cease-fire line in Jammu and Kashmir to the marshes of the Rann of Kutch in north-western Gujarat. On the evening of December 3, the Pakistani army launched ground operations in Kashmir and Punjab. It also started an armored operation in Rajasthan. In Kashmir, the operations were concentrated on two key points, Punch and Chhamb. The Chhamb area witnessed a particularly intense battle where the Pakistanis forced the Indians to withdraw from their positions. In other parts of Kashmir, the Indians made some small gains along the cease-fire line. The major Indian counteroffensive came in the Sialkot-Shakargarh area south and west of Chhamb. There, two Pakistani tank regiments, equipped with United States-made Patton tanks, confronted the Indian First Armored Corps, which had British Centurion tanks. In what proved to be the largest tank battle of the war, both sides suffered considerable casualties.

Though the Indian conduct of the land war on the western front was somewhat timid, the role of the Indian air force was both extensive and daring. During the fourteen-day war, the air force's Western Command conducted some 4,000 sorties. There was little retaliation by Pakistan's air force, partly because of the paucity of non-Bengali technical personnel. Additionally, this lack of retaliation reflected the deliberate decision of the Pakistan Air Force headquarters to conserve its forces because of heavy losses incurred in the early days of the war.

From the Diary of a Bangladeshi on March 27, 2008

Today marks 37 years of independence for a tiny country I love, a country that gave me birth before it was itself born, a country founded on the belief that freedom is precious and worth dying for, a country of brave martyrs and brave survivors, a country of unfulfilled promises called Bangladesh.

Thirty-five years ago, the Pakistan army unconditionally surrendered to the Indian Army at the Dhaka Racecourse in Bangladesh.

With the stroke of a pen, Bangladesh was born. That birth, however, came at an enormous cost. Before the Pakistan army and its local collaborators were finally subdued by the Indian Army, they had slaughtered up to 3 million Bengalis in nine months of madness.

This is the story of that slaughter. This is the story of genocide in Bangladesh.

In 1971, Bangladesh, then called East Pakistan, was part of a geographical monstrosity created by the British in 1947. Pakistan, as created by the British, consisted of West Pakistan and East Pakistan, separated by the vast expanse of the Indian land mass in the middle. East and West Pakistan spoke different languages and were culturally distinct. East Pakistan accounted for the majority of Pakistan's population, yet it was economically exploited and politically marginalised by West Pakistan.

Bengalis, the people of East Pakistan, were also persecuted for speaking their native language and for being either Muslims who had converted from Hinduism or for being Hindus. Pakistan, translated as 'The Land of the Pure', was intolerant of Bengalis because they were not 'pure' Muslims.

The tension between East and West Pakistan began to boil over in 1970 after West Pakistan's minimal response to the devastation wreaked by the cyclone of 1970 in East Pakistan. Nearly half a million Bengalis died as a result of the cyclone and the indifferent response by the Pakistani government.

In the midst of the tension, the Pakistani military rulers decided to hold the first democratic elections in Pakistan's history. The Awami League, representing Bengalis in East Pakistan, won the majority of seats in the National Assembly. However, the military leadership of West Pakistan refused to allow the Awami League to form a government.

The siege of East Pakistan by the Pakistan army had begun. War was now inevitable. On March 7, 1971, Sheikh Mujibur Rahman, leader of the Awami League, gave a speech at the Dhaka Racecourse that mobilised the Bengali nation for resistance. He began the speech with a call to arms:

The struggle this time is for emancipation! The struggle this time is for independence!

On March 25, 1971, the Pakistan army launched Operation Searchlight to 'eliminate' the Awami League and its supporters in East Pakistan. The goal was to 'crush' the will of the Bengalis. The killing began shortly after 10 pm. In the first 48 hours the orgy of killing had ravaged Dhaka city.

The Hindu population of Dhaka took the brunt of the slaughter. Dhaka university was targeted and Hindu students were gunned down. Mujib was arrested shortly after declaring Bangladesh independent. The rest of the Awami League leadership went into hiding and those that survived eventually fled to India. The genocide had just begun.

On February 22, 1971 the generals in West Pakistan took a decision to crush the Awami League and its supporters. It was recognised from the first that a campaign of genocide would be necessary to eradicate the threat: 'Kill three million of them,' said President Yahya Khan at the February conference, 'and the rest will eat out of our hands.' (*Robert Payne, Massacre [1972], page 50.*)

On March 25 the genocide was launched. The university in Dhaka was attacked and students exterminated in their hundreds. Death squads roamed the streets of Dhaka, killing some 7,000 people in a single night. It was only the beginning. Within a week, half the population of Dhaka had fled, and at least 30,000 people had been killed. Chittagong, too, had lost half its population.

All over East Pakistan people were taking flight, and it was estimated that in April some 30 million people were wandering helplessly across East Pakistan to escape the grasp of the military. (*Payne, Massacre, page 48.*) Ten million refugees fled to India, overwhelming that country's resources and spurring the eventual Indian military intervention. (The population of Bangladesh/East Pakistan at the outbreak of the genocide was about 75 million.)

But the will of the Bengali people was not broken on the night of March 25, 1971. On the contrary, while Dhaka burned, so did the illusion of a united Pakistan.

At 7:45 pm on March 27, 1971 Major Ziaur Rahman, leader of a rebel army unit in East Pakistan, broadcast Bangladesh's independence on Mujib's behalf. With the following words, the armed resistance to the Pakistan army began:

This is Shadhin Bangla Betar Kendro [Free Bangla Radio]. I, Major Ziaur Rahman, at the direction of Bangobondhu Mujibur Rahman, hereby declare that the independent People's Republic of Bangladesh has been established. At his direction, I have taken command as the temporary Head of the Republic. In the name of Sheikh Mujibur Rahman, I call upon all Bengalis to rise against the attack by the West Pakistani Army. We shall fight to the last to free our Motherland. By the grace of Allah, victory is ours. Joy Bangla.

Major Zia's broadcast from a small radio station in Chittagong was picked up by a Japanese ship in the Bay of Bengal. It was later rebroadcast by Radio Australia and the BBC.

Yahya Khan and the Pakistan army planned their genocide well. Yahya Khan aimed to crush the Bengali spirit once and for all. Before the crackdown all foreign journalists were expelled from East Pakistan. Only a handful managed to evade the Pakistani army.

One of them was Simon Dring. On March 30, 1971 he filed a chilling report of the massacre that took place in Dhaka on the night of March 25. Dring reported that in 24 hours of killing, the Pakistan army slaughtered as many as 7,000 people in Dhaka and up to 15,000 people in all of Bangladesh.

The Pakistan army employed tanks, artillery, mortars, bazookas and machine guns against the unarmed population of Dhaka. Their targets were students, local police, intellectuals, political leaders, Awami League supporters, Hindus and ordinary citizens. They carried out their ruthless killing spree with military precision.

Dring described the attack on Dhaka University as follows:

'Led by American-supplied M-24 World War II tanks, one column of troops sped to Dacca University shortly after midnight. Troops took over the British Council library and used it as a fire base from which to shell nearby dormitory areas.

'Caught completely by surprise, some 200 students were killed in Iqbal Hall, headquarters of the militantly antigovernment students' union, I was told. Two days later, bodies were still smoldering in burnt-out rooms, others were scattered outside, more floated in a nearby lake, an art student lay sprawled across his easel.

'Army patrols also razed nearby market area. Two days later, when it was possible to get out and see all this, some of the market's stall-owners were still lying as though asleep, their blankets pulled up over their shoulders.'

The 'old town' quarter of Dhaka city was singled out for destruction by the Pakistanis because of strong Awami League support there and because there were many Hindu residents in the area. Here is how Simon Dring described the attacks on unarmed civilians:

'The lead unit was followed by soldiers carrying cans of gasoline. Those who tried to escape were shot. Those who stayed were burnt alive. About 700 men, women and children died there that day between noon and 2 pm, I was told.

'In the Hindu area of the old town, the soldiers reportedly made the people come out of their houses and shot them in groups. The area, too, was eventually razed.

'The troops stayed on in force in the old city until about 11 pm on the night of Friday, March 26, driving around with local Bengali informers. The soldiers would fire a flare and the informer would point out the houses of Awami League supporters. The house would then be destroyed—either with direct fire from tanks or recoilless rifles or with a can of gasoline, witnesses said.'

After having massacred 15,000 unarmed civilians in a single day, the Pakistani soldiers bragged about their invincibility to Simon Dring:

'"These bugger men," said one Punjabi lieutenant, "could not kill us if they tried."

'"Things are much better now," said another officer. "Nobody can speak out or come out. If they do we will kill them—they have spoken enough—they are traitors, and we are not. We are fighting in the name of God and a united Pakistan."'

In the name of God and a united Pakistan, genocide had just begun.

The Pakistanis began their killing spree in the major cities of Dhaka, Chittagong and Comilla. However, as terrified Bengalis fled to the countryside, the Pakistani army followed. Pakistan began to fly in additional troops into Bangladesh to continue the genocidal campaign. The goal was the extermination of the Bengali nation.

Hindus in particular were targeted for extermination. Bengali Muslims, however, did not escape the Pakistani killing machine since Bengali Muslims were considered 'tainted' by their Bengali/Hindu culture. In the face of the ongoing massacres, a guerilla army formed under the leadership of rebel Bengali military officers and organised student activists.

This guerilla army, known as the Mukti Bahini in Bengali, fought a war of attrition with the Pakistani army until December 16, 1971. The Mukti Bahini received training and support from the Indian government as it resisted Pakistani occupation. The Pakistani army was constantly harassed by Bangladeshi resistance. In response the Pakistani army slaughtered more Bengalis.

The killing continued unabated throughout the summer of 1971. The army moved methodically from village to village, leaving a trail of destruction in its wake. In June the Pulitzer Prize-winning journalist Sydney Schanberg filed a number of eyewitness accounts from Bangladeshi towns for *The New York Times*. In response, the Pakistan army expelled him from the country on June 30, 1971.

Schanberg described the systematic subjugation and killing of Bengalis:

'Army trucks roll through the half-deserted streets of the capital of East Pakistan these days, carrying "antistate" prisoners to work-sites for hard labor. Their heads are shaved and they wear no shoes and no clothes except for shorts—all making escape difficult.

'Street designations are being changed to remove all Hindu names as well as those of Bengali Moslem nationalists as part of a campaign to stamp out Bengali culture. Shankari Bazar Road in Dacca is now Tikka Khan Road, after the lieutenant general governor of East Pakistan and whom most Bengalis call "the Butcher."

'Since the offensive began the troops have killed countless thousands of Bengalis— foreign diplomats estimate at least 200,000 to 250,000—many in massacres. Although the targets were Bengali Moslems and the 10 million Hindus at first, the army is now concentrating on Hindus in what foreign observers characterize as a holy war.

'Of the more than six million Bengalis who are believed to have fled to India to escape the army's terror, at least four million are Hindus. The troops are still killing Hindus and burning and looting their villages.'

When the burden of the killing became too much for the army, the Pakistanis enlisted and trained paramilitary units made up of non-Bengali Muslims and Bengali collaborators from right-wing religious parties. These paramilitary units, the al-Badr and al-Shams, worked as informers and assassins to augment the military's gruesome task of killing Bengalis. In June 1971 Sydney Schanberg reported on the formation of these units:

'Throughout East Pakistan the Army is training new paramilitary home guards or simply arming "loyal" civilians, some of whom are formed into peace committees. Besides Biharis and other non-Bengali, Urdu-speaking Moslems, the recruits include the small minority of Bengali Moslems who have long supported the army—adherents of the right-wing religious parties such as the Moslem League and Jamaat-e-Islami.

'Collectively known as the Razakars, the paramilitary units spread terror throughout the Bengali population. With their local knowledge, the Razakars were an invaluable tool in the Pakistani Army's arsenal of genocide.'

At the end of June 1971, Schanberg visited the town of Faridpur and reported on the persecution there:

'The Pakistani Army has painted big yellow "H's" on the Hindu shops still standing in this town to identify the property of the minority eighth of the population that it has made special targets.

'The campaign against the Hindus was—and in some cases still is—systematic. Soldiers fanned through virtually every village asking where the Hindus lived. Hindu property has been confiscated and either sold or given to "loyal" citizens. Many of the beneficiaries have been Biharis, non-Bengali Muslim migrants from India, most of whom are working with the army now. The army has given weapons to large numbers of the Biharis, and it is they who have often continued the killing of Hindus in areas where the army has eased off.

'However, army commanders in the field in East Pakistan privately admit to a policy of stamping out Bengali culture, both Muslim and Hindu—but particularly Hindu.

'In Faridpur—and the situation was much the same throughout East Pakistan— there was no friction to speak of between Hindu and Muslim before the army came.

'The army tried to drive a wedge between them. In April, as a public example, two Hindus were beheaded in a central square in Faridpur and their bodies were soaked in kerosene and burned.

'Still, there is no sign of a hate-Hindu psychology among the Bengali Muslims. Many have taken grave risks to shelter and defend Hindus; others express shock and horror at what is happening to the Hindus but confess that they are too frightened to help.'

For his part in exposing Pakistani atrocities in Bangladesh, Schanberg was promptly expelled from Bangladesh.

The Pakistan army and the Razakars did not stop at simply massacring Bengalis. They also took to raping Bengali women. During nine months in 1971, over 200,000 Bengali women and girls were raped. Many were taken as sex slaves and raped multiple times by the Pakistani army.

By December 1971 the genocide had decimated Bengali society. On December 3, 1971 the Indian Army formally joined the war. In 13 days the Indian Army delivered a humiliating defeat to the Pakistan army in Bangladesh. The army that had committed mass murder against an unarmed civilian population was decisively routed in less then a fortnight.

The Pakistan army, on the verge of defeat, was determined to wipe out Bengali culture in one final act of barbarism. On December 14, 1971, the Pakistan army unleashed the paramilitary units al-Badr and al-Shams to exterminate Bengali intellectuals. The goal was to find and kill Bengali political thinkers, educators, scientists, poets, doctors, lawyers, journalists and other intellectuals. The al-Badr and al-Shams fanned out with lists of names to find and execute the core of Bengali intellectuals. The intellectuals were arrested and taken to Rayerbazar, a marshy area in Dhaka city. There, they were gunned down with their eyes blindfolded and their hands tied behind their backs.

On December 16, 1971 the Pakistan army in Bangladesh formally surrendered. At the cost of three million dead the nation of Bangladesh was born. It was the most concentrated act of genocide of the 20th century.

Thirty-five years after the birth of the nation, many have forgotten the sacrifices of those who are no longer with us. But for those of us who survived, for our parents who kept us safe through the months of terror, there is no erasing the horrors of 1971. Bangladesh today has yet to exorcise the demons of 1971. (Mashuqur Rehman).

WORLD'S SEPARATIST MOVEMENTS

Following is the updated list of world's separatist movements:

- Azerbaijan

    - ◆ **Nagorno-Karabakh Republic**—Nagorno-Karabakh dispute from the Armenian viewpoint.

    - ◆ **Karabakh.org**—Nagorno-Karabakh dispute from the Azeri viewpoint.

- Belgium

    - ◆ **Vlaams Belang**—Flemish independence party. Founded by same persons who founded now disbanded **Vlaams Blok**.

    - ◆ **New Flemish Alliance (NVA)**—For an independent Flanders within a federal Europe. Split off from **Volksunie**.

    - ◆ **Spirit**—For decentralization rather than Flemish separation. Split off from **Volksunie**.

    - ◆ **Lijst Dedecker (LDD)**—Has Flemish independence written in its political program; has reached the Belgian electoral treshold and is seated in the Belgian parlement with 5 members, as of 2007/11/14.

- Bougainville

    - ◆ **Bougainville**—The Forgotten War in the South Pacific.

    - ◆ **Bougainville Independence**—A history of the island's struggle for freedom, from the World History Archives.

- o ◆ **Bougainville Updates**—Latest news on the struggle for independence.

- Britain

  - o ◆ **Sinn Féin**—This is the political arm of the Irish Republican Army, independence movement that won independence for most of Ireland, except for the counties now called Northern Ireland, which is still a part of the United Kingdom. They won independence mainly not through a program of direct military confrontation or bombing, but of assassination of British officials and their informants, a program that was depicted in the movie and book *Michael Collins*. They continue to agitate for unification of Northern Ireland with the rest of Ireland. The problem is that the majority of the people who live in Northern Ireland do not want to be united with the rest of Ireland. They do have a legitimate claim for ending discrimination against Catholic citizens of Northern Ireland, but not for unification, although the general unification of Ireland and Britain within the European Union is likely to make the issue moot. Nevertheless, their example is worth studying.

  - o ◆ **Scottish National Party**—Their current program is directed at independence within the European Union, which leaves many questions about what the relationship with England would be, but their support is growing, and the recently elected Labour government has promised the Scottish Parliament greater autonomy.

  - o ◆ **Scottish Separatist Group and The Scottish National Liberation Army**—The Scottish Separatist Group was formed in October 1995 by former members and supporters of the Scottish National Liberation Army. The SSG is a Scottish Republican and revolutionary nationalist group which supports the Scottish National Liberation Army politically. The SSG is an activist group which totally rejects the pseudo-nationalism of the collaborationist SNP and its allies.

  - o ◆ **Scots for Independence**—History, articles, and links.

o ◆ **Scottish Independence**—Scotland's move towards independence.

o ◆ **The Scottish Distributist**—Nothing short of independence for Scotland will do—free of both Westminster and Brussels.

o ◆ **Siol nan Gaidheal**—Cultural and fraternal organization supporting Scottish independence.

o ◆ **Scots Independence Tour**—The current situation, historical perspective, and prospects for the future.

o ◆ **The Campaign for Scottish Independence**—Prefer non-violent methods.

o ◆ **Cornish Stannary Parliament**—Kernow, also known as Cornwall, is a nation conquered by England whose original people were Celtic, like the Welsh and Scots, and are trying to defend their heritage.

o ◆ **Mebyon Kernow—the Party for Cornwall**—Cornish, Green, Left-of-center and decentralist.

o ◆ **Cymru Annibynnol—Independent Wales Party**—Seek Welsh independence.

o ◆ **Cymru 1400**—Welsh nationalist/republican movement that aims for a Welsh republic and to defend Cymru, its language and culture.

o ◆ **Plaid Cymru—The Party of Wales**—Welsh nationalist/republican movement, opposed to the National Assembly for Wales.

   ▪ ◆ **TribanCoch**—Journal of the Plaid Cymru membership.

   ▪ ◆ **Cymdeithas DJ**—Research and public education to preserve and promote the Welsh language (Cymru).

o ◆ **Welsh Distributist Movement**—Radical Right-wing alternative to Plaid Cymru.

- o ◆ **The Welsh Assembly**—Not the official parliamentary body, or a group seeking independence for Wales, but a group who oppose British membership in the European Union.

- o ◆ **Mec Vannin**—Political party advocating full republican independence of Mannin (the Isle of Man).

- o ◆ **Ulster Nation**—Campaigns for independence from both Great Britain and Eire.

  - ◆—Older site.

- o ◆ **Campaign for an English Parliament**—You thought England already had a parliament? They seek one separate from Scotland, Wales, Ulster, etc.

- o ◆ **English Democrats Party**—Seek separate English Parliament, constitution.

- o ◆ **Silent Majority**—Not so silent, also against membership of Britain in the EU.

- Canada

  - o ◆ **The Western Canada Concept**—Movement dedicated to building an independent nation of Western Canada.

  - o ◆ **Alberta Independence Party**—Party which advocates the independence of Alberta under certain circumstances.

  - o ◆ **British Columbia Separatist Movement**—Seek independence for the province.

  - o ◆ **BC Sovereignty**—Advocate independence of British Columbia.

  - o ◆ **The Republic of Alberta**—Dedicated to the secession of Alberta.

  - o ◆ **The Newfoundland Patriot**—Advocate independence of Newfoundland and Labrador.

o   ◆ **Ontario Independence League**—Advocate independence of Ontario.

o   ◆ **Cape Breton Liberation Army**—Comedy troup satirically "fighting" for the right of Cape Bretoners to separate from Nova Scotia and form their own province.

o   ◆ **Mouvement de libération nationale du Québec (MLNQ)**— They seek independence for Quebec, the predominantly French-speaking province of predominantly English-speaking Canada, mainly to try to prevent their assimilation into the larger English-speaking world. Unfortunately, it is not political union that produces that assimilatiion, and independence will not end it. The world is adopting English as its universal language, something that is no longer reversible, due to the global system of trade and communications. There are indications, however, of a conspiracy to promote Quebec independence to bring about a breakup of Canada and the admission of its English-speaking provinces as states of the the United States. There is already a strong movement for U.S. statehood in the Western provinces of British Columbia, Alberta, and Saskatchewan. British Columbia would have to change its name. This site is entirely in French.

• Chechnya

    o   ◆ **History of Chechnya, Past of the Chechen Republic**— History up to the Russia—Chechnya War of 1994-1996.

    o   ◆ **The Chechen War after the Fall of Grozny**—Report on the struggle in Chechnya.

    o   ◆ **Russia vs Chechnya**—Basics of the Russian-Chechen conflict.

• China

    o   ◆ **International Tibet Independence Movement**

    o   ◆ **Government of Tibet in Exile**—Official site.

    o   ◆ **Free Tibet!**—The world-wide movement to achieve freedom and justice for Tibet, occupied by China since 1959. Although these efforts are mainly nonviolent, we encourage the support of an armed resistance to back up the political efforts. See <u>Letter by Jon Roland</u>.

- ◆ **Free Tibet**—Old site.

- ◆ **National Democratic Party of Tibet**—Supports the restoration of Tibetan independence under a democratic framework.

- ◆ **Taiwan Independence Movement**—Advocate abandoning "one-China" farce.

- ◆ **Inner Mongolian People's Party**—Advocates freedom, democracy and human rights for the Mongols in Inner Mongolia currently under Chinese colonial rule.

- ◆ **Free Southern Mongolia**—Supports the Mongolian separatist movement.

- ◆ **Southern Mongolian Freedom Federation**—Statements published by the organization and photographs of protests which it has staged.

- ◆ **East Turkestan Information Center**—Advocates the cause of Uyghur (Uighur) independence.

- **European Union**—Not a nation yet and already it has separatist movements.

  - ◆ **UK Independence Party**—Seeks Britain's withdrawal from the European Union.

  - ◆ **Europe of Democracies and Diversities (EDD)**—Group of parliamentarians favoring a democratic Europe of independent nation-states.

  - ◆ **Europe of Nations**—Eurosceptic anti-Maastricht, anti-EU group (in European Parliament)

  - ◆ **Campaign for an Independent Britain (CIB)**—Coalition group which seeks the UK's withdrawal from the EU.

- ◆ **The Bruges Group**—Neo-conservative group of primarily British eurosceptics.

- ◆ **Eurosceptics across Europe**—Links to national anti-EU sites.

- ◆ **CAFE—Conservatives Against a Federal Europe**—Brits who don't want to live in a European Superstate.

- ◆ **The Democracy Movement**—A non-party campaign to keep the pound and stop the "European Superstate".

- ◆ **Congress for Democracy**—An all-party forum campaigning for an independent pound and against British entry to the single currency.

- ◆ **The Magna Carta Society**—Promotes the rights and freedoms of British subjects, assured for all time by the Magna Carta, argues all EU Law illegal in Britain.

- ◆ **The Eurosceptic**—Fighting for UK independence from the European Union.

- ◆ **The Free Britain Site**—Warns of the dangers to Britain from EU membership and abolishing the Pound.

- ◆ **TEAM—The European Alliance of EU-critical Movements**—EU-critical network of about 40 organisations in 14 countries in and outside the European Union.

- France

  - ◆ **Corsica Nazione**—Corsican national party.

  - ◆ **Partit Occitan**—The Occitan Party: its program, Charter, and claims.

  - ◆ **Union Démocratique Bretonne—Breton Democratic Union**—Advocates home rule for Brittany.

  - ◆ **Iparretarrak (IK)**—Armed group acting in the northern Basque Country.

- o ◆ **Nationalforum Elsaß-Lothringen—Forum Nationaliste d'Alsace-Lorraine**—National Forum of Alsace-Lorraine, the bilingual borderland between France and Germany.

- o ◆ **The Savoy League—La Ligue Savoisienne**—Savoy, one of the oldest nations in Europe, was annexed by France in 1860. The Savoy League, created in 1994, seeks to reclaim its independence.

- • Georgia—The country, not the state.

  - o ◆ **Abkhazia.org**—Coalition for a Democratic Abkhazia.

  - o ◆ **Abkhazeti.com**—Georgian side of the Abkhazian conflict.

  - o ◆ **Republic of Abkhazia (Apsny)**—Devoted to preserving Abkhazia's de facto sovereignty and promoting its international recognition.

  - o ◆ **Voice of Abkhazia**—The official radio station of the de facto government.

- • India

  - o ◆ **Jammu Kashmir Liberation Front (JKLF)**

  - o ◆ **Jammu Kashmir Liberation Front (JKLF)**—Alternate site.

  - o ◆ **Dalitstan Organization**—Seek independence for the Dalits, or black Untouchables, also known as Dravidians, the original inhabitants of the Indian subcontinent before the arrival and dominance of the caucasian Hindis.

  - o ◆ **Hezb-e-Mughalstan**—The "Party of Mughalstan", which seeks independence for Muslims, especially those in a band of territory from Kashmir to Bombay.

  - o ◆ **Mughalstan Nation**—Seek a sovereign and independent homeland for the Urdu-speaking Muslims of South Asia.

  - o ◆ **Free Tamil Nadu**—Seeks independence for the Tamil people of south India, and perhaps union with the Tamils of Sri Lanka.

- o ◆ **United Liberation Front of Assam**—Party seeking independence for this state.

- o ◆ **National Socialist Council of Nagalim**—Party promoting the independence of Nagaland and many of the surrounding regions in the northeast.

- o ◆ **Revolutionary People's Front of Manipur (RPF)**—Party promoting the independence of Manipur.

- o ◆ **People's Revolutionary Party of Kangleipak (PREPAK)**—

- o ◆ **Declaration of Independence of the Sikh Homeland**— Historical background and grievances of the Sikh population.

- Indonesia

  - o ◆ **Aceh Portal**—Acehnese Independence Movement for Northern Sumatra.

  - o ◆ **Free Papua Movement—Organisasi Papua Merdeka (OPM)**—Also known as Irian Jaya.

  - o ◆ **West Papua Niugini (Irian Jaya)**—Promote the fight for self-determination and independence for all West Papuan peoples.

  - o ◆ **East Timor Human Rights**—This page has links to several sites supporting independence for East Timor, which was invaded by Indonesia, and has since gained independence.

- Israel

  - o ◆ **Palestinian National Authority**, formerly called the Palestine Liberation Organization, since the agreement with Israel yielding administration to it of parts of the Occupied Territory resulting from the 1967 war. They are seeking an independent Palestinian state comprising all or most of that Occupied Territory, and some of them would also like it to include the rest of Israel as well. On the other side, many Israelis would like to keep the land as part of Israel. The trouble is that Palestinians already live there, and they can't figure out a way to get them to leave, and they don't want to extend full citizenship to them, because then Jews would be outnumbered in Israel. They are moving to some kind of agrement in which most of the land will become a Palestinian state, but whether they can agree on how much of that land will be included remains an open issue, and a potential source of continuing conflict and perhaps war in the Middle East.

- ◆ **Palestinian Liberation Organization**—National liberation movement led by Yasser Arafat.

- ◆ **Popular Front for the Liberation of Palestine**—Party advocating the destruction of Israel.

- ◆ **Azzam Publications**—This is an outlet for Islamic Jihad, which promotes its view of Islam, Palestinian independence, and opposes Israel and Western influences in the Islamic World.

- Italy

  - ◆ **Lega Nord**—Party advocating the independence of northern Italy, or Padania.

  - ◆ **The Two Sicilies: The Old Independent State of Southern Italy**—Southern Italy's answer to the Lega Nord.

  - ◆ **Sardinians in Italy**—Overview and chronology of the situation in Sardinia.

  - ◆ **Sardigna Natzione (Sardinian Nation)**—Sardinian nationalist movement.

  - ◆ **Secession fever in Italy**—Numerous separate areas are increasing their demands for autonomy from the central government in Rome.

- Kurdistan (Parts of Turkey, Iraq, and Iran)

  - ◆ **Kurdistan Democratic Party—KDP—Iraq**—One of the two main independence parties.

  - ◆ **Patriotic Union of Kurdistan—PUK**—Second of the two main independence parties.

- o ◆ **Kurdistan Regional Government—KRG**—De facto government in Northern Iraq.

- o ◆ **Kurdistan Kurdish Conflict**—Commentary from globalsecurity.org.

- o ◆ **Kurdish Information Centre**—National liberation movement.

- o ◆ **American Kurdish Information Network**—This is an arm of the Kurdish National Movement, which seeks a homeland, probably composed of parts of Turkey and Iraq, and perhaps of Iran.

- Madagascar

  - o ◆ **Merina Nation**—Seeks cultural preservation, autonomy, and perhaps independence for the original malayo-indonesian people of Madagascar.

- Mauritania and Sudan

  - o ◆ **Coalition Against Slavery In Mauritania and Sudan (CASMAS)**—Opposes abuses of black Africans by dominant Arabs in these countries, which is the issue in the genocidal civil war in Sudan, in which the people in the South seek independence from the North.

- Mexico

  - o ◆ **Ejército Zapatista de Liberación Nacional (EZLN) (Zapatista National Liberation Army)**—The Zapatistas seek justice for the aboriginal people of the State of Chiapas and parts of neighboring states, either through reform throughout Mexico or some degree of autonomy for the region. However, they are also becoming the voice for the oppressed throughout Mexico. The site is in Spanish, English, and French.

- New Zealand

  o ◆ **Maori Independence**—Struggle for "Tino Rangatiratanga" (absolute sovereignty) by the indigenous people of New Zealand.

- Philippines

  o ◆ **Moro Islamic Liberation Front**—Islamic separatist movement in the Philippines.

- Spain

  o ◆ **Euskal Herria (Basque Country) Journal**—This is the PR arm of the Congress for Peace in Euskal Herria (CPEH) and the Basque National Liberation Movement (MLNV), which seeks independence for a region of Spain centered on Guernica and San Sebastian, and spilling over into France. They speak one of the few remaining European languages that is not part of the Indo-European group, related only to a language spoken in a small region in central Asia.

  o ◆ **Peace in the Basque Country**—Official site of the Basque autonomous government.

  o ◆ **Links to the Basque conflict**—Directory by a communist group.

  o ◆ **Esquerra Republicana de Catalunya**—Seek autonomy for Catalonia.

- United States of America

  o ◆ **Alaskan Independence Party**—Seeks referendum with choice of statehood, independence, commonwealth, or self-governing territory.

  o ◆ **Alaskans for Independence**

  o ◆ **Free the Bear—California Secession and Independence**

  o ◆ **California Secessionist Party**

o ◆ **The Republic of Cascadia**—Advocates independence for the Pacific Northwest from both America and Canada, with a libertarian and pro-business perspective.

o ◆ **Cascadian National Party**—Advocate secession of the present states of Washington and Oregon from the United States.

o ◆ **Cascadia Confederacy**—Advocates independence of the Pacific Northwest region from the U.S. and Canada, with an anti-nationalist and anti-capitalist perspective.

o ◆ **State of Jefferson**—The rich history surrounding the events leading to the State of Jefferson secession movement of 1941. The State of Jefferson lives on in the hearts and minds of many residents of northern California and southern Oregon today.

o ◆ **Hawai`i—Independent & Sovereign**—Separatist movement of Hawaiian aboriginal people.

o ◆ **La Voz de Aztlan**—Separatist movement that seeks a *reconquista* (reconquest) by *chicanos* (ethnic hispanics of Aztec descent) of the Southwestern United States and creation of a new nation of *Aztlan* (legendary ancient homeland).

o ◆ **New England Confederation Movement**—Seek independence for New England states. Also see <u>New Hampshire Chapter</u>.

o ◆ **Second Vermont Republic**—Seek independence for Vermont.

o ◆ **South Carolina League of the South**—Seek independence through secession, perhaps for all of the Southern states of the 1861-65 Confederate States of America.

o ◆ **Republic of Texas**—This is one of several pages for the somewhat fractured Texas Independence Movement which has recently received a great deal of attention. We do not support the movement. Constitutional compliance throughout the United States is attainable. Independence is not necessary, and distracts from the cause of constitutional compliance. But they do raise a number of interesting issues.

o   ◆ **Provisional Government of the Republic of Texas—** Another Republic of Texas site.

o   ◆ **United People's Party (Partido Nacional La Raza Unida)—** Many of them seek to separate the part of the U.S. taken from Mexico from the U.S. and make it an independent Hispanic nation called Aztlan.

Some of the important separatist movements are discussed below:

The Basque Separatist Movement

If we study history of nations in this world, we will observe that throughout history, several empires have risen and fallen, cultures have prospered and eventually died away, and other people have taken their places. The Muslim Kings ruled India for almost 1000 years until they finally lost their political power. Though everything in history will eventually change as time goes on, the types of conflicts that arise have remained very much the same.

As I am writing this book to reflect the desire of Urdu-speaking people of Karachi for their own independence and autonomy, I would like to give the example of Spain, where in the north alone at least four different languages are spoken and different groups of people represented. These groups have also long desired independence, or at the least increased autonomy, though their approaches to achieve this goal are varying. Perhaps the most interesting region is the Basque region on the French border. Though the official political party uses peaceful methods to achieve their aims, they are overshadowed in the media by the ETA, which uses widespread violence to gain attention. The conflict between the Spanish government and the Basque people, particularly the ETA, has existed for a very long time, but recently has been very eventful due in part to the Franco regime and more drastic measures from the opposing sides. Kosovo's recent independence must have also played an important role in some way to spark the freedom tendencies in this Spanish region.

What is the Basque Separatist Movement?

Basque Country in a region on the border between France and Spain, the majority of which is located in northern Spain. This is the central region of Basque conflicts, but it has united with Navarra, in northern Spain to the east of Basque Country to form what is considered the Basque Separatist Movement. The Basques are a very old culture, often thought to be one of the original European cultures. Their land is very hilly, which allows them to remain relatively isolated from the rest of Europe, though in the Middle Ages they did embrace Roman Catholicism. They are such a diverse and complex people, that entire museums have been devoted to defining their particular identify.

The Basque separatist movement can be simply summarized as the desire of the Basque people to achieve greater independence. There are varying degrees of separatist supports, ranging from those who simply want increased autonomy, to those that demand total independence from Spain. They believe that because the Basque region and culture is much older and so drastically different from Spain's, they should be allowed to form their own country. As one Spanish reporter puts it,

> [The ETA and Basque Separatist Movement] wants to establish an independent socialist Basque state straddling northern Spain and the southern end of France's Atlantic coast. The Basques consider their culture distinct from those of their neighbours and speak a language unlike any other in Europe. The Basque language (called Euskara) is believed to predate the arrival of the Indo-European languages to the continent, of which French, Spanish, German, Icelandic, Welsh, Serbo-Croat and almost all others are the modern descendants. The Basque region, home to large fishing ports, heavy industry and wealthy banks, has historically been one of the richest in Spain.

The Basque Separatist movement began as an idea, and eventually evolved into a movement and the foundation of a political party. However, in the past half-century it has evolved into a powerful sentiment among many people, and continues to cause hostile sentiments between the Spanish government and Basque citizens.

History of the Basque Separatist Movement

The movement first arose at the end of the nineteenth century under the leadership of Sabina de Arana y Goiri. After his death, the group was granted autonomy by the Republican government, which lasted through the Spanish civil war (1936-39). When the Franco regime eventually won the war and took power, he made sure that the Basque people suffered for having supported the Republicans. In April 1937, Franco had German aircraft bomb Guernica, a thriving Basque town, killing 1,000 people. The tragedy has been forever immortalized in a painting by Pablo Picasso, called "Guernica", that depicts the pain, horror, and anguish felt by those that experienced the bombing and others around the world. This was the first tangible sign of the hatred Franco felt toward the Basque people, but it was certainly not the last.

Shortly after the war ended, Franco further repressed the Basque people. Not only did he take away every sign of autonomy that they had so painstakingly worked to gain, but he strictly prohibited the Basque language and culture. The people were no longer allowed to speak their native language, which until then had been very widespread and inescapable in daily life. Also, they were not allowed to practice any customs or traditions that had been celebrated for generations before them. Furthermore, the majority of Basque intellectuals were imprisoned and tortured for their political and cultural ideas[2].

These unjust and blatant discriminations against the Basque people infuriated them, making them even more desperate to achieve some degree of autonomy. Throughout the 40s and 50s, Basque political parties tried negotiation, protests, and many other non-violent methods to achieve limited autonomy. It was not until the late 1950s that any group had any success.

In 1959 the Euskadi Ta Askatasuna (ETA) was formed. The name means "Basque for Basque Homeland and Liberty" in the native tongue. The ETA originated as a faction of the Basque National Party (BNP) and split over non-violence policies. The BNP had always been rigidly opposed to any form of violence, no matter what the justification. However, the ETA strongly disagreed with that and that thought violence was necessary to achieve their goals. In 1966 the ETA further divided into two significant groups based primarily on their goals and methods. The first group had very Marxist-Leninist ideals, and favored sabotage and assassinations to gain complete independence. The other group considered themselves to have more national ideas and, though they approved of violence, they did not support it as much as the other group. In addition, they merely favored autonomy, rather than total independence.

Tensions between the Spanish government and the ETA reached their height during the 1970s. In 1973, the ETA used a car bomb to assassinate Prime Minister Luis Carrero Blanco, who Franco had just appointed as his successor. When Franco died in November of 1975, he had still not chosen another successor. This left the country in the hands of King Juan Carlos I, who began to work with politicians and labor groups to bring about Spain's transition to democracy. During this time, the Spanish government divided Spain into seventeen distinct regions all with varying autonomy, one of which was the Basque region, in the 1978 constitution. The Basque region was granted many liberties, most notably the permission to elect its own parliament and form its own police force, both of which were completely independent of the Spanish government, and was granted more control over education and tax raising powers.

At the end of the 1970s the ETA had gained some sympathy and even popular support due to its struggles and repression under the Franco government. However, in the 1980s, they convinced anyone who was sympathetic toward them that it was undeserved. 1980 is considered to be the ETA's bloodiest year yet, when one hundred and eighteen people were killed. In 1987 the ETA detonated a bomb in a Barcelona supermarket, killing twenty one shoppers. It was the single bloodiest act of violence from the ETA even to this day. All they did was to apologize for the "mistake". However, during that time, the ETA regained some popular support when former Interior Minister Jose Barrionuevo and former Secretary of State Rafael Vera were found guilty of masterminding actions in the so-called "dirty war" that the Spanish government was waging against the ETA. Upon their conviction, killing of ETA members became unjust in the eyes of the public, transforming their victims into martyrs for the cause of Basque liberation.

Recent Developments in the Quest for Independence

The last decade has seen a great deal of action from the ETA, as well all increasingly dramatic response from the Spanish government. A poll conducted in September of 1991 showed that thirty three percent of Basques favored separatism, yet it still was not achieved. In 1992, the ETA created a worldwide panic when they threatened that the 1992 Olympic Games in Barcelona would be a chief site for violent attacks. However, these threats never materialized[9]. Later in 1992, the ETA, desiring independence above all else, requested a conditional truce so that they could gain increased autonomy. However, the Spanish government refused to negotiate with them, adding to further heightened tensions.

In 1995 the ETA attempted to assassinate Popular Party opposition leader Jose Maria Aznar using a car bomb. Luckily, Aznar's car was protected by armor plating, which ultimately saved his life. Later that year, Spanish police foiled an ETA plot to kill King Juan Carlos while he was visiting Majorca. In 1996 Aznar won the elections, making him prime minister. Because he failed to secure an absolute majority, he was forced to negotiate a weak minority government in the Basque and Catalonian regions, as well as the Canary Islands. He granted them further increased regional autonomy and doubled the amount of national income tax given to regional governments from fifteen percent to thirty percent[10].

In 1997 the ETA further shocked the world when it was blamed for the murder of a police officer using a car bomb in Bilbao. The assassination took place just fifteen feet from a high school with over 2,000 students, which shocked and appalled the world. The risk of this act in its proximity to so many children, secured the image of the ETA as barbaric and stopping at nothing in the minds of many people. Whereas previously, Spanish citizens could empathize for the Basque country because they had been severely repressed, the ETA's violent and increasingly risky actions erased any hope of sympathy from all directions. Previously, the only people at real risk were political officials and leaders. Though there had been threats that would affect the public, this was the first time that they actually materialized.

In July of that same year Basque town councilman Miguel Angel Blanco Garrido, a minor official in the local popular party, was kidnapped. The kidnappers, presumed to be members of the ETA, demanded the transfer of ETA prisoners being held in Spanish prisons. Two days after the government refused the request, Garrido was killed by his abductors[11]. This prompted over six million Spaniards to flood the streets in a spontaneous protest against the ETA and their widespread use of violence. From 1968 until that point, ETA violence had claimed over eight hundred lives and had wounded thousands more[12].

To contrast this period of extreme anti-ETA sentiments, later in July 20,000 people marched through the streets of San Sebastian in support of Basque independence. In October, the Guggenheim museum opened in Bilbao, and was described as "a new branch of the New York-based Guggenheim Museum, a critically acclaimed architectural masterpiece"[13]. Its opening served as a stark contrast to the ETA hatred that was so predominant throughout Spain and the world.

Achieving the Goal of Peace

The first serious aims at peace began in 1998. On September 19, 1998, the ETA declared an unconditional cease-fire. They set no specific conditions or criteria to be met, except that if they were attacked the hostilities would resume. This was the first time that the group has suspended all attacks for an indefinite period of time. In 1996 there had been a brief cease-fire for a predetermined length of time and with specific conditions, but nothing like the current cease-fire. Interior Minister Jaime Mayor Oreja noted that the truce would be welcomed with "happiness and relief," but also pointed out that past ETA cease-fires had always ended in renewed violence. One possible reason for the cease-fire was to open negotiations addressing an independent state with Northern Spain and Southern France. It is also believed to be due in part to the Lizarra Declaration, which was a statement signed by over two dozen political groups including the Basque Nationalist

Party and the Herri Batasuna (a branch of the ETA), and called for formal peace talks and an end to expressions of violence. The four-page cease-fire announcement also referred to the Northern Ireland peace accord forged in April 1998, which may have raised ETA expectations for a political solution to the ongoing conflict. However, all attempts at a peace talk were rejected by Aznar until the ETA formally renounces all forms of violence. Only then will they negotiate, Aznar has said.

In December of 1999, the cease-fire was called off. Many believe that both sides grew increasingly suspicious and believed that the other side was not playing fair. The ETA said that they called off the cease-fire because they were frustrated by the lack of political movement toward greater autonomy. It was called off in a "belligerently worded communiqué which accused Madrid of intransigence in its refusal to consider self determination for the Basques"[16]

In August 2002, the Spanish parliament voted two hundred ninety five to ten in favor of seeking a total ban of the Basque political party known as the Batasuna, which is not historically affiliated with the ETA. The Batasuna has been targeted for refusing to condemn an ETA attack that killed a six year old girl on August 4, 2002. The Batasuna has not been implicated in the death itself, but because of its lack of condemnation is considered to have links with the ETA that justify its abolishment. According to Luis de Granded, a member of the ruling Popular Party, "Batasuna is a mask of ETA … that justifies ETA's crimes". Judge Baltasar Garzon, the presiding judge in the Supreme Court aspect of the conflict, said that the Batasuna are "part of [the] ETA and that as a result it was associated with 'crimes against humanity'". However, not all parties agree with this opinion. Basque Nationalist Party speaker Inaki Anasagasti said that "our party will vote unanimously 'No' because we disagree on the method and we don't think it's the solution". As for the Batasuna party itself, it denies it is the political wing of ETA but pointedly refuses to condemn attacks claimed by or blamed on ETA

The ETA and Basque Separatist Movement Today

Through all its acts of violence, desires for freedom, attempts at peace talks, and many other feats, the ETA remains an active political organization. About half of the Basque population is thought to be in support of independence and half against it, fueling continuing disagreements. In Basque country, many people are still afraid of the ETA because they fear what will happen to them if they speak freely about politics. The Spanish people are becoming very tired of living in fear not only for their own lives, but for the lives of their leaders as well. For this reason, there is a great deal of pressure on the Spanish government to end the violence and impose peace that the ETA can agree on.

Though the movement is still very active, its supporters have changed and its foundations have been changed slightly. The movement is primarily supported by young people who were raised in a democracy where Spain is a member of the European Union, allowing them to enjoy the advantages of any other industrial European country. They want to separate because they cannot find a way to express their nationalism without confrontation, and the confrontation inevitably includes Spain. In the opinion of Xavier Mas De Maxas, "there's a cultural war going on. I mean, the young Basque street agitators ... are against Spain because they've been taught that everything coming from Spain is bad, (that) Spain is an oppressive force and (that) it's occupying this land without any legitimacy".

A culture's desire for independence is certainly not something new to the world. Nearly every culture has been a part of some group or nation that was ruled by another political party, and more often than not those cultures desire autonomy and independence. However, the thing that makes the Basque's case so exceptional is many of the circumstances surrounding it. First of all, they are considered the oldest group in Europe, and it is ironic that they should be governed by a younger culture. Furthermore, the Basque Separatist Movement gave rise to the ETA, which has proved to be exceptional in various ways. Not only do they utilize and even recommend violence to achieve their means, but they do so in a way that is nearly savage. In general, they restrict their terror to military and political officials. However, on the occasions that is has expanded to include the general public and even children, the ETA never seems to show any real remorse. This makes it very hard for anyone to sympathize for them, much less support them.

In my opinion, Basque Country deserves independence regardless of the possibility that it will have widespread repercussions throughout Europe. But we must not forget that Kosovo's independence has proved that legitimate right of independence should not be ignored. Moreover, there should not be double standards. If USA and certain countries of EU had supported formation of Kosovo, they should also support formation of Basque Country.

Lesson for the Urdu-speaking people in Pakistan

The best lesson which the Urdu-speaking nation in Pakistan can learn from the Basque Separatist Movement is that the Urdu-speaking nation should also transform its single political force called MQM-Muttahida/Mohajir Qaumi Movement into "Jinnahpur Liberation Movement" to facilitate liberation of Urdu-speaking people from cruel control of Pakistani establishment.

WHAT MQM SHOULD DO NOW

As it has been established that Pakistan is a 100% failed state and in view of the fact that living under military siege of Pakistan army in the disguise of an artificial democracy which has brought the same old faces of corrupt and cunning politicians from Punjab, time has come for the urdu-speaking nation to get up and acquire their own independent country called Republic of Jinnahpur. In order to achieve this task, there are many hurdles. However, impossible is nothing. Either we fail to prepare or prepare to fail. Urdu-speaking nation cannot afford to remain in such a situation that makes them rather a third class citizen in Pakistan. They are treated as "untouchables" like in India. They have no province of their own. They dont have enough representation in the Pakistan National Assembly according to their population simply because the powerful political parties from Punjab and Sindh want to restrict their entry into mainstream politics. The illiterate land owners representing the rural dynasty of Pakistan do not want educated urdu-speaking people to outclass them. These illiterate landlords, *jagirdars* and cunning feudals want to keep their socalled superiority intact by depriving people of Pakistan from educational prosperity. Recently, Pakistan's Supreme Court invalidated minimum educational requirement of a Bachelor's degree to contest elections. They dont want urdu-speaking nation to spread their message of awareness among the masses and therefore these land lords and *jagirdars* are biggest advocates of status-quo in order to keep their control on the entire system of governance. Pakistan Army is the military arm of such elements which desire their own supremacy all over Pakistan. They dont want an educated urdu-speaking person to destroy their plans of dictatorship whether military or civil.

I, therefore, suggest that MQM being the single political force of urdu-speaking nation of Pakistan should do the following acts immediately:

1. TO FORM JINNAHPUR LIBERATION MOVEMENT IMMEDIATELY WHICH SHOULD COMPRISE OF URDU-SPEAKING YOUTH, INTELLECTUALS, ARTISTS, BUSINESSMEN, STUDENTS, RELIGIOUS SCHOLARS, POLITICIANS, WRITERS & POETS, JOURNALISTS, MEMBERS OF CIVIL SOCIETY, EDUCATIONISTS AND PEOPLE FROM ALL WALKS OF LIFE WITH A DEFINED MISSION TO ACCELERATE

MOVEMENT FOR ACQUIRING AN INDEPENDENT COUNTRY CALLED REPUBLIC OF JINNAHPUR;

2. TO ORGANIZE A MASSIVE PLEBISCITE AND TAKE VOTES FROM URDU-SPEAKING NATION TO CONSOLIDATE THEIR DESIRE FOR AN INDEPENDENT COUNTRY CALLED REPUBLIC OF JINNAHPUR;

3. TO COORDINATE WITH USA SENATORS, EU MEMBER STATES AND THE WORLD'S TOP HUMAN RIGHTS ORGANIZATIONS IN ORDER TO MAKE THEM AWARE ABOUT THE DEMANDS OF URDU-SPEAKING NATION LIVING IN PAKISTAN AND THEIR RIGHTS OF EXISTENCE WITH A SPECIFIC IDENTITY UNDER THE BANNER OF REPUBLIC OF JINNAHPUR;

4. TO APPROACH UNITED NATIONS TO SEND PEACE KEEPING TROOPS TO KARACHI IMMEDIATELY TO AVOID YET ANOTHER "OPERATION CLEAN UP" BY PAKISTAN ARMY ON THE PRETEXT OF ELIMINATION OF TERRORISM AND SABOTAGING THE MOVEMENT FOR INDEPENDENCE;

5. TO FILE OFFICIAL APPLICATION WITH THE OFFICE OF THE SECRETARY GENERAL OF THE UNITED NATIONS TO RECOGNIZE INDEPENDENCE OF REPUBLIC OF JINNAHPUR AND REQUEST FOR MILITARY AS WELL AS DIPLOMATIC ASSISTANCE OF THE UNITED NATIONS;

6. TO APPROACH MUSLIM WORLD AND DISSEMINATE INFORMATION TO THEM ABOUT THE POLITICAL RIGHTS OF URDU-SPEAKING NATION AND NEED FOR AN INDEPENDENT COUNTRY FOR THEM;

7. TO ORGANIZE CONFERENCES, PRESS BRIEFINGS, SEMINARS, WORKSHOPS, MEETINGS AND FORA IN DIFFERENT PARTS OF THE WORLD IN ORDER TO CONVEY MESSAGE TO THE WHOLE WORLD ABOUT THE IMPORTANCE AND NEED OF AN INDEPENDENT COUNTRY FOR URDU-SPEAKING NATION IN SOUTH ASIA FOR PEACE AND HARMONY IN THE REGION;

8. TO APPLY FOR MEMBERSHIP TO ALL REGIONAL AS WELL AS INTERNATIONAL ASSOCIATIONS, GROUPS, TREATIES, CLUBS, UNIONS AND ORGANIZATIONS (TRADE OR OTHERWISE) ON BEHALF OF REPUBLIC OF JINNAHPUR;

9. TO FORM A GOVERNMENT-IN-EXILE OF REPUBLIC OF JINNAHPUR WITH IMMEDIATE EFFECT IN ANY EU COUNTRY OR USA OR INDIA;

10. TO APPROACH PARMANENT MEMBERS OF SECURITY COUNCIL OF THE UNITED NATIONS TO SEEK THEIR CONSENT AND APPROVAL FOR FORMATION OF REPUBLIC OF JINNAHPUR THROUGH A UN RESOLUTION BY PRESENTING TO THEM ALL FACTS AND FIGURES IN SUPPORT OF THE IDEA OF AN INDEPENDENT COUNTRY FOR URDU-SPEAKING NATION IN SOUTH ASIA;

What is a Plebiscite

A plebiscite is a popular vote on a proposal which includes the entire populace. Voters are asked to either reject or accept the proposal, with the outcome of the plebiscite determining the fate of the proposed measure, action, constitution, or other political proposal. A plebiscite should not be confused with a general election or regular voting, as no party candidates are included in it.

In a democracy, a plebiscite serves a valuable function. It allows legislators and citizens alike to place laws directly in front of the citizens for judgment. A plebiscite does not offer alternatives, asking voters to make a yes or no answer. This is not always a bad thing, especially when the proposal is clear cut. The term is also used in the context of major national political decisions, such as a those which result in the changeover of a government, the ceding of territory to another nation, or a bid for independence from a colonial power. In other words, this is a a vote by the people of an entire country or district to decide on some issue, such as choice of a ruler or government, option for independence or annexation by another power, or a question of national policy. In the case of urdu-speaking nation living in Pakistan, plebiscite shall refer to option for independence.

What is Government in Exile

According to Wikipedia, A **Government in Exile** is a political group that claims to be a country's legitimate government, but for various reasons is unable to exercise its legal power, and instead resides in a foreign country. Governments in exile usually operate under the assumption that they will one day return to their native country and regain power. In accordance with this definition, Government of Republic of Jinnahpur in Exile shall be formed in any country which may grant permission to do so.

Some other Governments in Exile:

- The Government of the Autonomous Republic of Abkhazia, a pro-Georgian government claiming to represent the breakaway autonomous republic of Abkhazia is currently located in the Georgian-controlled part of this region, the Kodori Valley.

- The administration of the Belarusian National Republic exiled since 1920 and currently led by Ivonka Survilla in Toronto, Canada. See History of Belarus: BNR.

- The National Coalition Government of the Union of Burma is led by Sein Win. It is composed of members of parliament elected in 1990 but not allowed by the military to take office. It is based in Rockville, Maryland, U.S.A.

- The Republic of Cabinda was invaded by Angola in the year 1975. Cabinda had been a Portuguese protectorate, while Angola had been a colony.

- Chechen Republic of Ichkeria. The government is largely based in Western Europe, Arab nations, and the United States. Some members are fighting in the rebel movement against the Russian Army.

- The Progress Party of Equatorial Guinea has proclaimed Severo Moto Nsá "President" in Madrid exile.

- Sahrawi Arab Democratic Republic (SADR) of Western Sahara is head-quartered in the Tindouf region in Algeria but controlling the Free Zone in the eastern part of Western Sahara.

- The Republic of Serbian Krayina Government in Exile was led since 26 February 2005 in Belgrade by the remains of the Government of the Republic of Serbian Krajina after Croatian forces pushed out the internationally unrecognized entity in 1995 during Operation Storm at the end of the Croatian War of Independence.

- The Republik Maluku Selatan, in exile from the South Moluccas, Indonesia, in the Netherlands since 1950.

- The <u>Central Tibetan Administration</u> of the <u>Dalai Lama</u>, a government in exile (based in <u>Dharamsala</u>, <u>India</u>), which claims to represent the people of <u>Tibet</u>.

- The <u>Royal Lao Government in Exile</u>

- The <u>Government of Free Vietnam</u> based in <u>Garden Grove, California</u>

International law recognizes that governments in exile may undertake many types of actions in the conduct of their daily affairs. These actions include:

- becoming a party to a bilateral or international treaty

- amending or revising its own constitution

- maintaining military forces

- retaining (or "newly obtaining") diplomatic recognition by sovereign states

- issuing identity cards

- allowing the formation of new political parties

- instituting democratic reforms

- holding elections

- allowing for direct (or more broadly-based) elections of its government officers, etc.

Accordingly, the Republic of Jinnahpur's government in exile shall also undertake all the above-mentioned actions immediately.

JINNAHPUR'S FUTURE ROLE

JINNAHPUR AS A MODERATE STATE

It shall be widely accepted that Republic of Jinnahpur should be a moderate state beyond mere demographic criteria. That is to say, it must be more than a state of Sunni or Shia Muslims already living in city of Karachi under siege of military dictatorship of presently undivided Pakistan. In order to be a moderate state, it must be built upon principles based on anti-extremism in terms of religion or sect, including what are commonly considered to be religious principles of certain Muslim sects like Sunni-ism and Shia-ism. On the other hand, to pose this as a matter of religion and state is to adopt a terminology which is in itself problematic in the local tradition and to phrase the issue of the relationship somewhat falsely by putting it in Western terms, whereby religion is the province of mosques/churches and religious scholars called Ulema (clerics), and where any close relationship between religion and state would have to provide for some kind of formal recognition of the role of the mosque or its clerical leadership in the polity. Let us then try to approach the question from an indigenously Urdu-speaking perspective which, while it does not solve all the problems inherent in the issue by any means, offers us an alternate way to conceptualize the matter and which may help us to better confront it in reality.

THE THREE PILLARS

The classic Islamic polity is organized around three important factors of authoritative expression, namely Quran, Hadith and Fiqah. Traditionally each of these pillars derives its authority directly from some combination of Divine and popular sanction. Over the generations, the bearers of each of these pillars have changed. Today, it is in the hands of the radical clerics and, as a result of modernity, is shared by certain academics and intellectuals, de facto if not de jure.

Republic of Jinnahpur as a moderate polity shall have manifestations of all three of these pillars, carrying on the tasks of its governance. From a traditional point of view, the Ulema (clerics) shall continue to be the teachers of Quran, indeed in Jinnahpur more faithful to the Urdu-speaking tradition unlike a Punjabi or Pathan tradition than perhaps in any other community in South Asia because of the scope of their jurisdiction.

The first conclusion that we can come to is that, while Republic of Jinnahpur as a state shall be formally democratic and secular, providing equal support to all religions and no special recognition to any, as a polity it is indeed a moderate one even if ambiguously at times and ambivalent about its Muslim identity in various crucial ways. It also means that the strengthening of the Jinnahpur's religious character of being an Islamic country as a polity need not, indeed should not, mean the strengthening of the power of radical religious intellectuals.

In this respect, there shall be some substantial progress to be made soon after independence of Republic of Jinnahpur as a country. As we all know that today's undivided Pakistan is housing millions of radical religious clerics who are free to move and say whatever they like within the jurisdiction of Pakistan, this will cease to continue in Jinnahpur.

The bitter and cruel Martial Law of late General Zia-ul-Haq, which marked the beginning of radical Islam from the soil of Pakistan in the disguise of Tablighi Jamaat, accelerated this trend on the pretext of preaching of Islam in and outside Pakistan. Under the nose of General Zia-ul-Haq and supervision of Military Establishment, the Tablighi Jammat deliberately tried to introduce newest religious expressions into the life of the state, albeit through a kind of civil religion rather than through traditional religion. Umra and taking of Qaris and Naat readers on official foreign trips became quite like a tradition during Zia regime. But, then, in many respects the very character of Islam being that of a civil religion, linking religious and political matters, made this new trend as an exploitation of religious symbols for political purposes. This trend has not changed since then in today's undivided Pakistan. Republic of Jinnahpur will be free from such hypocrisy.

From another perspective, it can be said that in the Republic of Jinnahpur, there will be a strong majority of Urdu-speaking Muslims who would like to have a positive relationship with the Quran and Hadith. They will never tolerate radical leaders who may show them the way nor models to follow. There is every chance that the processes of secularization will continue unabated in the Republic of Jinnahpur so that the vast majority of Urdu-speaking Muslims will indeed be non-extremist by virtue of their birth on a truly secular soil.

THE TRUE URDU-SPEAKING SCHOOL OF THOUGHT

At the very least, Republic of Jinnahpur shall produce a Socio-Islamic school of thought that shall be equipped to cope with the contemporary world, that is to say, religious scholars who shall have a proper general as well as Islamic education and who know how to speak to the Muslim public. Today, it is fair to say that there are no non-extremist religious scholars being trained in Pakistan who meet this standard. The tragedy of Lal Masjid and suicide bombings in undivided Pakistan are glaring evidence of Pakistan's failure on the religious front also.

NON-TRADITIONAL ISLAM IN JINNAHPUR

In Republic of Jinnahpur, there shall be no discrimination against Reform and Conservative organizations for purposes of worship or anything else. Since both movements have a strong clerical dimension, their attention shall be turned to securing recognition for their scholarly achievements rather than being given to the training of a generation of Conservative Muslims.

Moreover, in Republic of Jinnahpur, where the daily expressions of religion shall be in the hands of true Muslim scholars and the State shall not play a clerical role in true sense, this shall avoid extremism at government level and hence shall promote moderate thinking and policy making on the priciples of a free approach.

THE EXISTENCE OF RELIGIOUS PARTIES

Statehood shall, in many respects, be Jinnahpur's ultimate test. The purpose of the establishment of the Republic of Jinnahpur, shall be to allow freedom of speech, freedom of religious beliefs and freedom of religious activities within the jurisdiction of Jinnahpur's boundaries. In such a state, the HUMANITY will inevitably be stronger than RELIGIOUS IDENTITY. Hence, the political structure of Jinnahpur shall reject an active religious presence in the political arena. It is difficult to see how that presence could be manifested in Jinnahpur's political system other than through religious parties. Needless to say, this explanation for religious parties presented on the highest plane shall be made even more real by the very practical reasons of securing legislative and financial support for religious institutions, needs, and expectations on a day-to-day basis.

This does not mean that the future of the religious parties function-ing within the jurisdiction of presently undivided Pakistan shall also be assured in Jinnahpur. The future of Jinnahpur shall be clouded by the breaking away of its traditional members to *Maulvis* and *Religious Cults* like Tablighi Jamaat. However, still, it would be quite premature to assume that it will disintegrate unless the number of religious followers drops so precipitously that the state is left to turn secular with a vengeance.

About Religious Legislation

One of the attributes of statehood shall be the restoration of the political arena as a major decision-making forum for matters of religious concern in the public domain. Under such circumstances, it shall become inevita-ble that vital questions such as those surrounding religious standards will become political questions. The fact that they have is another sign that, with all its ambiguities and ambivalences, Jinnahpur shall be a moderate Muslim state even in a traditional sense.

On the other hand, to say that is not to suggest that every situation which in the abstract calls for religious legislation should lead to such legisla-tion. Before a decision is made, there shall be many considerations which shall come into play. First and foremost is the issue of consequences. For example, on the latest round of the "Who is a Moderate Muslim" issue, in the narrow sense the legislation shall be almost unexceptionable. But in the larger sense of the preservation of the unity of the Urdu-speaking people in a situation in which the legislation will not do anything to change matters for the better and will only precipitate Muslim disunity, one would hardly consider it to be wise. Prudence is also an Islamic value, one that the Muslim people have not always practiced. Invariably, when it has not, disaster has ensued.

Today, the struggle over religious legislation has been exacerbated because of a major shift that is taking place in the Muslim countries. Until recently, virtually all Muslims whether from Indonesia or Malaysia, no matter what their particular stance with regard to religious belief and practice, had grown up in traditional environments. Hence they had a certain understanding of and respect for tradition even if they no longer observed or even were militantly opposed to traditional Islam.

Today, paradoxically, at a time when militant secularism has greatly declined, a new generation has grwon up which, while it is more likely to acknowledge a belief in Allah (God) and the appropriateness of some religious practices, has little or no personal experience with traditional Islam. It is a generation that fits into the contemporary world of consumerism in which convenience is a most important value. They are the ones who want cinemas and places of entertainment to be open Thursday night and Friday and who would like to be able to do their shopping on their free day. For them, these are matters of individual choice and they resent interference with their convenience. Thus the consensus around certain publicly enforced standards of observance is rapidly breaking down.

Not surprisingly, those in favor of maintaining such standards and who feel that the face of the society as a whole would be changed for the worst if matters are merely left to individual choice, now seek to reinforce the maintenance of those standards through appropriate legislation, which is opposed by the other side. This situation is analogous to what occurred in the United States in the early 20th century. During the 19th century, people of all levels of religious belief and practice accepted the Protestant norms in society with regard to such matters as Sunday observance, temperance, the content of the school curriculum, and the like. When that consensus broke down early in the 20th century, Protestant fundamentalists sought to restore it through legislation. Even when they succeeded in getting such legislation enacted, as in the case of Prohibition or laws prohibiting the teaching of evolution in the schools, their victories were temporary because the majority of the population and the temper of the times was opposed to them. The end result was to dismantle even the tradition of Sunday closing for the convenience of the new consumers.

That is likely to be the fate of legislation in Republic of Jinnahpur which shall reflect the imposition of the will of the Majority on the minority. Hence those in favor of that legislation should think twice before pressing for it. At the present time the majority Urdu-speaking people is not opposed to the maintenance of public observance in the institutions of the state. They want freedom of choice in other areas.

Quality of Relationship with Neighbouring Countries

The Republic of Jinnahpur shall have a well-defined policy framework in the matter of its relationship with its immediate neighbouring countries like Sindhudesh, Balochistan and other countries in the region like India, Iran and Afghanistan apart from Pakhtoonistan and Punjabistan (representing remaining part of Pakistan). This policy framework shall be based on the same principles of "Integration Without Accessation" as followed by European Union Member countries. Similarly, Jinnahpur shall also be an active member of SAARC (South Asian Association for Regional Cooperation) and continue to have cooperation with other SAARC member countries in the following areas:

1. Agriculture and Rural Development;

2. Health and Population Activities;

3. Women, Youth and Children;

4. Environment and Forestry;

5. Science and Technology and Meteorology;

6. Human Resources Development; and

7. Transport.

JINNAHPUR'S MILITARY COOPERATION WITH INDIA

India's relations with the newest country on the world's map, that is, Republic of Jinnahpur shall be a very important factor for the future of South Asian region. Jinnahpur's security and safety shall also safeguard the security and safety of India for the sole reason that the changes in the South Asian geo-strategic environment shall compel India to establish full diplomatic relations with Republic of Jinnahpur as soon as Jinnahpur is formed in order to make sure that Pakistan's nuclear arsenal is destroyed immediately by using the soil of Republic of Jinnahpur. As it is an established fact that transparency often lacks in the issues related to nuclear and missile development programmes of a country, safety and security of the strategic capabilities lies primarily on the wisdom of the possessor state. In Pakistan, the vulnerabilities to the overstretching desire of acquiring non-conventional capabilities have achieved multidi-mensional threatening postures. The world community needs to ponder over the potential risks of nuclear threats that may emanate from nuclear Pakistan. Therefore, the formation of Republic of Jinnahpur shall pro-vide an opportunity to destroy Pakistan's nuclear arsenal with the help and assistance of India and USA.

Pakistan is estimated to have an arsenal of 30 to 55 nuclear weapons, with 24 to 48 nuclear warheads based on highly enriched uranium (HEU). Pakistan's official claim is that these nuclear weapons are not assembled and thus comparatively safe. They insist that the fissile cores are stored separately from the non-nuclear explosives packages, and that the war-heads are stored separately from the delivery systems. General Mirza Aslam Beg, former chief of army staff, once told a reporter that "mat-ing them would take two to three days." This, however, would seem to contradict the other claim of ready-to-use weapons—a claim made more than once in relation to India.

According to experts, Pakistan's primary reliance on HEU makes its fissile materials particularly vulnerable to diversion. HEU can be used in a rela-tively simple gun-barrel-type design, which could be within the means of non-state actors who intend to assemble crude nuclear weapons.

The security of Pakistan's nuclear arsenal became a major concern of the Washington-headed West, which had been far less bothered about South Asia's nuclear fate despite all its lip service to the cause of non-proliferation, in the days following 9/11. Within two days of the trag-edy, Pakistan's military, under the watchful eye of a Musharraf favorite, Lieutenant-General Khalid Kidwai, relocated the weapons described as the country's "crown jewels" to six "secret locations." General Musharraf was then claimed to have sacked his intelligence chief and other offi-cers and detained suspected retired nuclear weapons scientists including Abdul Qadeer Khan on a false pretext, in an attempt to "root out extrem-ist elements that posed a potential threat to Pakistan's nuclear arsenal."

Lt.-Gen. Kidwai has ever since been a regular visitor to Washington, pre-sumably with a mission to offer periodical reassurances about the security of Pakistan's nuclear weapons. Islamabad, however, has also consistently claimed that it was not ready to compromise security by cooperation with even the George Bush administration in this regard.

But serious doubts have been raised about the much-vaunted secrecy. The known links of Pakistan's intelligence agencies, past and present, with the Taliban and other extremists do not constitute reassurance in this regard. A CNN report, obviously based on official briefing, said that Washington and the Pentagon knew of Pakistan's secret nuclear sites. The motive behind the disclosure has been a matter of debate in intelligence circles. Whatever may be the case, in my opinion, the only way to get rid of Pakistan's nuclear arsenal is through a direct missile attack which can only be possible from the soil of Republic of Jinnahpur.

PROPOSED UN RESOLUTION

IN CONNECTION WITH
REPUBLIC OF JINNAHPUR

Following is the proposed UN Resolution in connection with the formation of Republic of Jinnahpur:

Recognizing the inalienable right of all people to self-determination and independence in accordance with the principles of the Charter of the United Nations and of the Declaration on the Granting of Independence to Colonial Countries and Peoples, contained in its resolution 1514 (XV) of 14 December 1960,

Having examined the report of the Special Committee on the Situation with regard to the Implementation of the Declaration on the Granting of Independence to Colonial Countries and People relating to the question of Republic of Jinnahpur,

Having heard the statements of the representatives of India, USA and Israel, as well as those of General Assembly resolution 1514 (XV) of 15 December 1960,

Bearing in mind the responsibility of the world community to undertake all efforts to create conditions enabling the people of Karachi to exercise freely their right to self-determination, freedom and independence by forming Republic of Jinnahpur and to determine their future political status in accordance with the principles of the Charter and the Declaration, in an atmosphere of peace and order,

Mindful that all States should, in conformity with Article 2, paragraph 4, of the Charter, refrain in their international relations from the threat or use of force against the territorial integrity or national independence of any State, or from taking any action inconsistent with the purposes and principles of the Charter,

Calls upon all States to respect the inalienable right of the people of Karachi to self-determination, freedom and independence by forming Republic of Jinnahpur and to determine their future political status in accordance with the principles of the Charter of the United Nations and the Declaration of the Granting of Independence to Colonial Countries and Peoples,

Calls upon the Government of Pakistan to continue to make every effort to find a solution by peaceful means through talks between the Government of Pakistan and the Mohajir Qaumi Movement and Jinnahpur Liberation Movement representing the urdu-speaking nation living in Karachi and other cities in Sindh province,

Appeals to all the political parties in Pakistan to respond positively to efforts to find a peaceful solution through talks between them and the Government of Pakistan in the hope that such talks will bring an end to the strife in province of Sindh and lead towards the orderly exercise of the right of self-determination by the urdu-speaking nation living in Karachi and other cities in Sindh province for the formation of Republic of Jinnahpur,

Strongly deplores the military presence of the armed forces of Pakistan in Karachi,

Calls upon the Government of Pakistan to desist from further violation of the territorial integrity of urdu-speaking nation and to withdraw without delay its armed forces from Karachi in order to enable the urdu-speaking nation living in Karachi and other cities of Sindh to exercise freely their right to self-determination and independence by forming Republic of Jinnahpur,

Draws the attention of the Security Council in conformity with Article 11, paragraph 3, of the Charter, to the critical situation in Karachi and recommends that it take urgent action to protect the territorial integrity of Republic of Jinnahpur and the inalienable right of its urdu-speaking people to self-determination,

Calls upon all States to respect the unity and territorial integrity of Republic of Jinnahpur,

Requests the Government of Pakistan to continue its cooperation with the Special Committee on the Situation with regard to the Implementation of the Declaration on the Granting of Independence to Colonial Countries and Peoples and requests the Committee to send a fact-finding mission to Karachi as soon as possible, in consultation with the political parties in Pakistan and the Government of Pakistan.

WILL WATER DIVIDE PAKISTAN?

Yes, water will divide Pakistan. Water has a great historic importance. Noah, the apostle of Allah was helped by Allah with water when Allah showered the entire world with water and drowned the enemies of Allah in water. Rain fell on the earth for a period of forty days and nights. The waters flooded the earth for a hundred and fifty days, and every living thing on the face of the earth was wiped out. As the waters receded, the Noah's ark came to rest on the mountains of Arafat. Noah AS and his family continued to wait for almost eight more months while the surface of the earth dried out.

Similarly, in the story of Ismail AS, son of Abrahim AS, water has very important significance too. One day, Abraham woke up and asked his wife Bibi Hajara AS to get her son and prepare for a long journey. In a few days Abrahim AS started out with his wife Bibi Hajara AS and their son Ismail AS. The child was still nursing and not yet weaned. Abrahim AS walked through cultivated land, desert, and mountains until he reached the desert of the Arabian Peninsula and came to an uncultivated valley having no fruit, no trees, no food, no water. The valley had no sign of life. After Abrahim AS had helped his wife and child to dismount, he left them with a small amount of food and water which was hardly enough for 2 days. He turned around and walked away. His wife hurried after him asking: "Where are you going Abrahim, leaving us in this barren valley?" Abrahim AS did not answer her, but continued walking. She repeated what she had said, but he remained silent. Finally she understood that he was not acting on his own initiative. She realized that Allah had commanded him to do this. She asked him : "Did Allah command you to do so?" He replied: "Yes." Then his great wife said: "We are not going to be lost, since Allah Who has commanded you is with us."

Abrahim AS invoked Almighty Allah thus: *"O Our Lord! I have made some of my offspring to dwell in a valley with no cultivation, by Your Sacred House (the Ka'ba at Mecca); in order, O our Lord, that they may offer prayers perfectly (Iqamat as salat) so fill some hearts among men with love towards them, and O Allah provide them with fruits so that they may give thanks. O our Lord! Certainly, You know what we conceal and what we reveal. Nothing on the earth or in the heavens is hidden from Allah."* (Ch 14:37-38)

Ismail's mother Bibi Hajara AS went on suckling Ismail and drinking from the water (she had). When the water in the water skin had been used up, she became thirsty and her child also became thirsty, She started looking at Ismail AS tossing in agony. She left him, for she could not endure looking at him, and found that the mountain of As-Safa was the nearest mountain on that land. she too walked on it and started looking at the valley keenly so that she might see somebody, but she could not see anybody. Then she descended for As Safa and when she reached the valley, she tucked up her robe and ran in the valley like a person in distress and trouble till she crossed the valley and reached the mountain of Al Marwa. There she stood and started looking expecting to see somebody, but she could not see anybody. she repeated that running between Safa And Marwa seven times.

The prophet Muhammad (pbuh) says: "This is the source of the tradition of the Sa'y (rituals of the hajj, pilgrimage) the going of people between them (As-Safa and Al-Marwa). When she reached Al Marwa (for the last time) she heard a voice and she asked herself to be quiet and listened attentively. She heard the voice again and said: "O whoever you maybe! You have made me hear your voice; have you got something to help me?" She saw an angel at the place of Zam zam, digging the earth with heel of Ismail AS till water flowed from that place. She started to make something like a basin around it, using her hand in this way, and started filling her water skin with water with her hands and the water was flowing out water she had scooped some of it. That water is called Abe Zam Zam i.e. The Water of Zam Zam which is still flowing and shall continue to flow till the doomsday. Hence, in this story, water's significance has been proven yet again.

Story of Musa AS known as Moses in Christianity also tells us about role of water in his life. When Moses was born, he was sent down a river in a basket because Pharoah had ordered all Jewish male children to be killed and thrown into the Nile River. Similarly, in Judaism, the Festival of Passover is derived from the story of the ten plagues and the exodus of the Jews from Egypt. The Pharaoh's army chased them through the desert towards the Red Sea. When the Jews reached the sea they were trapped, since the sea blocked their escape. It was then that a miracle occurred. The waves of the Red Sea parted and the Israelites were able to cross to the other side. As soon as they all reached the other side the sea closed trapping the Pharaoh's army as the waves closed upon them. Then as the Israelites watched the waters of the Red Sea sweep away the Pharaoh's army they realized they were finally free. Water has lot of significance in the story of Moses also.

Story of Yahya AS (known as John in Christianity) is also related to water in some way. There are quite a number of traditions told about Yahya AS (John).

Ibn Asaker related that one time his parents were looking for him and found him at the Jordan River. When they met him, they wept sorely, seeing his great devotion to Allah, Great and Majestic. In Christianity, Yahya AS is popularly known as "John, the baptist". The reason is Yahya AS used to clean the sins of the people with the water of Jordan River. Hence, in this story of Yahya AS (John), water's importance has emerged again.

Finally, the story of Hazrat Imam Hussain AS (grand son of Holy Prophet of Islam Hazrat Muhammad SAW) tells us about the desert of Karbala (Iraq) where his children were thirsty as well as the women and the men. The brutal soldiers of Yazeed bin Mawiyah (both father and son are the famous hypocrites according to Islamic history) prevented Hazrat Imam Hussain AS and his people from the Euphrates water. Hazrat Imam Hussain AS had a 6 months old baby prince Hazrat Ali Asghar AS who was crying aggressively for water and Hazrat Imam Hussain AS took him to Yazeed's army asking for water just for the baby prince Hazrat Ali Asghar AS, instead they threw towards baby prince Hazrat Ali Asghar AS a dart which struck the baby prince Hazrat Ali Asghar AS on his neck and martyred him instantly. Imam Hussein AS then took the blood of his baby in his hand and threw it to heaven asking Allah to witness what these people had done to baby prince Hazrat Ali Asghar AS who belonged to the family of their holy prophet SAW. In this story, water is also there. Those who listen to this story, shed tears which is also water and shall continue to shed tears till the doomsday.

Water's Role in Dividing Pakistan

The Government of Pakistan seems all set to announce the construction of a mega dam, most probably the Kalabagh Dam on Indus River over the fierce opposition by two of the federating units, the NWFP (Pakhtoonistan) and Sindh. If it does so, the proposed Kalabagh Dam would be one of the two most controversial water projects in the country—the other being the under-construction Greater Thal Canal. Both the projects shall pave way for the disintegration of Pakistan.

The opponents of Kala Bagh Dam argue on the basis of the following points:

1. There is no extra water for any new dams or reservoirs in the Indus River System. During the past few years there has been scarcity of water in the country and even the present dams have not been filled to capacity even though it is said that they have lost capacity due to silting. The lower riparian province has suffered immensely due to the damming of Indus River. It can't afford any more losses;

2. Provincial assemblies of the three federating units have unanimously rejected Kalabagh-Dam;

3. Indus River System Authority, IRSA, rejected the Kala Bagh Dam on October 22, 1996 on the basis that: a) The Dam will be silted rather quickly. b) Its short life: 22–30 years. c) Poor performance. d) Comparatively lower electric generation-capability;

4. The short life of the dam and a diminished power generation potential would result in huge losses to the country's exchequer. It is economically infeasible;

5. The dam will displace a large number of people and inundate fertile lands in the NWFP (Pakhtoonistan) and Sindh. Many more acreage will be lost because of water logging in Mardan, Swabi, Charsadda, Pabbi, Nowshera, Dhoda, Kharmatoo and other areas. It will also cause land degradation in the Peshawar valley and affect the sweet water aquifers in Karak and Lakki Districts;

6. Additionally, the inhabitants of the low lying areas on both sides of rivers Indus, Sawan, Kabul and Tui will have to be shifted and given new houses and lands for settlement. These inhabitants are in hundreds of thousands and this will incur a heavy expenditure;

7. It will cause backpressure in the River Kabul, resulting in the increase in water logging;

8. Nowshera, a sizeable city of the Frontier Province (Pakhtoonistan), will be threatened with termination or severe water logging, as it will stand 24 feet below the height of Kalabagh storage.

9. Several bridges and roads including the Attock-Talagang road on river Sawan and the Kohat-Rawalpindi road and the Peshawar-Rawalpindi road on river Indus besides some railway tracks and other infrastructure will be submerged by the Kalabagh-Dam;

10. The Sui gas line between Peshawar-Rawalpindi and Rawalpindi-Kohat will also sink in the Kalabagh dam;

11. The Mardan and Swabi SCARP projects will be affected;

12. Possible backwater effects on the Ghazi-Barotha project;

13. The dam will need about 19.5 MAF (for storage and the proposed irrigation canals) water. That will further strain the availability of water in the country espe-

cially for Sindh and Balochistan. Some recent statements say that the design will be changed and no canals will be built. But nobody in Sindh believes it as Wapda and federal authorities have a long history of broken promises and hypocrisy.

14. If the dam is built, there will not be any water available for downstream Kotri (Sindh) in the future. As a result the Delta and the Katcha areas in Sindh will be destroyed and the sea intrusion will cause annual losses of millions of dollars to the Sindh economy;

15. As the Dam will sit on a fault area, any earthquake can cause a disaster. Its proximity to Khewra salt mines only magnifies the problem;

16. Other adverse effects: a) Deleterious impact on environment, ecosystem, biodiversity, habitat, wetlands and subsoil aquifers b) Intensification of drought and desertification c) Acceleration of poverty in the lower riparian province with increased rural to urban migration d) Drinking water problems e) Progressive, illegal decreases in share of Sindh in Indus River System waters, as is already the case;

17. Sindh will continuously be blackmailed, as water taps will be controlled upstream;

Following is the article of Shaheen Rafi Khan about Kalabagh Dam which gives an idea how such a dam is useless and simply a political weapon of Punjab with an ulterior motive to enslave Pakhtoonistan, Sindh and Balochistan:

The Kalabagh dam is controversial for many reasons. A key reason has to do with the decision making process, which is highly centralized, politically coercive, and technically flawed. Regrettably, when the need is for broad-based stakeholder consultations, the existing trend is towards even greater centralization. For instance, the rotating chairmanship of the Indus River System Authority has recently been converted into a permanent appointment, provincial resolutions against Kalabagh have been given short shrift, the Council of Common Interests (CCI) has consistently ignored the matter and community concerns continue to be met with blatant disregard. Small wonder then that the political leadership in the smaller provinces and civil society are up in arms against Kalabagh.

In this essay, we critically examine four contested aspects of the Kalabagh dam. These relate to: water availability; environmental impacts; food and energy; and technical and financial feasibility. The work of colleagues is gratefully acknowledged.

Water availability is an over riding concern. Is surplus water available to justify the Kalabagh project? WAPDA itself—the generic source—has sown confusion on this issue. It cites two average flow figures: 123 MAF (million acre-feet) and 143 MAF. The first calculation is based on a 64-year period (1922-1996) and includes both wet and dry cycles. The second estimate is based on a much shorter and wet cycle period of 22 years (1977–1994). Since the total requirement (inclusive of the additional allocation of 12 MAF under the 1991 Water Accord), is calculated at 143 MAF, there is a clear short fall of 20 MAF if we use the first estimate. This means Kalabagh may remain dry every 4 out of 5 years.

Even the higher flow figure (143 MAF) overlooks certain factors. The first of these is system (evaporation and seepage) losses. If such losses increased from 6.2 MAF post Mangla to 14.7 MAF post-Tarbela, presumably, they will be even higher post-Kalabagh. This would have adverse implications for inter-provincial water distribution. New irrigation infrastructure appears untenable in view of these losses, since the increased upstream off-takes would be at the expense of downstream flows. This concern is also ignored when presenting Kalabagh as a replacement for Tarbela. Tarbela is projected to lose 5.3 MAF of its storage capacity by the year 2010. Since Kalabagh would, essentially, be replacing this loss, the Right and Left Bank canals would divert even more of Sindh's allocations than they presently are. In addition, illegal off-takes would also tend to be exacerbated.

Consider now the environmental implications of constructing yet another large dam on the Indus River ecosystem. A catalogue of existing degradation provides the context for future environmental impacts of dams like Kalabagh. Degradation of the Indus delta ecosystem, as a result of reduced water outflows, is already a highly visible phenomenon. The present level of silt discharge, estimated at 100 million tons per year, is a four-fold reduction from the original level before large dams were constructed on the River Indus. The combination of salt-water intrusion (some reports show this as 30 km inland), and reduced silt and nutrient flows has changed the character of the delta considerably. The area of active growth of the delta has reduced from an original estimate of 2,600 sq. km (growing at 34 meters per year) to about 260 sq. km.

The consequent ravages to the ecosystem have been exceptionally severe, in particular to the mangroves, which are its mainstay. They sustain its fisheries, act as natural barriers against sea and storm surges, keep bank erosion in check and are a source of fuel wood, timber, fodder and forest products, a refuge for wildlife and a potential source of tourism. Without mangroves and the nutrients they recycle and the protection they provide, other components of the ecosystem would not survive.

The direct and indirect benefits of mangroves are enormous. In 1988, Pakistan earned Rs.2.24 billion from fish exports, of which shrimps and prawns constituted 72%. Additional income is generated from fuelwood, fodder and forest products was another Rs.100/-million. Not only is this revenue at risk from mangrove loss, but the physical infrastructure required to replace the natural protection provided by the mangroves (dykes, walls) would entail enormously high capital and maintenance costs.

The health of mangroves is directly linked to fresh water inflows. Releases below Kotri barrage in most years and excluding floods average 10 MAF. Of this, little or none actually reaches the mangroves. The rest is lost due to evaporation or diversions. According to the Sindh Forestry Department, about 27 MAF is required to maintain the existing 260,000 ha. of mangroves in reasonably healthy condition. This is 27 MAF more than currently available, a situation which has contributed to ecosystem instability and mangrove loss. Within the framework of the Indus Water Accord, an additional 12 MAF would be diverted for upstream dam construction—including Kalabagh. This would reduce existing sub-optimal flows further and aggravate an already critical situation.

A community of about 100,000 people, residing on the northern side of the Indus Delta, depends on the mangroves for their livelihood. The prevailing view is that being under privileged, such communities are prone to degrade their environment. However, it is difficult to fathom why poor communities should endanger the very basis of their existence. The more likely explanation is that community practices have not changed, but they appear unsustainable because the resource base has begun to degrade. Communities are more often the victims than the agents of such degradation are. The real culprits are water diversion; biological and chemical water contamination and large-scale commercial practices, compounded both by institutional ignorance and complicity in such practices.

Mangrove loss is only one among the many manifestations of "biodiversity deficits" emerging along the entire length of the Indus River ecosystem. The ecosystem has been severely fragmented over time by its extensive network of dams, canals and barrages, resulting in threats to a variety of species and organisms, the most notable among them being the Indus dolphin and the 'palla' fish. Both can be classified as indicator species, as their impending loss represents the loss of a way of life, characterized by interdependence between communities and their environment.

Another myth firmly embedded in the minds of our planners is that large dams are the perfect flood prevention devices. The evidence for Pakistan shows otherwise; that its large dams not withstanding, there has been no reduction in the incidence and intensity of floods nor in the associated losses in lives, crops, livestock and infrastructure. There is no seeming pattern to the floods other than the fact that they could have coincided with wet cycles. In actual fact, the severity of flood impacts appears to have increased after the two major dams, Tarbela and Mangla, were constructed.

In actual fact, the shrinking of the riverbeds due to water diversions reduces their absorptive capacity and hence enhances the danger of flooding. River ecosystems have a natural capacity to deal with floods and these natural processes provide many benefits. Flood plains, wetlands, backwaters are commonly referred to as nature's sponges; they absorb and purify excess water as a hedge against lean periods. They act as spawning grounds for fish and wildfowl. The floods themselves replenish agricultural soils. Communities living around these areas adapt to this natural rhythm and use its bounty to ensure reliable and sustainable livelihoods. It has also been pointed out that dams don't prevent floods, they merely create 'flood threat transfer mechanisms'. The solution is to work with communities, rely on their knowledge and to supplement their flood mitigation and coping strategies.

Two of the most commonly cited arguments in favor of large dams relate to food security and energy. Such arguments have become increasingly compelling in the light of perceived threats to food security and the recent furor surrounding the private power projects. We examine both of these arguments in turn. Additional water from Kalabagh can enhance crop production in three ways: by irrigating new land; by enhancing cropping intensity on existing land; or through yield enhancement. The first option appears tenuous. It is claimed that Kalabagh will irrigate close to an additional million hectares of barren land, and bring Pakistan closer to wheat self-sufficiency. However, the reports of the National Commission on Agriculture and the National Conservation Strategy suggest otherwise. They indicate that available cultivable land is almost fully utilized, leaving little scope for extensive cultivation. Between 1952 and 1977, about 80% of the increase in total cropped area was due to the cultivation of new land. Since then, this proportion has fallen dramatically, with double cropping accounting for the bulk of the increase. The reports suggest that in addition to the water constraint a very tangible land constraint exists as well.

Crop production can also be increased through cropping intensity increases or crop yield enhancements. Both are water dependent and establish an a priori justification for Kalabagh. The NCS report states that at present 12.2 million hectares of land are available for double cropping while only 4.4 million hectares are being double cropped—clearly water is the constraining factor. With respect to yield enhancements, water is again required in large quantities by the high yielding seed varieties (wheat, cotton, rice, maize) and for its synergetic effects upon chemical inputs.

However, a critical choice needs to be made here. Does one opt for additional water, or can the same results be achieved through improved water use efficiency? Higher water retention in the system risks aggravating an already massive problem of water logging and salinity. In fact, the controversial and exorbitantly expensive ($780 million), 25-year National Drainage Plan project has been launched to mitigate its impacts. Kalabagh is bound to add to the problem, not only in its immediate environs but also where new irrigation infrastructure is to be situated.

A clearly preferred choice is to use existing water more efficiently, and to focus on the necessary institutional changes for its equitable distribution. Some of the proposed measures are canal and watercourse rehabilitation, land leveling, improved on-farm water management and, at the policy level, switching demand based management while protecting the needs of the poor small farmers. These are clearly win-win solutions as they are relatively low cost, efficient, equitable and environmentally friendly.

After the recent commotion over private power, the government began to hype up Kalabagh as an alternative source of cheap and clean energy. In the process, it switched adroitly from its earlier position that energy demand had been overstated, to one where it now posits a deficiency in supply. However, the cheap energy argument is becoming increasingly untenable—both financially and technically. Donors such as the World Bank and the Asian Development Bank are unlikely to provide concessional funding for Kalabagh. This reflects their commitment to the thermal based private power projects, as well as the censure they have faced for getting embroiled in projects with major environmental and resettlement costs. And even if concessional funding was available, it is still not clear that hydel unit costs would be lower than thermal, once these costs are factored in.

At this point, the whole debate appears to be moot since the government is scampering for funds to keep the economy afloat against the backdrop of sanctions. Even so, renewed policy statements suggest there is a resolve to proceed when the situation permits. Apart from the political compulsions, there is an inertial aspect to this decision as well. Institutional and financial paralysis inhibits the scope for energy conservation, efficiency improvements and diversification. The options have been identified often enough: on the supply side these are reduction of transmission and distribution (T&D) losses and renewable energy development technologies (solar, wind, biomass). On the demand side, both technical and economic options exist for energy conservation. While these have been employed to some extent (tariff increases, energy efficient lighting), the efforts are a far cry from the kind of sustained initiatives launched in some South Asian countries, such as Thailand, where revamped energy supply systems are part of a larger network, with linkages to R&D, the private sector and trade facilities.

The title of a study "Tarbela Dam Sedimentation Management", carried out by TAMS-Wallingford (March 1998) is self-explanatory. It shows that a de-silted Tarbela would yield the same irrigation benefits as Kalabagh, but at one-seventh the cost in net present value terms. The study states that, "replacement of [irrigation and energy] benefits by constructing a new dam and reservoir down stream is feasible, but will be expensive, environmentally damaging and socially harmful. An alternative option cited is the construction of new outlets at the Tarbela Dam that will enable sediment to be flushed from the reservoir.

The proposed Tarbela Action Plan is based on computer simulations of sediment flows. These simulations were designed to determine whether flushing was technically feasible and could be used to enhance long run storage capacity and to predict future sedimentation. Based on these simulations, a three phased action plan was proposed. The implementation of this plan would ensure long term and sustainable storage with only a small annual reduction in capacity. The estimated increase in retention at 6 MAF is exactly what the Kalabagh reservoir is designed to hold.

Our conclusion is that the burden of proof is on those who advocate building the Kalabagh Dam. Our findings show that it is not economically, socially or environmentally viable. Also, the proposed benefits are based on faulty or misunderstood premises and, in any case, there exist in each case more viable and cost effective alternatives. The End of article.

On December 31, 2006, four progressive parties in Punjab united to protest against the proposed dam. The rally, held in Lahore, was charged by police, and activists of the four parties—the National Workers Party, the Labour Party Pakistan (LPP), the Pakistan Mazdoor Mehaz and the Mazdoor Kissan Party—were beaten.

Farooq Tariq, an organiser of the rally and national secretary of the LPP told *Green Left Weekly* by phone: "The LPP opposes the dam because it will deny Sindh its share of water and turn it into a desert. We oppose the construction of big dams on environmental grounds. Furthermore, this dam will benefit the Punjab ruling class and will add to the exploitation of Sindh. All provinces except the Punjab have repeatedly opposed the construction of this dam. This democratic verdict should be taken as a referendum and the dam abandoned. "For the dam to proceed, especially under an unelected, military dictatorship, is a violation of all democratic norms." Two days earlier, protesters at Jehangira, 60 kilometres east of Peshawar, closed the Grand Trunk road between Peshawar in the NWFP and the country's capital Islamabad for seven hours. That rally was organised by the Awami National Party (ANP) and was attended by representatives of almost all political parties, including the Pakistan People's Party, an ally of Musharraf. The Mutehida Majlas Amal, a coalition of Islamic fundamentalist organisations that was in power in NWFP (Pakhtoonistan) in the last regime, also sent representatives to the rally.

ANP president Asfandyar Wali Khan told the rally: "Pakistan and Kalabagh dam cannot co-exist". He said that proceeding with the dam against the wishes of three provinces could lead to a "1971-like situation", referring to the civil war that saw east Pakistan split off to form Bangladesh. "We are opposed to the disintegration of the country, but if the establishment is bent on drowning its own people—then we will choose how we want to die", he said.

In my opinion, water will play an important role in disintegration of Pakistan.

DIVIDE PAKISTAN TO ELIMINATE TERRORISM PETITION 2001

I had written the following petition in September 2001 exactly few days after 9-11 as I was of firm opinion that Pakistan was the most dangerous country involved in international terrorism. Almost after 7 years, people around the world have understood and believed that Pakistan is a dangerous country and its involvement in protecting terrorists is thus confirmed and verified by circumstantial evidence:

To: Civilized Nation

Dear Civilized Nation

I am writing to you as I believe that you can play a very significant role in reshaping of the geography of South Asia in order to combat international terrorism. The entire terrorism network has been managed by terrorist forces stationed in Pakistan under the safe umbrella of Government of Pakistan. These terrorist forces have taken the shelter of Islamic identity in order to implement their dangerous designs of dominating South Asia and make it an Islamic territory altogether thereby driving out Christians, Hindus and Sikhs living in India. The ultimate scheme was first made during the lifetime of late General Zia-ul-Haq who can be termed as the main actor towards this direction. The said General Zia-ul-Haq took advantage of the then Afghan-Russian war and made it possible to develop a terrorist network in the region by sponsoring extremist Islamic groups and providing them all necessary military training and ammunition. The atomic program of Pakistan was also part of this endeavor. However, General Zia-ul-Haq died in a military plane crash in 1988 and there was the beginning of a new democratic era in Pakistan. But this democracy was itself fake in the sense that same old faces appeared to rule the country for their own monetary benefits. Consequently, Pakistan became yet another victim of terrorist forces which acted from the strong base of Pakistan Army which has been the main principal of all terrorism in the South Asia. It was Pakistan Army which does not want any peace in the region so as to keep the region under stress in general and to keep India being their hostile neighbor under a constant military threat.

The coming back of Pakistan Army in power through General Pervez Musharraf from the back doors on October 12, 1999 was yet another attempt to continue with the same old plan of Islamic domination in South Asia as masterminded by late General Zia-ul-Haq. This conspiracy had enjoyed assistance of China as China needed a strong Pakistan to keep an eye on India so that India should not become any problem for China in her traditional desire to win the regional supremacy which may pave way for her becoming another super war.

Pakistan is the central headquarters of all terrorist activities under the authoritative command of Inter-Services Intelligence (ISI) an organ of Pakistan Army who have been sheltering Islamic terrorists organizations in the country through military as well as financial support. Their objective is simple that is to rule the region under an Islamic system of their own brand and elimination of non-Muslim communities and culture. They believe that unless they use power they cannot fulfil their ambitions and as such they have found terrorism as the most convenient method for accomplishment of their political agenda. In order to promote this terrorism through religious recognition and some historic significance with a view to make it attractive for the youngsters, they misinterpreted the concept of Jihad (holy war) and since the Muslim masses living in that region are totally illiterate and ignorant about their own religion, they were misguided by the help of hypocrite Islamic scholars who motivated and induced the foolish young Muslims to fight against non-Muslims. These fools did not even think that if it was the question of Muslim and Non-Muslim, then they should also fight China being totally out of the religious orbit. But, in that case, their brains do not work because it is but China itself which is assisting the Pakistan Army in such activities. Hence, the entire phenomenon is not to propagate the Muslim beliefs but to conquer the whole world through the assistance of China. Pakistan right now is the puppet of China and therefore it has become inevitable to address this issue on top priority.

Chinese experts in connivance with the Pakistan Army have worked very intelligently to use the religion of Islam as a tool very useful to be used for extracting cheap fighting force in the name of holy war. On the other hand, the whole Pakistan Army getting salaries in millions of dollars per annum is not coming forward for this s-called Jihad simply for the reason that they know that it has nothing to do with any Jihad but to implement certain long-term political plans. It is, therefore, very essential to focus from a different angle without wasting any further time on Osama Bin Laden who is nobody but a well-trained puppet of Pakistan Army being used extensively for the purpose of masterminding the terrorist schemes and implementing them through the technical co-operation of Pakistan.

Inter Services Intelligence Agency (ISI) is the real government in Pakistan. In the present situation it is the ISI, which is devising the self-made covert policies for the Government and also ensuring its implementation. It is part of the ISI's well-established policy to organize violent pro-Taliban protest demonstrations against the United States in the provinces of Sindh, Balochistan and NWFP (North West Frontier Province) and keep the province of Punjab away from these demonstrations and strikes. After the terrorist attacks of 11th September 2001, the United States and the international community declared in clear words that we would now see that "who stands with us or against us". The United States and international community assured the Pakistani rulers that if they extend co-operation to United States and international community in the war against terrorism, Pakistan would get the legitimate fruits of such co-operation. After these assurances of the International Community, the ISI conspired to activate the religious and so-called Jihadi groups on their payroll to use the provinces of Sindh, Balochistan and NWFP (North-West Frontier Province) provinces as their battleground against United States and International Community. This conspiracy to use the minority provinces was aimed to give the United States of America and the International Community a completely wrong impression that people living in these provinces are against USA while the real situation is totally different. Pakistan Army through its terrorism network called ISI has made an attempt to tarnish the image of small provinces of present Pakistan on one hand and on the other to deceive USA and the International Community. It is a bitter truth that the province of Punjab is the hub of all the fanatical and so-called Jihadi groups and the Headquarters of all the fanatical and extremists groups are situated in different cities of the province of Punjab like Lahore, Multan, Jhang, Faisalabad and Nankana.

The ISI's "game" to deceive the United States and international community would not last long and this act of deception would reach to its logical conclusion. When that happens the world would know who actually benefited by deceiving others and who lost, whereas who was deceived by whom and who was hoodwinked.

It is not understandable as to why the Americans are not addressing the real issue. The real issue is Pakistan itself. In Pakistan, there is no religious disintegration right now. Rather all the religious groups are having mental equation when it is about the religion. There is no conflict among them if it is about Islam. Although they advocate a different Islam which was never the one introduced by Muhammad Bin Abdullah in Mecca some 1500 years ago, yet they are together under the supervision of ISI. ISI has sponsored this new brand of Islam with ulterior motives and to implement its hidden agenda. This new brand of Islam does not enjoy any recognition from the Muslims who really believe in Muhammad. It is indeed unfortunate that Islam has always been victimized throughout by the people who terms themselves as Muslims. Muhammad's Islam was hijacked even in his own lifetime when there were people who disliked Muhammad's relatives and wives. Such miscreants even accused Muhammad's wife Ayesha of adultery. People like Amir Mawiya hated Ali, the nephew of Muhammad so much so that Ali wrote to him several letters condemning Amir Mawiya to be a hypocrite. The revenge came exactly 50 years later when son of Amir Mawiya called Yazeed killed Hussain brutally who was the grand son of Muhammad and son of Ali at the place called Karbala (Iraq). The shia sect of Islam condemn this brutal murder of Hussain and do not recognize Ami Mawiya as Muslim for this arbitrary act of his son Yazeed. Today, Iran is the shia state while a large number of Shias live in Iraq also. It was one of the evil designs of late General Zia-ul-Haq that he made Pakistan a difficult place for shias and the formation of certain militant religious organizations was yet part of this plan. Today we have yet another Yazeed bin Amir Mawiya called Osama Bin Laden and several followers who have changed the very fabric of Islam in the new century. These are religious demons representing the Satan and not Islam.

It is, therefore, necessary to disintegrate Pakistan if we want to collapse the terrorists' network altogether. Unless we destroy the root cause of the whole terrorism tree, we will not be able to eliminate terrorism from the region which has been transformed into a centralized processing unit working under an integrated system not conveniently accessible unless Pakistan is divided in at least four parts. It is essential to divide the northern part of Pakistan into two countries that is Punjabistan and Pakhtoonistan. The Punjabistan will be on the eastern side and the present province of Punjab can be converted into Punjabistan while the North West Frontier Province (NWFP) having its borders with Afghanistan should be made another country called Pakhtoonistan. The new Pakhtoonistan will be a country loyal to the international comity of nations and shall not harbor any terrorists within its geography. Punjabistan shall not have any access to terrorist camps now being run by Pakistan Army in Afghanistan and NWFP as Pakhtoonistan will be a hurdle between Afghanistan and Punjabistan. The Pakistan Army mainly belongs to Punjab and hence the creation of Punjabistan and Pakhtoonistan will break the integrated network between Afghanistan and ISI (Pakistan Army).

On the southern part of Pakistan, two new countries Sindhudesh and Jinnahpur can be made. The Sindhudesh will comprise of Sindhis living in the province of Sindh while Jinnahpur will be a country to house the urdu speaking immigrants from India who had migrated from India after partition of 1947. The population of urdu speaking community living in Karachi (the main commercial city of Pakistan) is around 15 Million. This new country called Jinnahpur can be a secular state of its own kind. The idea is that some 10 million Christians from India may also voluntarily migrate to Jinnahpur to form a pure secular state in South Asia so as to keep a political balance in the region. In Karachi alone (which will be transformed into a new country called Jinnahpur), we can have as many churches as we want along with awarding rights of preaching Christianity and Islam in parallel terms. There will be no extra-ordinary religious resistance in Karachi for the sole reason that the new countries Pakhtoonistan and Punjabistan will have no immediate links with Jinnahpur and as such the terrorist network would not be effective at all. The preaching groups like Tablighi Jamaat (Muslim Preaching Organization based in Raiwind near Lahore-Pakistan) will no more be as effective as now after losing their linkage with their country-wide network. This linkage can only be broken through disintegration of Pakistan. The religious schools called Madressas will no longer be connected with each other. The so-called religious scholars will be confined to their own areas of birth and permanent residence and shall not freely move to other cities in the region presently called Pakistan. Jinnahpur will be a purely secular state with a significant Christian population. We can have permanent airbases of

USA and other military set-ups in Jinnahpur to keep a sound military control in the region to safeguard the entire humanity from the threats of terrorism.

The geography of South Asia has to be revised to combat the terrorism and to prevent further loss of lives in the name of Jihad. The region has become very dangerous to spark 3rd world war and if not checked at this hour of need, country like Pakistan, which has attained nuclear technology due to assistance of China, can become dangerous for the whole humanity. Today we have some loyal people in Pakistan Army who would prefer to favor anti-terrorism drive initiated by the Americans. But what about the religious groups within Pakistan Army which are equally responsible in promotion of terrorism in the name of Islamic domination and are still busy to destabilize the international efforts towards the direction of elimination of terrorism altogether. How can such religious groups destroy their own puppet government called Taliban whom they helped right from its inception and are still harboring their leaders and terrorists like Osama Bin Laden. They may come into power and remove General Pervez Musharaf from his present status. What the Americans will do when a more religious-minded foolish army man captures power in Pakistan? Will they think of bringing back of democracy in Pakistan? It will be too late at that time. It is therefore better to act now.

Pakistan should be divided into four parts as immediately as possible under the supervision of United Nations in the best interest of humanity. This would not be any sort of denying any sovereign country of its right to exist. Pakistan is comprised of five nations and there is no problem in giving these nations their new countries to enable them to have a more realistic identity of their own. This is necessary to eliminate the roots of terrorism completely. This geo-political surgery has become inevitable to save the humanity from the cruel hands of terrorists who will come again to strike and they have no other place to hide and conspire but Pakistan.

I request the entire humanity to join me in this campaign of disintegrating Pakistan in the best interest of the whole humanity. If we break Pakistan today, we are disintegrating the entire terrorist network headquartered in Pakistan. This terrorist network works through a very technical integration in terms of Islamic militant groups, Islamic preaching organizations and Islamic schools called Madressas. A divided Pakistan will destroy the spinal cord of the terrorism and there will be no training camps, no more Osamas and no more threat to humanity.

Say YES to this petition and support international fight against terrorism and against those who harbor terrorists and their supporters. Disintegration of Pakistan will pave way to divide the forces busy to make new designs to conquer the world through terrorism. A divided Pakistan will bring peace to the region and shall facilitate destruction of terrorist training camps and elimination of terrorism altogether.

SYED JAMALUDDIN

SEPTEMBER 2001

http://www.petitiononline.com/PAK47/petition.html

jamal_ics@yahoo.com

THE END

978-0-595-51453-3
0-595-51453-7

www.ingramcontent.com/pod-product-compliance
Lightning Source LLC
Chambersburg PA
CBHW030310290526
45785CB00001B/292